Corra Harris

Lady of Purpose

Corra Harris

Lady of Purpose

By JOHN E. TALMADGE

UNIVERSITY OF GEORGIA PRESS
Athens

To My Sons
BILLY AND PETE

Contents

Illustrations

CORRA HARRIS
From Corra Harris Papers, University of Georgia Library

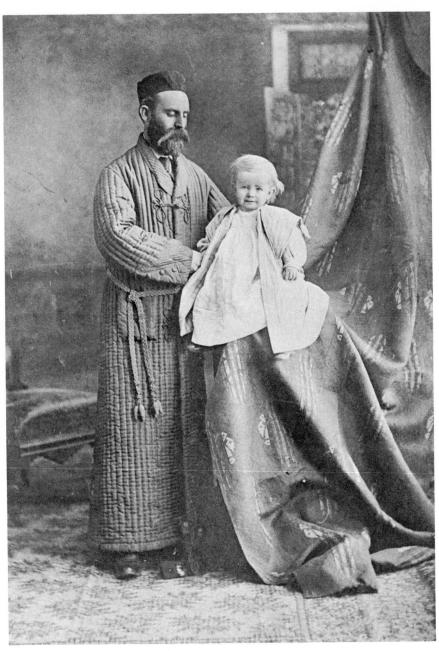

LUNDY H. HARRIS AND LITTLE LUNDY
Courtesy of Emory University Library

FAITH HARRIS LEECH
From the portrait by Ella Hergesheimer
Courtesy of The Parthenon, Nashville, Tennessee

CORRA HARRIS IN LIVING ROOM OF VALLEY HOME. Courtesy of the Atlanta *Journal*

Preface

I BECAME acquainted with Corra Harris through the slow process of reading, literally, thousands of her letters. When Dr. Edwin Everett, head of the English Department at the University of Georgia, suggested I do a biography of her, she was only a name to me. I knew the title of only one of her books, *A Circuit Rider's Wife,* and I had not read it. I had heard she taught a course in "Evil" at Rollins College, and I seemed to remember that her husband had committed suicide. That was all. Certainly I began my research with an open—perhaps I should say an *empty—* mind.

First I read her two autobiographies and the limited biographical material available—a master's thesis, a few articles, and a serial in an Atlanta newspaper. From those sources I got the picture of an amiable, witty lady forced by financial needs into writing, and, even after considerable success, untroubled by literary ambitions. In her autobiographies she appeared to harbor no grudge against the Methodist Church, which she felt had treated her clergyman husband unfairly, and she reported with commendable brevity his death and that of her beloved daughter. It was a pleasant, entertaining story, but hardly a promising framework for a biography. I was about ready to agree with the book publisher who thought that Mrs. Harris had told all that needed to be known about her life. But I moved on to her vast correspondence which had until then remained largely undisturbed in our library, and in other libraries from Rollins College to Harvard University.

As I worked my way through the letters and talked with a few older people who had been with the Harrises in their times of trouble, I became gradually aware of a different story and a more complex woman. My most revolutionary discovery was that in her writings Mrs. Harris had adroitly cloaked the enormity of her

ix

personal tragedies. Such concealment was understandable and forgivable, but, as I read other letters, I saw that she had employed the same technique to safeguard her hard-won literary reputation, her profitable business dealings, and the admiration of her many readers. A common definable motivation had ordered her strenuous life, from the thoughts of early childhood to the making of her final will. I could not mistake or ignore the thesis that had emerged for my biography.

The number of people who have helped me, in various ways, to complete this book is larger than I had supposed. I am especially grateful to Mr. John D. Harris and Brigadier General Frederick M. Harris, nephews of Mrs. Harris, for permission to use her papers at the University of Georgia Library. That collection has been the main source of information for the biography. My old friend Dr. Thomas H. English obtained for me permission to investigate the Warren A. Candler Papers at Emory University. Mrs. Mary K. Davis, Assistant Curator of the Emory Special Collections, made it a pleasure to work with those papers. Mrs. Harry Fine and Mr. Arthur Dakin made available the Paul Elmer More Papers at Princeton University. Mrs. Joseph Whitehead of Carlton, Georgia, loaned me the letters of Mrs. Harris to Mr. A. W. Mathews. The following libraries and historical societies gave me permission to use Harris letters from various collections: Rollins College, Hamilton Holt Papers; Pennsylvania Historical Society, George Horace Lorimer Papers; University of North Carolina, Arthur T. Vance Papers; Lilly Library, University of Indiana, Upton Sinclair Papers; Yale University, William Lyon Phelps Papers; Harvard University, Walter Hines Page Papers.

Many people gave me information about the three Harrises and tried to answer my questions: Mrs. Bettie Rains Upshaw and Mrs. Trannie Rains Smith of Rydel; Paul Akin and Dr. H. B. Bradford of Cartersville; Mrs. Donald McClain, Harold Patterson, Dr. Goodrich White and Mrs. Nathan Goodyear of Atlanta; Mrs. Arthur Booth of Athens; Herbert Wilcox of Elberton; E. L. Adams and William Cantrell of Young Harris; Mrs. Lester Lane of Cornelia; Charles Neal of Demorest; Mrs. Robert Mintz of Rockmart; and Mrs. Adell Dickey of Oxford. Fortunately in my research I could count upon the interest and assistance of two good friends: my colleague Dean William Tate, a neighbor to Mrs. Harris, and Mrs. Carrie Weems of Silver Spring, Maryland, a kinswoman of Professor Lundy Harris. Four people who furnished me with important information have died since I talked with them: Reverend Nathan Thompson of Anderson, S. C., Mrs.

Linnie Anthony Crowe of Cartersville, Miss Effie Morgan of Nashville, Tenn., and Dr. Charles C. Jarrell of Oxford, Ga.

Here at the University of Georgia I have several people to thank. Dean Gerald Huff and Dr. Robert McRorie of the Graduate School, and Drs. Edwin Everett and Robert West, heads of the English Department, arranged research time for me. The receipt of a research award, donated to the University of Georgia by Mr. Leroy Michael and the late Mr. David Michael, furnished me with financial assistance. Again I am indebted to Mr. W. Porter Kellam, Director of the University of Georgia Libraries, and to his assistants Mr. John Bonner, Mrs. William Tate, and Mrs. Christine Burroughs for obtaining material from other libraries and directing me to information obtainable on our own shelves. Mrs. Grace Weinman checked and augmented the bibliography, and Professor Corliss Edwards and Dr. Richard Peake saved me many tedious hours by reading and summarizing Mrs. Harris's miscellaneous journalism. Mr. Ralph Stephens, Director of the Georgia Press, helped greatly to get the manuscript in shape for publication.

I have taken full advantage of my wife's reliable editing and proofreading, but her most valued assistance came in our discussions of Corra Harris—which have continued down to the writing of this preface.

1

· · · · ·

· · ·

·

The Circuit Rider Takes a Wife

IN THE late afternoon of February 8, 1887, several buggies and
carriages drove out of Elberton onto the Old Peterborough Road
in northeast Georgia. About five miles from town they turned off
into a driveway lined with cedars. The kin and friends of Tinsley
White and Mary Mathews White were gathering for the wedding of
Corra Mae, the Whites' older daughter, to the Reverend Lundy
Harris, a preacher from Banks County. As the procession drove up
to the rather dilapidated two-story house, more than one husband
must have chuckled at the thought of Tinsley getting a preacher
for a son-in-law.

Inside, the guests were greeted by a tall, sturdily-built girl.
Corra wasn't a beauty, even in her wedding dress; her face was too
large and heavy. Yet when she began to talk, her lively grey eyes
made you forget she wasn't pretty.

The women, however, as well as the men, were more interested
in the man she introduced them to. He was a handsome fellow
with dark blue eyes, a straight nose, and a ruddy complexion.
Standing next to Corra he didn't look tall, just about her height,
but when she moved away he didn't seem short. Perhaps it was the
way he carried himself. He was pleasant enough when you were
talking with him, but as the room began to quiet down for the
ceremony, a sort of brooding look came into his eyes, as if he were
thinking of something a long way off.

The bride, however, kept her mind upon the scene around her.
In her autobiography she described in detail the people and the
room. As she and Lundy stood before black-bearded Atticus Haygood, Methodist Bishop and former President of Emory College,
the old parlor seemed "to glow like the very heart of love" from
the busy fire and softer candle lights. Outside the windows ever-
green boughs stirred in the deepening twilight. Gradually Corra
became aware of her mother in the shadows behind Haygood and

1

was puzzled by "a strange, foreboding look in her eyes." But many years would elapse before the daughter wrote of the wedding in her autobiography. By that time she could easily believe she had read prophecy in her mother's look.[1]

Corra White was too self-confident to have suffered misgivings. She came of strong-willed ancestors, of Cavalier strain on her father's side and of Puritan on her mother's. Like both branches of her family she was willing to fight for what she wanted.

Tinsley Rucker White, her father, was descended from Virginia stock that had settled in Elbert County after the War of 1812. His father William Bolling White was famous for his cool courage. Once he had driven alone a hundred miles bringing a hundred thousand dollars with him to launch a new bank. As a state senator and friend of Alexander Stephens he had stood with the Whigs in the bitter political battles that divided Georgia before the Civil War. William had married Mildred Rucker of the family that had given his home town the name of Ruckersville. The Ruckers were a brilliant, unpredictable clan famous for oratory and warm tempers. Its chieftain Joseph Rucker, Tinsley's uncle, who had ruled his many acres like a medieval baron, was benevolent enough if given his way in all things. The family was as well known for its wit as for its fearlessness. A Rucker attorney is said to have prosecuted a case so belligerently that when it ended, the defendant invited him to the woods for further discussion. Rucker went willingly, returned badly beaten and, from then on, declared that if he "went to the woods again it would be with a woman." The men of the family handled their religious affairs with the same nonchalance. Corra Harris declared that her father prayed like "one god treating personally with another God." [2]

The blood of the Ruckers and Whites ran strong in Tinsley's veins. In 1861, at the age of seventeen, he walked to Virginia and enlisted in Lee's army. Wounded in his first battle, he returned to service after a brief recuperation and fought through to the Appomattox surrender. He would never mention Gettysburg among his battles, believing that any man who fought there should have at least one scar to show. Tall, spare, and hawk-eyed he could have posed in later life for "The Confederate Veteran." He acted the part too. During World War I he sneered at a nephew for fighting in trenches and just escaped apoplexy when a newspaper writer suggested that veterans donate their bronze crosses to be cast into cannon for killing Germans.[3]

Tinsley's immediate family could seldom have complained of dullness, although he himself became periodically bored with farming and family life. His daughter told how he would leave home to market a year's crop and return the next morning blissfully drunk and completely unperturbed that his cotton money had found its way into the pockets of soberer poker players. Drink, however, was not essential to raise his voice or spirits. At the mention of Shakespeare or the War Between the States, he would make the room resound with his recitations and orations. His escapades were long remembered in Elbert County. Gallantly he refused to surrender some early love letters even after the writer's husband took a long-distance shot at him. At the insistence of his wife he carried his county for Prohibition by the practical expedient of voting a horde of Negroes befuddled by his own corn liquor. In good times and bad he was equally incorrigible.[4]

Corra's maternal ancestors, on both sides, also had come from Virginia, settling first in Wilkes County before going on to Elbert. They were, however, a different breed from the Ruckers and Whites. The Mathews men became physicians, preachers, and merchants—reliable citizens and soldiers. Not given to histrionics they devoted themselves quietly and steadily to their families and occupations. Dr. Albert Clark Mathews, Corra's grandfather, was highly respected both for his professional skill and business judgment. But for all their sobriety and steadiness the Mathews were also a prideful stock. One travelled all the way to Washington to challenge President John Adams for a political slight.[5]

In her writings Mrs. Harris had little to say about her maternal grandmother's family, the Woottens. The single reference found is not complimentary. She admitted a physical resemblance to the women of that branch, but was glad the resemblance ended there, for she had found them "mealy mouthed . . . at the expense of truth." A kinswoman of Mrs. Harris has given more favorable information. The Woottens were descended from a famous English family, a branch of which immigrated to Virginia and came from there to Georgia. Like the Mathews, the Wootten men were respected as soldiers and as citizens. Dr. Albert Mathews obviously thought more of the women than his granddaughter did. When Sophia Wootten Mathews, Corra's grandmother, died, he married her cousin, Eliza Julia.[6]

The union between Tinsley White and Mary Mathews was not consummated—or maintained—without difficulty. Dr. Mathews was not attracted to Tinsley as a prospective son-in-law and persuaded at least one preacher not to marry the couple. They eloped and lived for a while with a kinsman of the groom. Dr. Mathews finally accepted his burden and turned over to them a small house in his backyard. He even helped Tinsley to buy Farmhill. The following statement in his will reveals that his financial resources were strained to keep the property in his son-in-law's possession: "I have already done more for Mrs. White than I am now able to do for my other children." [7]

When Mary White came to understand her father's objections to her marriage, she did not return to her parents, but took charge of the family's fluctuating fortunes and even tried to wean Tinsley from the bottle. Her efforts produced at least a spectacular show. In the first act Tinsley would march unexpectedly into the living room and proceed to toss and catch the delighted Corra and her sister Hope, their shrieks punctuating his bass laughter. With some difficulty Mrs. White would disengage the children and send them to bed. Then followed an interval in which Tinsley slept and the two girls waited eagerly for the second and final act. They would be summoned to the parlor, which was reserved for such occasions. Their mother marched in followed by a subdued, white-faced Tinsley. Mrs. White would order all to kneel while she prayed for the sinner until he wept and assured God and those present of his repentence. Also given to dramatics, Corra would add her wails to the uproar. When Mrs. White finally accepted Tinsley's pledge, he would immediately regain his superb self-confidence and wipe his eyes on a convenient window curtain. [8]

Gradually Corra became aware that the family was paying for their entertainment. Mary White would put the household on an austerity budget so that eggs and butter could be sold to stores and neighbors. In time Dr. Mathews would have to help again. [9]

Corra had decided, but different, feelings about her parents. She boasted that she had inherited her father's spirit. If her brain was dissected, she said, it would be found to contain his "beak-like nose." But her mother's courage and will were not lost upon her. In old age she would wonder if she had become the woman her mother would approve of. Perhaps she summed up best her feelings for her parents when she said that she believed everything her mother said, but preferred what her father said without believing it, "because it was nearer kin to my own thoughts, not yet said." [10]

Mrs. White took over the rearing and instructing of Corra—a duty Tinsley cheerfully relinquished. Unquestionably she helped to shape the girl's mind. She read and interpreted the Bible to Corra who learned to love its dramatic stories and stately rhetoric. She absorbed also something of her mother's steady, concrete faith and retained it throughout her life. No doubt she listened with less pleasure to Mary's long discourses on how the Mathews had never produced any women but "good" women, for at that time Corra considered herself anything but good. Sometimes the talks between mother and daughter were not so amicable. Corra was headstrong and given to tall tales, and Mary's sermons on lying might well be emphasized with a vigorous switching. Such punishment may have done little good, but it certainly did no harm. Corra was too healthy-minded to brood or suspect her mother of injustice.[11]

Even as a child Corra took pleasure in the physical world. She loved the bustle of Farmhill: the plowing, milking, cotton picking, especially the killing of hogs when the barnyard had turned white with the first frost. On winter afternoons she could lie content for hours before a blazing fireplace, waiting for the lighting of candles at dusk. She loved to feel warm and safe.[12]

Her inquisitive mind directed her to exciting adventures and, often, to subsequent punishment. She tried to fill up the Farmhill well, "set" a batch of eggs under her bed-covers, and sported a corset which she found uncomfortable and difficult to remove. Sometimes, when bored, she would frighten herself by wondering if a shooting star might not come through her window, or whether a cloud shaped like a polar bear might not suddenly start growling. She would beg the Negroes to tell her stories, but not the one about the pool of blood which never dried up on a nearby grave. She even developed a dislike for cemeteries and funerals. The hymn "Shall We Gather at the River?" was beautiful all right, but she wasn't ready to leave Farmhill yet.[13]

Her sister Hope, first regarded by Corra as "a pious fraud," later became a ready partner in mischief, and a tough opponent in a fight. Once when the two had been separated, punished, and told to kiss, Hope whispered in her ear "Come outside and we can finish it." But Corra liked to be alone at times. It was so pleasant to lie in the big front lawn and look up at the wide sky. Why, she was directly under its highest point! That meant she had been born in the exact center of the universe. Perhaps God intended her to be a very important person. It was a pleasant thought.[14]

These early speculations may have been the root of a purposefulness which developed steadily through the years of her uneven schooling. At an old Field School she shared a tree house with the other children, and later at the Elberton Female Academy, which she attended when Tinsley's pocketbook permitted, she played the ancient "wishing game" with the girls and admitted that she, too, was wishing for a handsome husband. But she apparently in-

dulged less and less in these common diversions. The principal of
the old Field School remembered her not only as a serious, obe-
dient student, but one who helped him keep the other children in
order. A classmate at the Female Academy recalled years later
that the girls considered Corra White a little "queer" because she
made no close friends and took no interest in clothes. Nor would
she join in students' pranks, although she was not above laughing
at them. At Sunday School Corra was one of only two girls who
could be persuaded to conduct the class. By her own admission she
had no childhood sweethearts.[15]

Seldom did her report card show a mark below "A." She took
especial pains with her writing. Professor A. J. Noyes of the
Female Academy praised her compositions, and an elderly kinsman always thought of her as a girl "writing at something."
Undoubtedly her most helpful teacher was Mary Heard, a well-
educated spinster who permitted Corra and Hope to attend tutor-
ing lessons she was giving a neighborhood girl. She encouraged
Corra to read good books but denied her claim in later life that
these books included Paley's *Moral Philosophy* and Hopkins' *Evidences of Christianity*. When an old lady, Miss Heard wrote
Corra, "I have only pleasant memories of you as a pupil," but she
regretted that her former student still did not show proper respect
for facts.[16]

At fifteen Corra White expected to take up school teaching
within a year or two. She would have to make her living; Tinsley's
habits and farming obviously were not going to improve, and
Mary White would be hard put to keep a roof over them and give
Hope and Albert, the youngest child, an education of sorts.
Teaching was about the only job open in those days for Southern
girls of respected families, and Corra seemed suited for her work.
She was well-read, communicative, and dependable, and, what
was equally important, she was large and fearless enough to keep
a class in hand. In fact, she was ready to take over at fifteen. Mrs.
White, however, had been thinking about the matter. Albert
Mathews, her younger brother, was principal of a school over in
Banks County, just north of Elbert. Why not send Corra over to
study under him for a year. It was arranged.[17]

Corra soon felt at home in the Old Salem Community. Uncle
Albert knew everyone and was proud to introduce his bright-faced
niece. She would arrive early at the frame school house and watch
the younger children appear, some walking, others on mules behind fathers or older brothers who would set them down and
return to farm work. The larger boys would scurry about getting

a fire started inside against the January cold, and others would bring drinking water from the nearby spring. As the Principal's niece Corra felt important. On Sundays she would go with him to the Old Salem Meeting House. Perhaps there Mathews introduced her to Lundy Harris, an Emory College friend living with his mother at Banksboro.[18]

Corra immediately became interested in the handsome, grave-eyed man. Of course he was older than she was—and she rather wished he did not have that beard—but he was kind, very intelligent, and *so* goodlooking. Undoubtedly she asked Uncle Albert questions about Mr. Harris. He did not tell her everything.[19]

Lundy Howard Harris came from two lines of clerical ancestors. Four generations on his father's side had produced Methodist circuit riders; the great-great-grandfather was said to have been ordained by John Wesley. Little else has been found about them. Wesley Harris, Lundy's grandfather, married a lame girl, and John, his father, was described as "a man of considerable culture for the times in which he was reared." A capacity for pity and a love of learning were traits that Lundy too would evidence throughout his life.[20]

Mary Parks, Lundy's mother, was also descended from Methodist clergymen. William Justice Parks, her grandfather, had given up Indian fighting to battle for the Lord. William, Jr., and Harwell, his brother, had heard and answered "the call." The Parks were men of unshaken faith and sound judgment. A preacher once said that the North Georgia Methodist Conference always needed the common sense of at least one Parks.[21]

Lundy Harris was born at McDonough, Georgia, in 1858, and grew up in the bare atmosphere of Methodist parsonages during the Civil War and Reconstruction. In those barren days a boy could easily believe his preacher father that a Christian must place his hopes on the world to come. John, the "cultured" father, must also have taken over his oldest son's education—there was little to be had elsewhere—for in 1872 Lundy entered Emory College at the age of fourteen.[22]

Lundy did well at the small Methodist college in the pines of Oxford, Georgia. But as a journalist of that day said, at Emory there "was nothing to disturb the peace of mind necessary to . . . temperate and harmonious development." Young Harris became proficient in Greek under the instruction of John M. Doggert, a man said to have "given consternation to the students by the new and thorough methods" he used in teaching that subject. Besides acquiring a love of Greek language and literature, Lundy obtained a sound general education, graduating with both the B.A. and the M.A. degree in 1876.[23]

But Lundy's peace of mind was disturbed at Emory—by religion. With Methodism in his blood, and living in the atmosphere of a church school, he could hardly have remained indifferent to the "revivals" that periodically stirred the campus. At one of those outbursts of faith, he followed his friend Warren Candler to the altar rail. His venture down the church aisle was undoubtedly prompted by the man appealing from the pulpit: Atticus Greene Haygood, President of Emory, and Lundy's mentor. Religion became a burning issue for Lundy. In an address at the Few Literary Society he described eloquently a painting of the Crucifixion hanging in an Italian church. Spectators, he said, could almost catch "the whispered 'it is finished' from those trembling, bruised lips." A classmate of Lundy's recalled that at times he would brood over the sin and indifference of the world. After graduation he stayed on first as Haygood's secretary and later as instructor in Emory's new Sub-Freshman Department. Although no longer a student he attended the President's lectures on "Evidences of Christianity." Haygood, according to his biographer, collected proof for his thesis "in an effort to convince himself of the truth he so eloquently taught others." He could, of course, have discussed his subject more frankly with Lundy who was, by 1879, living in the Haygood home.[24]

In April of 1882 Warren Candler, busy with pastoral duties at Sparta, Georgia, received a disturbing letter from R. J. Burden, a fellow student in Emory days. Burden came straight to the point.

Our good friend Lundy Harris is in trouble. He is in great trouble. I do not know whether you have heard it or not, but briefly he has overtaxed his strength by hard study which has precipitated neuralgia and doubtless other ailments of a nervous character which have superinduced the use of opiates, which have in turn suggested the use of stimulants. While in a state of semi-faintness from the former, he took an overdose of the latter and became intoxicated, very intoxicated.[25]

Burden went on to say that Harris had resigned from the church and offered his resignation to the faculty. What he did not say—perhaps did not know—was that Mrs. Haygood had administered the "overdose" of whiskey from the family medicine chest. What Lundy had done after the prescription took effect is not known.[26]

Candler tried to help his distraught friend, but Lundy's distress grew heavier. He appealed to Dr. W. W. Evans, his physician and

Haygood's brother-in-law, to say that he had suggested whiskey for the neuralgia. Evans declared he had no recollection of advising that medication. Then Haygood accepted Lundy's resignation and remained quiet about who had supplied the "medicine." Convinced that every man's hand was against him, Lundy left Oxford and refused Candler's offer of the principalship of the Sparta Academy. At one point he threatened to ship as purser on an ocean freighter. Reluctantly he allowed his Uncle Harwell Parks and Candler to dissuade him and finally accepted, later in the summer, a teaching position at the Sparta school. He disappeared from existing records until January of 1885 when Corra met him in Banks County.[27]

In her autobiography Mrs. Harris declared it was years later before she learned of Lundy's disgrace. Had she been told the story during those wonderful days at Salem, it would not have changed her feeling for him. She was in love. If Lundy had problems, she could help him solve them. Perhaps Lundy became aware of the girl's superb self-confidence. Troubled, indecisive men are often drawn to strong women.[28]

As the day drew near for Corra's return home, she and Lundy spent more time together, walking through the pine woods, arguing over books, discussing many things. The night before she left, Lundy told her they would be married when she was old enough. She agreed.[29]

Back in Elbert County she enrolled for a final term at the Female Academy and then taught in a country school. At times she became bored waiting for Lundy to declare her of an age for marrying. He wrote at intervals, and she amused herself by trying to imitate his lucid penmanship.[30]

In March of 1886 Harris made a solemn decision and then wrote Candler. He was going to enter the Methodist ministry. He explained that he had continued to lead "a moral life," but had finally realized he could only find spiritual peace "in preaching Christ." Mrs. Harris has left no account of when she received the news. It could hardly have startled her. Lundy's ancestors had served the family church for over a hundred years. He could be expected, sooner or later, to follow in their steady footprints.[31]

2

. . . . .
. . .
.

Circuit and Campus

MRS. HARRIS's honeymoon was a twenty-mile train ride from Elberton to Hart County where Lundy served the Redwine Circuit. Although she was known in her lifetime, and afterwards, as "the Circuit Rider's Wife" and her most famous book carried that title, little is known about her highly-publicized experience in backwoods Protestantism. As will be shown later, her novel cannot be taken as autobiography in spite of her claims.

The scenes and people she came to know there must, however, have resembled those in her story. Bascom Anthony, who rode another Georgia circuit, has left an account of his ministry very like the one Mrs. Harris gives of her fictional characters. Like Anthony and his wife, the two Harrises subsisted on his meager salary, suffered physical hardships, lived under the stern code of rural Georgia religion. Lundy, too, had distant churches to service —two in mountain districts—which could be reached only by buggy over rutted roads and through streams often swollen by winter rains. Corra went with him; each of his churches expected to see his wife on every trip. They must have spent many a night in a one-room cabin already crowded with parents and children. Their great social occasion was a "dinner-on-the-ground" where the preacher's wife was counted on to stuff herself with heavy food and praise those who provided it. The wife must never be absent from the women's meetings, or from church services, held twice on Sunday and one night during the week. It was a stern test for a seventeen-year-old bride reared in a home managed by a competent mother and enlivened by a tipsy, exuberant father.[1]

Mrs. Harris once boasted that she had always kept herself and Lundy presentable and well-fed, however small his salary. Her resourcefulness and stamina, inherited from her mother, received their first test on the Redwine Circuit. Her sense of humor, a gift from Tinsley, also stood her in good stead. She derived more

10

amusement than irritation from the carping of church stewards and the gossip their big-bosomed wives shared with her. Also, she was rebellious enough to take pleasure in the local sinners so roundly criticized by the self-appointed saints. She came to understand those rows of weather-beaten men and women who sat quietly in church, their eyes fixed pathetically on the pulpit, but who became shouting maniacs under the spell of an emotional sermon. This understanding would be put to use when she began to write her first stories.[2]

A bride learns a great deal about her husband during the first year of married life, and the Harrises' year on the Redwine Circuit was bound to have made Mrs. Harris aware she had married a complex man. Lundy was earnest about his profession and strangely determined to know God's will. He took minute pains with his sermons. When he finally hit upon a subject, he would ask Corra if she thought he could handle it. She soon learned she must not give her assurance readily, or he would decide she had not considered the question and would promptly tear up his paper. Sometimes he would open his Bible at random and take the text that met his eye as a command from God. Yet, as concerned as he was with religion, he had not forgotten his Emory classroom and his Greek books. Perhaps the illiterate atmosphere of the circuit prodded his memory of that life he had thrown away. As Mrs. Harris has pointed out, the dichotomy in his character was made evident in his desire to write two books: a Greek grammar and a life of Christ. She wondered if he could ever bring these two urges into harmony.[3]

In her autobiography Mrs. Harris reports, almost humorously, her first experience with Lundy's "loss of the witness of the spirit" during that first year. As she explains it, he "had stubbed his toe, spiritually speaking, against some little transgression" and doubted his fitness to conduct a forthcoming revival. After she had given him a common-sense lecture, he apparently regained "the witness," for he preached a most successful sermon that evening. She explained in *A Circuit Rider's Wife* that all Methodist preachers who were not hypocrites go through "those recurrent down-sittings before the Lord." Yet, a few years later another Methodist preacher tells how Lundy, during his early ministry was barely restrained from confessing publicly that he was unworthy of his calling and "almost spoiled everything by his abnormal self-consciousness." One remembers how freely Lundy had acknowledged his drunkenness at Oxford.[4]

As 1887 drew to a close Mrs. Harris put Lundy's religious

quandaries and her own churchly duties more and more out of her mind. Her first baby was coming due. In October she returned to Farmhill, and on Christmas Eve a daughter was born in the gentler surroundings of the mother's old room and attentive Negro servants. The child was named Faith. Even in those first days Faith showed promise of inheriting the aristocratic beauty of her father.[5]

Just before the baby came Lundy arrived from a meeting of the North Georgia Conference bringing good news. Next year he would be assigned to a church in Decatur where he would share the charge with Atticus Haygood, who had resigned the presidency of Emory. It is impossible to gauge Mrs. Harris's feelings about the Haygoods at that time. Whenever she did learn that Mrs. Haygood had given Lundy the unfortunate dose of whiskey, she became their implacable enemy. Lundy, on the contrary, forgave both Haygoods when he entered the ministry. But even if Mrs. Harris knew the full story in 1887, she would have welcomed their move. She was ambitious for Lundy, and in Decatur she could rear Faith with more comforts and necessities at hand.[6]

The year at Decatur must have passed without remarkable incidents, for Mrs. Harris does not mention it in her writings. If Lundy was plagued by neuralgia during that time, he must have let his wife prescribe instead of Mrs. Haygood. In 1888 Warren Candler, who had followed Haygood as Emory's president, offered Harris an adjunct professorship in Greek. There can be no doubt of his or his wife's reaction to this offer. A return to Emory would mean for Lundy that his escapade had been forgiven, and the Greek grammar might become a reality. Mrs. Harris was glad to separate him from too intimate a connection with religion. In addition she considered a professor a considerable cut above a minister. She would always have great respect for education.[7]

Lundy found that Emory and Oxford had changed little during his absence. Seany Hall, a monument to Haygood's persuasive ways with Yankee philanthropists, had replaced Old Main, but around it were grouped the same squat wooden buildings. Back in the pines the professors' white-framed houses looked a little more dingy. The atmosphere of the campus had remained rural. In the afternoons black-bearded professors passed the small library on their way to political discussions and checker-games at the Oxford grocery stores. The students clung to their country pleasures in and outside the classrooms. Desks carried the marks of their pocket knives, and floors of their tobacco juice. On the lawns outside squirrels still dodged whizzing rocks. The senior class "possum and 'tater' supper" remained a cherished tradition.[8]

The college was dedicated to solid, respectable Christianity and as much education as was possible. Even the more learned professors—such as Morgan Calloway in English, Mansfield Peed in mathematics, and J. M. Bonnell in natural science—were all good Methodists. In addition Calloway was an authentic Confederate veteran who had stopped a Yankee bullet. The faculty had its "characters," but even they performed within bounds. Julius Magrath, Professor of French, was a Polish Jew, but he had become a Methodist and frequently expressed a desire to convert his fellow Hebrews. In Greek H. A. Scomp had an equally worthy ambition: to drive strong drink from Georgia. With that in mind he had published a ponderous tome entitled *King Alcohol in the Realm of King Cotton*. At times young Henry Bradley of the science department came a little too close to unorthodoxy when his turn in the college pulpit came, but then Warren Candler would bring things back to normal the following Sunday.[9]

Candler dominated the scene with his eye on both faculty and students. His small, sturdy figure left legends in its wake. As the college annual put it, "the jay is the only individual in Oxford that Shorty does not rule." His discipline was, however, tempered by a mordant wit. When he appeared late for his chapel service one morning, the students shouted, "Cut, cut." Gravely climbing to the pulpit, Candler explained that he had been delayed by a search of the text, "Kish said to Saul, 'Go find the asses.'" "Like Saul," he said, "I have found them." [10]

Mrs. Harris once declared that she was "just a little feminine creature at Oxford rocking Faith's cradle." It was a description contrived to support a point she happened to be making.[11]

When Mrs. Harris reached Oxford, she immediately set about becoming a member of the community and college. She worked hard on the old Allen House which Lundy rented, arranging the furniture, painting the fences, planting flower and vegetable gardens. Fortunately she found it easy to make friends with Miss Net, Candler's level-headed wife. Soon the two ladies were exchanging home-grown vegetables and borrowing chairs from each other to seat the Ladies' Missionary Society. With Miss Net as a sponsor, Mrs. Harris was readily accepted. She did what a professor's wife was supposed to do. The meetings of the Ladies' Society must have bored her, but she did enjoy the eccentricities of its more ancient members. One elderly lady must be gently contradicted when she lamented that she was "a luke-warm Christian," and another demanded that a certain chair must be kept vacant when she could not be present. But the worst of them were more genteel and lively than the farmers' wives on the Redwine Circuit.[12]

She encouraged Lundy's students to call, fed them cookies, promised to intercede with her husband for the less studious. They crowded her Sunday School class where they giggled over her light interpretations of the Scriptures. She hoped none of them ever carried her Biblical criticisms to Warren Candler. Some of the local ladies disapproved of her popularity. Mrs. Harris was said to have kissed a new boy when he called. And she let students escort her to night services in the chapel, although she was not much older than some of them. Perhaps this gossip finally reached Mrs. Harris, for a few years later she wrote Mrs. Candler that she had decided to let no more boys in need of mothering "take refuge beneath the shelter of my kindness." [13]

On the whole she managed to respect the unwritten law that Emory was a man's world, but on one occasion she could not resist entering. Detecting a young professor's plagiarism in the college magazine, she aired her find to the student editor. Next she brought the matter to Candler, taking the precaution, however, to ask him not to tell Lundy. Candler willingly consented. He had an equal distaste for college scandal and meddling faculty wives. [14]

The nature of her boredom is evidenced in a prank she played one night in Lundy's absence. Putting on a pair of his trousers and blacking a moustache on her upper lip, she put a cigar in her mouth and strolled over to the home of Bishop Haygood who had retired in Oxford. As a concession to her sex she did not light the cigar. On opening the door Haygood was horrified at the sight of his visitor. [15]

Restless with so much spare time on hand, she began to do some writing. The pile of stories and articles in her desk began to grow. She found a home for only two of her manuscripts—two "nightmare stories." The Atlanta *Constitution* accepted "Darwinkle's Dream," and the New Orleans *Picayune* "Nicodemus Topinglow." Since she left no dates of their publication, they have not been located. In 1892 Thomas Nelson Page visited Oxford, and Mrs. Harris asked him to read one of her stories. He returned it with the comment that he had "read things not so good in magazines." Page was famous for his kindness. [16]

Mrs. Harris did not stay by Faith's cradle or, later, by her side, but she became and remained a devoted mother. The pink-and-white baby grew into a lovely child. Even then Mrs. Harris was awed by the girl's delicate beauty. She was delighted to learn that her slender daughter could hold her own in a stand-up fist fight with the neighborhood boys. Faith had a quick mind and—thank God—a common sense attitude towards religion. In Sunday

School she had calmly announced she had never had a religious experience, and she refused to read the church's children's magazine after her mother pronounced it nonsense. Faith was going to to be a wonderful woman—and yet she had inherited more from her father than his looks; she had an inquiring mind and sensitive feelings.[17]

Lundy kept busy and seemed reasonably happy. Everyone told Mrs. Harris what a wonderful teacher he was. The boys admired the way he corrected their blackboard exercises without referring to the textbook. They appreciated his interest in them; he would stop one on the campus, inquire about his reading and suggest additional books. He was the "fairest" professor on the campus, but he didn't take any nonsense. Once he thrashed a prominent alumnus' son for being "a general good-for-nothing." Students fulfilled their required chapel attendance by waiting for his turn in the pulpit. When he preached, they never exercised their privilege of scraping their feet if his sermon grew long. He was popular, too, with faculty and townspeople, but Mrs. Harris wished he wouldn't spend so much time with blind George Stone and youthful Henry Bradley. But he had never been impressed by important people. In a grocery store discussion he had taken Warren Candler to task for criticizing Rudyard Kipling's vulgar diction.[18]

Lundy spent a great deal of time also with Bishop Haygood. Haygood, broken in health and heavily in debt, had come back to Oxford for his last days. In January of 1895 he ordained Lundy a deacon. The old teacher and his favorite pupil spent many hours together. Unfortunately Lundy left no record of their conversations. Early in the next January a student brought a note to Lundy in his classroom and watched a look of "sudden terror" come over the professor's face. Haygood had suffered a stroke and was dying. On into the night Lundy sat by his bed until death came. As he described his vigil, "I stood by his couch and looked upon him as he drifted slowly away among the shadows." [19]

Religion was still heavy on Lundy's mind. A month before Haygood's death he wrote a Christmas article for the college magazine elevating his faith at the expense of his classical learning. "Christianity means hope," he declared, "while paganism . . . means, at bottom, despair." Was he arguing with himself? A student who heard him preach got that impression from his sermons.[20]

At the end of ten years the Harrises seemed content in Oxford. They had moved into the Scomp house which Lundy was buying with monthly payments. When Candler was made a bishop in

1898, Mrs. Harris in congratulating Mrs. Candler remarked that "we will stay under the green leaf shadow of village life, more sheltered than you will ever be again." There could, of course, have been resignation in her voice, but she did say, years later, that Oxford had been the "Eden" of her married life.[21]

Over the quiet years changes had taken place in the family circle. She had borne two sons. One died at birth, and two-year-old Lundy, Jr., did not have Faith's sturdy constitution. William Albinus (Al), Lundy's second brother, had married her sister Hope, bringing the two families even closer together. Al had maintained the family tradition by also entering the ministry. Brilliant, eccentric Henry, the third brother, had studied four years at Emory. He and his homespun friend Nathan Thompson had spent much time at Lundy's home, a sizable part of it at Lundy's table. After graduation the two had left to serve circuits in Texas.[22]

Just before the Harrises came to Oxford, Corra's mother had died. Her last days had not been spent in the house she struggled to save: Farmhill had been swept away in the tide of Tinsley's debts. After her death, he had married again over the objections of another father-in-law.[23]

Mrs. Harris would hardly have been displeased that Tinsley had found a second wife to look after him. She had enough responsibilities already: little Lundy's health, Faith's education, and Lundy's queer religious ideas. She could never be quite sure what was going on in his mind. As Emory Commencement drew near, she was glad to see the school year end. Lundy had worked too hard, taking over ailing Morgan Calloway's classes in addition to his own work and preparing an address for the Commencement exercises.[24]

College closed, the students disappeared, and Oxford grew quiet in the early summer heat. On June 7, 1898, Mrs. Harris returned from the village to find a note from Lundy. It has not been preserved, but a family friend remembered two sentences in it.

I have gone to Texas. There is a man there who has the spirit.[25]

3

· · · · ·
· ·
·

Pilgrim in a Barren Land

BY THE time Mrs. Harris had finished reading Lundy's note, frightening questions were crowding her mind. Had Lundy gone crazy? He might be headed for Texas . . . he might be headed by now in any one of a hundred directions. What was she to do? Almost no money in the house and bills owed all over Oxford. Would Scomp foreclose the mortgage if she could not pay the next installment? The news would soon be all over Oxford that Lundy had left her. It was cruel of him.[1]

She hurried over to Warren Candler's. She had to talk to somebody. Candler listened gravely and gave her two pieces of advice: she must lean heavily upon him and be careful what she said in her distraught condition. Still numbed by the shock she returned home, but by then her mind was working on her problem.[2]

During the next two days she tried to stay busy. She sold her treasured camera to Henry Bradley and settled some small bills with the money. Branham's Grocery Store agreed to wait for payment. She waited to see Scomp till she could decide whether it would be better to sell or keep the house. Next she wrote Lundy's two brothers. There was no reason why they should not help, especially Henry who had boarded free at their house most of the time he was at Emory. She reminded him of that fact in her letter. Al, now holding a pastorate at Rockmart seventy-five miles north of Oxford, might be able to advise her. He wasn't as visionary as Henry—or Lundy.[3]

Al wrote back immediately. She must come at once to Rockmart, he said, and bring the two children. Lundy had undoubtedly lost his mind, Al thought. Corra should get Warren Candler to advertise in the newspapers asking anyone who had seen her husband to get in touch with her. She began to pack. The silent house had become unbearable. Only three friends had called since Lundy had deserted her.[4]

17

Candler was out of town; so before leaving for Rockmart Mrs. Harris wrote him, probably to his new residence in Atlanta. Carefully she explained why she must locate Lundy: she could never rest easy till she found him, and if "something happened to him" she must know, so that she could collect his insurance. She had to be practical about such things for the sake of the children. While she was on that theme, she said that she was looking for work and hoped Candler might be able to help her there.[5]

On June 17 an unsigned card appeared in the Atlanta *Constitution* saying that Professor Lundy Harris had disappeared from Oxford and his family was appealing to the public for any information on his whereabouts. The announcement explained that it was feared "a long, hard term of work and the strain of commencement have all contributed . . . to his mental unbalancing." Even with this explanation the card must have made bitter reading for Mrs. Harris.

That same day brought the first news of the runaway. From Dripping Springs, Texas, Henry Harris wrote his sister-in-law that Lundy had just arrived there after walking twenty-five miles across the desert from Austin. On the way, "he broke down, possibly fainted . . . and saw sights he takes for revelations." After reporting Lundy's alarming experience, Henry calmly announced that his brother was leaving for Nathan Thompson's at Moore, a hundred miles from Dripping Springs. It is to be hoped that Henry arranged for some sort of transportation.[6]

Before leaving Dripping Springs Lundy wrote Candler. He said he would let Candler decide whether the letter should be showed to Corra; he had lost the right to communicate directly with his wife. Lundy explained that when he had lost his hold on God, he had decided to seek out Henry and Nathan Thompson who "know a great deal about God" and might be able to help him. His plans for the future were indefinite; he would probably come back to Georgia, but he could not say when. God was leading him along an unfamiliar road, but, he hastened to add, "I do not ask where it goes, so long as I can see Christ walking before me." In closing he sent an ominous message to "the holiest men and women" Candler knew.

Tell them I have given up all to follow him . . . he has shown me strange and terrible things and is showing them. Tell them to pray that my reason may not give way till I have come to a complete knowledge of his will.[7]

Candler forwarded Lundy's letter to Mrs. Harris and heard from her immediately. The tone of her reply vacillated back and forth between relief and bitterness. "I could sing," she wrote, "just to know he is alive." She wanted him home, but she would not allow him to suffer the humiliation of an arrest. She would not, however, go to him. Obviously hurt that he had taken his troubles to Henry and Nathan instead of to her, she declared she could no longer trust herself "to a man who . . . flies to the ends of the earth to consult two of the greatest cranks this country has ever produced." She respected Lundy's hunger for God, but she also had a religion and "it does not partake of the tramping, confessing order." Nothing, she assured Candler, could destroy her love for her husband, but she was not willing to bind herself and her children "to a wild-eyed scheme that must go out in the dark of some night and leave me alone." Moreover, she did not have the money—nor would she borrow the money—to go seeking a man who might that very day be begging bread at the backdoor of some Texas farmhouse. "Tell me what to do," she begged Candler.[8]

The following day she wrote again enclosing a letter from Henry which explained Lundy's "wild-eyed scheme." Whatever it was, Mrs. Harris wanted no part of it. She would be willing to join Lundy in Texas, but only after he had "time to rest from the burden of association." In the meantime, she said, "I think alone I can manage to pay what we owe and live besides." Again she begged Candler to help her find work.[9]

On either June 20 or 21, Lundy appeared at Nathan Thompson's front door. Thompson was startled. The face of his old professor was frightening. "Nath," he whispered, "the Devil has got me." Thompson put a comforting arm around him. "I've got you," he said.[10]

Henry Harris arrived close on his brother's heels. The three clergymen settled down to long theological discussions, and were waited on and fed by Nathan's young wife. Nathan and Henry did not find it easy to bring Lundy back into the fold. He had picked up a lot of queer notions—some of them almost "Romanish." Earnestly he begged them to read Thomas a Kempis's *Imitation of Christ*. It was a wonderful book. If they hadn't kept an eye on him he would have slipped off and fasted or done some other penance. Then there was something which Nathan referred to in his letters to Candler as "that Austin business." Lundy insisted he had to go back there and confess to the city authorities that he had broken some "civil law." Gradually, however, in the cheerful atmosphere of his two friends and at Mrs. Thompson's inviting table, he became calmer and "more reasonable." [11]

Meanwhile back in Georgia a group of more realistic clergymen was discussing Lundy Harris. Candler and Al Harris received Corra's consent to sending W. P. Lovejoy, a resourceful presiding elder, to bring Lundy back home. Lovejoy and Candler raised the money for the trip.[12]

When Lovejoy reached Thompson's, he found his mission a bit difficult. He reminded Lundy of his obligations to his wife, children, church; all to no effect. Lundy declared he had forfeited the right to see his wife . . . he was going to wait further on God's will . . . when he did go home he was going to work his way . . . he would be beholden to no man for charity. There was silence for a while. Suddenly Lundy turned to Nath. "Ought I to go?" he asked.

Nathan nodded. "It's time you started thinking about other people," he said. Lundy puzzled a moment as if that thought had not occurred to him. Then he gave in.[13]

In Rockmart Mrs. Harris had set herself to write a letter she must write to Candler before Lundy returned. She had learned what Lundy wanted to confess to the Austin authorities. Perhaps Al Harris had told her. In a letter to Candler two days earlier Al reported he "had tried to prepare Corrie for what she may possibly have to accept" when her husband appeared. Mrs. Harris had learned that this news had also reached Candler, and she was afraid it might already have affected his friendship for Lundy.[14]

Her letter gives no details of Lundy's misdemeanor but leaves no doubt of its nature. She begged Candler not to believe that her husband was "a deliberately unchaste man." He was innately virtuous in the manner of a woman. But, also like a woman, when he sinned he went "mad with sin." The nagging memory of his drunken spectacle at Oxford years ago had finally driven Lundy to "the Austin debauch," which, in turn, would haunt his future. She urged Candler not to desert his old friend. Society would probably cast her husband into "outer darkness," but she was "waiting for him with the same courteous respect, the same reverence, the same love that has carried me through the long years." [15]

Her next letter to Candler described Lundy's homecoming on June 25. When the knock sounded, she opened the door and held out her arms. He drew back. She must not touch him, he said, until she heard "the details of his crimes." Without answering she led him into the dining room and prepared tea. Completely at ease, he talked of Texas—its climate, architecture, and people. It was like listening to a man who had returned from an interesting vacation. When tea was finished, she suggested a walk. Not until they were some distance from Al's house did she say, "If you feel obliged to torture me with details, as you call them, I think I can listen; only it will just cause me needless pain. My way and heart are fixed."[16]

Lundy thought a minute and then said, "That relieves me from the necessity of telling you." As they took up their walk, he began his story with his departure from Austin.[17]

His description of the journey lost nothing in Mrs. Harris' retelling.

His tramp from Austin to Dripping Springs was the climax. He realized himself 'a tramp,' every tie was broken, his hold on God the slightest tenure. He began to shriek and cry as he went along to every living thing to pray God to save his soul. At last, as he staggered on, he came to the place where he could go no further. The sun seemed to burn through his brain. He lay down; a numbness came on his left side. Just before he thought he was about to die, a man came by in a wagon and took him up. Lundy told him his name, told him to notify Henry in case he should die.[18]

That night in the farmer's cabin he tossed, restless and feverish on the hard bed. Suddenly "a vision" emerged from the dark.

. . . two devils crawled up out of hell and looked at him and laughed horribly. . . . The vision changed. An endless procession of Christs passed by him in the shadowy gloom. He prayed that one might look at him, that he might know from the face whether or not he might hope, but as each image went by the face of Christ was slightly averted. . . . Then followed a long procession of sorrowful women. He looked for me among them. Had he seen me he would have concluded that my sorrow had killed me; in God's mercy he did not see it.[19]

When he paused in his narrative she was ready with a soothing explanation. The visions, she assured him, had no mystical or religious significance. He had undoubtedly suffered those same hallucinations during his "delirium tremens" at Oxford. Any physician would tell him that such images remained in the brain. The burning desert sun had revived them. Lundy seemed satisfied.[20]

That night as she lay in bed by his side, she heard him sit up and begin to mutter. Pretending sleep she waited. Lundy sank back in bed and moved closer to her. Still breathing regularly she put her arms around him. He gradually relaxed. In the morning he told her that the two devils had reappeared during the night, but when she took him in her arms, they had disappeared.[21]

It was just as well that Mrs. Harris shut off the details of Lundy's "crimes." Once started on a confession, he might have revealed that she had more to forgive than "the Austin debauch"; and she already had enough to bear and explain. At what time she learned the extent of his disgrace is uncertain. Certainly she knew of these additional "sins" before the fall of 1899, but a talk she had with Lundy at that time must be considered at this point.

In December 1898 frail Little Lundy died and was buried next to his brother in the old Oxford cemetery. The following October Mr. Harris visited the graves of his two sons. When he returned to Rockmart, Mrs. Harris went down to Atlanta for a short stay with Mrs. Candler. While there she heard the disquieting rumor that Lundy's recent journey to Oxford had been made to confess something that would ruin prominent ladies in the community.[22]

On returning home Mrs. Harris confronted Lundy with her news and later reported her findings to Mrs. Candler. Calmly, stroking her hair while he talked, he said "he had never thought a thought or done a deed that would reflect upon any white woman, married or single, in Oxford, Midway or Covington . . . there had been no white woman to confess about." Greatly relieved Mrs. Harris reported proudly to Mrs. Candler that Lundy had not been disturbed to hear the rumor. "He fears only the loss of God," she said.[23]

Harris had previously confessed to his wife, to Candler, and to several Methodist brothers that he had sinned with Negro women before his flight to Texas. At that time he made no mention of white women. When Mrs. Harris heard the rumor she feared he had not revealed the extent of his infidelity. Two days after their talk Lundy wrote to Candler confirming his confession and denying the rumor; he said he never wronged a white woman in Oxford, but "I have been intimate with certain Negro women." [24]

What seemed to trouble Harris more than his sins was the attitude of his friends towards them. His Methodist brothers had evidently thought that the race of the women involved lessened the gravity of his sins. "As I see it," he wrote Candler, "my conduct was as criminal before God as if a white woman had been it [sic]." [25]

Lundy Harris was beyond the comprehension of his devoted friends. Like them, he had grown up in rural Georgia, studied at Emory College and served the Methodist ministry, only to emerge as a strange, lonely figure in their common church and surroundings. His religious impulses, almost medieval in their intensity, were disturbed by modernistic doubts. His brilliant reputation as a teacher had been ended by his carnal sins committed while in search of God. Finally, and strangest of all, he had willingly confessed his sins and sought atonement through what Lovejoy described as "Romanish penance." Forced to explain a man they could not understand, his friends readily declared, among themselves, that Lundy was crazy. How else could they account for his outrageous conduct? Henry Harris thought overwork and the desert trek had aggravated his tendency to brood; Nathan, that the people back home had made him think "too much and too deeply." Al Harris probably spoke for the group when he said it was incredible that people could "be glad that our friend or kinsman were crazy, and yet I feel more and more the lifting of a load as my conviction deepens that he is insane." [26]

What Lundy's friends could not seem to grasp was that if he was mad, it was the madness of a soul who had lost God—a religious hungering rare in the modern world. His letter from Dripping Springs to Candler asked people to pray that he would find God before losing his mind. After returning to Rockmart he bravely faced the question of whether he had been insane and decided that if he had, then "my banishment from God drove me mad." Nowhere does he say that his carnal sins drove him insane or caused God to desert him. His doubts must have preceded his immoralities. [27]

Did Lundy's spiritual difficulties stem from a doubt of God's existence? It seems more likely that he lost faith in the divinity of Christ, and without this faith he saw God as an impersonal, even cruel, force in a hideous universe. As he told Candler, he would continue his search for God so long as he could see Christ leading the way. Whatever the psychological interpretation of his "vision," the line of Christs, with sorrowful, averted faces, is significant. A poem of Lundy's, written later during another troubled period, gives weight to this suggestion.

IN THE FAR FORGOTTEN LANDS

In the far forgotten lands,
By the world's last gulf of night,
Gasps a naked human soul
Writhing up and falling back,
Screaming for a God that cares.

In the far forgotten lands,
By the world's last gulf of night,
Bat-like creatures vex the gloom,
And whisper as they shudder by,
"Is there any God that cares"?

In the far forgotten lands,
By the world's last gulf of night,
Walks the cross-stained Nazarene,
Searching ever for his own,
On the crumbling edge of Hell.

In the far forgotten lands,
By the world's last gulf of night,
There he wanders all alone,
Dragging bleeding souls from hell,
With the whisper, "God does care." [28]

For Lundy's friends, the surest proof of his insanity was the admitted relationship with disreputable women. Al Harris was convinced that his brother was "crazy morally" but only suspected that he might be "mentally crazy." Lundy's conduct is indeed difficult to explain. Insanity is too facile an answer. A more convincing explanation seems to lie in statements he made during two discussions of his moral lapses. He told Candler that the confession of his Oxford sins was to "expose my spiritual difficulties in their most complicated and aggravated and heinous form," and on the train back from Texas he warned Lovejoy he would continue to obey God's will "even if what I might do should drag wife, children, friends and the whole church to the depths of shame." It appears that Lundy expected to travel the dark woods and then the Inferno so that disgrace and suffering would drive him to seek until he found God. C. G. Jung says that a man may feel that "indulgence in sin will teach him to know from what he needs to be saved." Jung explains that the sinner will suffer in the knowledge that he is sinning.

And yet he may feel that he has never been truer to his innermost nature and vocation, and hence never nearer to the Absolute because he alone and the Omniscient have actually seen the situation.[29]

In a report on Lundy to Candler, Nathan Thompson observed, "He's a funny fellow, ain't he?" Nathan's colleagues, in graver diction, came to the same conclusion.[30]

Determined from the first to defend Lundy and, if possible, to insure his future, Mrs. Harris could not so readily fall back upon the plea of insanity. The stigma, for her and him, would be as unbearable as his desertion. Before any news came from Texas she insisted to Candler that her husband was no more insane than he had been for the past twelve years. When she learned of "the Austin debauch," she faced the cruel choice of judging him either insane or deliberately unchaste. She insisted he was naturally virtuous, but at the same time she refrained from declaring him insane. In commenting on his religious "plans" she admitted that they might have their source in a diseased mind: "I believe they *have*," she said, "But I do not *know* it." [Italics hers.] After his return she intimated that physical ailments—exhaustion, fever, and a painful spine—had contributed to his mental state. If there had been insanity, it had been a temporary condition. "Lundy," she assured Candler, "is saner than he has ever been since I have known him." [31]

Pride and self-interest cannot account entirely for Mrs. Harris's hesitancy to declare her husband insane. She, alone, seemed to grasp the driving force of religion upon his life. Even before she could be certain that Lundy was in Texas, she declared that he "was seeking God with the same idea of repentance that drove the old monks into the desert." She knew also how little hold the world and people had on him. He was solitary by nature, she warned, and would always be listening for the voice of God calling him to follow.[32]

This clearer understanding of Lundy, gained through the tragic experience they shared, set her more firmly against his views and ways. His religion, his conduct, and his attitude towards his family, all went against the grain of her character and brought out sturdy traits already evident in her. The substance of her letters to Candler veers back and forth from unbreakable loyalty to her husband to frantic resentment at what he had done to her.

Lundy, she once declared, was superstitiously afraid of God, while she was not. Hers was "a sensible God," who did not demand that even sinners make spectacles of themselves. Always fearful that Faith, with her Harris beauty, might have inherited Lundy's brooding mind, she took care to instill in her daughter "the distant sky-blue God of my family." She would not, however, try to change Lundy's faith; it would be "like asking him to give up his hope of heaven." She could only hope to keep it within reasonable bounds.[33]

Mrs. Harris might acknowledge that Lundy had left her to seek God, and attribute his "Austin debauch" to remorse for past sins, but she made no secret of the humiliation she felt he had brought upon her and their family. His desertion would cause people to look upon her as "a woman of shame instead of a respectable wife." Bitterly she pictured him begging for food at the back-door of some Texas farm house, and her relief that he had not ruined "some prominent Oxford family" was apparently stronger than her concern over his having ruined lesser women in that community. Lundy's letter to Candler admitting his Oxford infidelities reveals his complete indifference to social distinctions. The Harris family, Mrs. Harris pointed out later to Faith, lacked badly the wisdom "to make strong, effective friends"—a wisdom, she went on to say, "in which I have always been particularly flush." When Lundy began to appear more normal in the quiet of Rockmart, Mrs. Harris took on the additional worry of whether he had closed all doors to their few influential friends.[34]

Even if Lundy found work, however, Mrs. Harris would continue to be haunted by the fear that he might lose, any day, the "tenuous grip" he held upon God. Already he was tramping the streets of Rockmart "like an Eastern hermit, a stranger upon earth, expecting . . . to hear the voice of God calling him to the East or West." Any day she might find a note awaiting her at Al's. And then, that more horrible thought: suppose the voice did not come? She might find him "dead and bloody by his own hand. . . ." Bravely she faced the prospect of never knowing peace again.[35]

She was resolved that whichever of the tragedies fell, she would be better prepared than she had been back in Oxford. First of all, she must find work. She could not continue to live on Al's charity. So far her frantic efforts for employment had produced nothing. The railroads did not train women in telegraphy. There were teaching opportunities, but Lundy must be given the first chance at them. She had given up the possibility of taking boarders in her Oxford house; the people there might not want her back. Her first thought had been that Clark Howell of the Atlanta *Constitution* might give her a position. His refusal had discouraged any further attempts in that field. She continued to ask Candler's advice and help.[36]

As anxious as she was for work, she could not give much time to the search. She had taken over complete management of the family. The Oxford home must be sold, and Faith prepared to live with Mary, Lundy's young sister, in Cuthbert. Above all, she must direct her husband's life. "He needs a strong hand to guide him," she wrote Candler. She feared she was not equal to her many responsibilities, but she set about assuming them.[37]

4

. . . . .
. . .
.

The Strange Ways of Providence

BY THE spring of 1899 Mrs. Harris was living under less pressure. She had, at least, taken her family off Al Harris's charity and established it in a routine of sorts. Lundy was teaching at Rockmart Institute, and she at a country school. They had rooms in the Institute's dormitory. Faith was still living with Mary, Lundy's young sister, at Cuthbert, attending the school where her aunt taught. Things were better, but Mrs. Harris knew she was only keeping her problems at arm's length.

For the present she could feel easy about Faith. Thank goodness Mary had taken the child out of their troubled household. She had absorbed all that happened, saying little, but with her face quiet and sad like the face of an older person. Well, she did not propose for Faith's life to be ruined. Her daughter was going to a good college some day where she could be with nice girls. But where the money was coming from only the Lord knew. She was making thirty dollars a month, and Lundy forty—when the Institute could find that much.

She had almost lost her mind while Lundy was out of work. He had been desperate to find a job and had kept repeating that he must support his family like any decent man. But he would not ask anyone respectable to hire him. He thought of becoming a farm hand, a store clerk, an army nurse, a sailor. He had been fortunate to get the place at the Institute, and he would not have gotten that if Warren Candler had not helped him without letting him know. Principal Kelley had preferred Corra for the position, but she knew Lundy would be shamed at the thought of her earning his bread.[1]

Lundy was doing a good job at the Institute; but the people of Rockmart were uneasy about his teaching their children. Rumors began to reach Mrs. Harris. Lundy was said to have talked wildly while visiting a sick pupil. One day a boy had hooted at him on the street, the same way the children in Oxford used to hoot at "Whiskers" Smith. And Lundy was doing nothing to help the situation. He would not associate with anyone except poor or unfortunate people. Silently he walked the streets "like a stranger on the earth." Often Mrs. Harris returned to her room expecting another note saying that he had "heard the voice of God calling him to the East or West." If that happened she would be no better prepared for what would follow than she had been at Oxford. A Rockmart girl watched Mrs. Harris crying at her dormitory window one afternoon.[2]

In her autobiography Mrs. Harris tells how one morning in early April of 1899 she followed Lundy into the Rockmart church where he prayed daily. Hiding in a back pew until he left she then offered a prayer of her own. She prayed in an Old Testament temper asking God "to confound our enemies and send us friends and help." It was the same tone Tinsley used in talking with the Lord.[3]

Things began to happen. On April 12, fifty miles south of Rockmart, a Negro named Sam Horse brained Alfred Crandall, a white farmer, with an axe and, according to Mrs. Crandall, raped her by the side of her dead husband. On Sunday, April 23, a mob dragged Horse from jail, emasculated him, and burned him alive. The Northern press poured denunciations upon the lynchers. The New York *Independent,* a liberal, crusading magazine, used articles by a Northern and a Southern clergyman, besides a scathing editorial by Editor William Ward, to express its indignation.[4]

A day or so later Hamilton Holt, associate editor of the *Independent,* burst into Dr. Ward's office. A Georgia woman, he said, had written in a wonderful attack on their lynching pieces. Oh, yes, a rabid Southern viewpoint, but the woman could write. Ward began to read. "The Negro is the mongrel of civilization; he has married its vices and is incapable of imitating its virtues." *That* would set the teeth of the magazine's readers on edge. The prose stayed clear and solid down to the end. "Will you men of the North who mold the sentiments of your people, place your sympathies wholly on the side of these beasts, passing without a word over their crimes to a bitter denunciation of our avengers?" Dr. Ward nodded as he passed the letter back to Holt. They must get it into the next issue.[5]

When Mrs. Harris opened her *Independent* of May 18, there it was: "A Southern Woman's Viewpoint," signed, Mrs. L. H. Harris, Rockmart, Ga. Her joy was heightened, not dampened, by the editor's comment, "We believe that Mrs. Harris's statements are the result of local excitement." Obviously the *Independent* expected her article to stir resentment; she had read the magazine enough to know it welcomed controversy. A bright straight road seemed to have opened suddenly before her. It looked even brighter a few days later when Dr. Ward wrote asking to see more of her writing. "The Lord," she decided, "certainly does know how to answer prayer." [6]

She obliged Dr. Ward immediately with an article on "Negro Womanhood." In it she sought to discourage social workers seeking to improve the race. Religion and education, she declared, could do little to improve the Negro woman. Reared in an atmosphere of promiscuity, usually raped by father or brothers before reaching puberty, she grew up expecting no pleasure but sexual relations. It was strong stuff, even for the *Independent,* and its editor explained to his readers he was running it "not because of its intrinsic value, but for the view it gives of the white men and women it represents." A heated response from readers prompted the editor to announce in the following issue that he "could not begin to print the admirable letters that came to us in indignant reply to Mrs. Harris's impeachment of Negro womanhood." [7]

Mrs. Harris was as pleased as the editor with the number of tempers she had ruffled. But one of the letters forwarded gave her pause. The anonymous writer—a Negro, she decided—wanted to know how a white woman came to know so much about the sexual habits of Negro men. She asked herself if Dr. Ward and Holt could be wondering too. Immediately she asked Candler—her ever-present help in trouble—to write Holt that she was a respectable married lady. Shortly afterwards, she received a letter from Holt, assuring her of his respect. He added that he was going to pay for anything else of hers that he published. [8]

In spite of this welcomed prospect, she could not get "The Negro Child" to Holt until October. Back came a ten-dollar cheque, which she proudly recorded in a notebook. With the publication of this third article she may have considered that the Negro's depravity had been fully established; at any rate, she began a series on the Southern whites. In the first two articles she made a thoughtful analysis of the basic differences between Southerners of each sex, and their Northern counterparts. [9]

Several interesting subjects caught her attention after December of 1899, at which time Professor Harris accepted a position at Young Harris College in the Georgia mountains. During her year there she came to understand and admire the rugged, slow-speaking natives. Three of the clearest character sketches she would ever do are found in "The Poor Man in the Mountains," "Country Doctor in the South," and "The Circuit Rider in the South." [10]

A larger opportunity on the *Independent* presented itself in December of 1900, and she moved quickly. When Maurice Thompson, its literary editor, retired because of health, she offered to do some book reviews until his successor could be found. Holt tested her with *An English Woman's Love Letters,* an anonymous work which was stirring a minor controversy. He never regretted his decision. In her review Mrs. Harris maintained a balanced judgment. She grew lyrical over the author's style but indignant over her frank revelations. Primly Mrs. Harris warned that the *Letters* were indecent enough to challenge Rousseau's *Confessions.* Holt claimed the *Independent* never received so many compliments on a review.[11]

During her ten years on the magazine Mrs. Harris never lacked assignments. Her problem became the time necessary to do them. Holt estimated she did twelve hundred book reviews for the *Independent.* She became also a valued source for editorials, short stories, and surveys of fiction. The editors pressed her hard: "Can stand 10 editorials . . . as fast as you can write them"; "the theme for the short story is good"; "I am printing your stuff as fast as I can." Somehow she managed to meet deadlines, while running a house, keeping an eye on Lundy, writing long letters to Faith. Once she declared she was "the tiredest person" on earth, but her only complaints to the *Independent* editors were for cutting her articles or delaying their publication. She warned one that if he kept holding her reviews to four hundred lines, he was going to hear from her. Or as she put it, he could relegate her "to the peanut gallery" but she would never "sit quietly there." [12]

A conservative, moralistic viewpoint colored her literary criticism. Writers of the realistic school affronted her like a personal insult. She declared that they taught "the futility of life with a zeal that is diabolical" and possessed minds that resembled "bits of 'pisen' fly-paper laid out to catch strictly modern ideas." This antagonism was genuine and not adopted to produce controversies for the *Independent.* Her inheritance and upbringing had made too much impression for her to accept alien ideas, however popular.[13]

This decided bent of Mrs. Harris's mind made it difficult for her to judge a book impersonally, and her exuberant nature tempted her, at times, into an extravagant style. But when she came to grips with a book, she could always find something intelligent or at least interesting to say. In reviewing *The God of His*

Fathers, she declared that Jack London "gathers up every situation in his fists, squeezes the blood out of it on the snow, scatters the bones of his heroes, and goes on to the next tragedy." She was perceptive enough to recognize in *Bismarck's Love Letters* that the Iron Chancellor prized highly his wife's "innocent nature." Even when Mrs. Harris indulged in rhetorical flourishes she could still make a point, as when she decided that "William Dean Howells . . . can no more interpret the mob mind of America than he can get drunk and paint the town red." [14]

Modern fiction, according to Mrs. Harris, was in an unhealthy state. Its symptoms were the "fungus characters" and "diseased romances" which portrayed "sentimental vice" and identified "the soul with the stomach." The cure she prescribed was a return to the older themes of "mother, home and heaven," and a shift in setting from the corrupt cities to the wholesome countryside. She insisted that neither in fiction nor in life did anyone have "a right to commit adultery, even if everything Darwin says is true." If novelists could not be shamed into reforming, then they should be made to qualify for an author's license attesting to their decent imagination and moral responsibility. It is hardly surprising that Mrs. Harris came to rank Will Harbin and F. Hopkinson Smith above Jack London and Henry James. [15]

Such reviews and articles embroiled her with well-established writers, but she met them head on. Her criticism might be fallible, but there was nothing wrong with her courage. Thomas Dixon, author of such robust fiction as *The Clansmen* and *The Leopard's Spots,* called in person to see if he could charm her into taking a more charitable attitude toward his novels. When she failed to respond, he grew irritated and remarked how closely Mrs. Harris resembled Jeanette Gilder, a fellow-critic more celebrated for brains than for beauty. Mrs. Harris bided her time. When goodbyes were being said, she told Mr. Dixon he did not look at all like the man she had imagined from reading his fiction. She had expected him to have a masculine head and fanatical face; certainly not "a woman's head and a pretty, effeminate face." Mr. Dixon could certainly conclude that his visit had not won him a friend. [16]

Mrs. Harris found Jack London harder to handle. Deciding that an article by "the hobo novelist," as she called him, reflected upon her moral character, she wrote demanding that he sign a typed apology, which she enclosed. Unfortunately his article, her letter, and the proposed apology have not been preserved, but London's reply throws light on the altercation. With mock distress he insisted she had read outrageous meanings into his innocent article; he feared she, and not he, had been "guilty of obscenity." He asked permission to keep her letter as a sad reminder that women are more evil-minded than men. In closing he begged her not "to sweat over respectability . . . it is so bourgeois." Later Mrs. Harris met London at a New York party, but did not re-open the discussion.[17]

Social reformers also irked Mrs. Harris, especially those like Upton Sinclair, who used the South to make unfavorable comparisons. She reserved some choice epithets for Sinclair: he was a "fly-blown genius," "a buzzard novelist," "the grandson of abolition prejudices." In 1907 he tried to appease and enlighten her with an invitation to Helicon Hall, his social project for rehabilitating the unfortunate. She repaid his hospitality by an article in the *Independent* which announced that Mr. Sinclair's charitable hostelry "sheltered more ungrateful guests and ignoble spies than any other home in New Jersey." The host could, but did not, point out that she had qualified for both categories. Two years later, however, she goaded him beyond endurance. In reviewing Sinclair's *The Advance of Civilization* she stated as fact a rumor that he had served as a butler in a rich man's house to collect damning material for this book. Sinclair published a heated denial, called her—not very originally—"a buzzard critic," and suggested she be starved in a garret until she developed humanitarian feelings. To Mrs. Harris's disgust, Holt decided not to publish either of her sarcastic "apologies."[18]

In debate her tactics were to attack with bold invective an opponent's position, and, if necessary to bolster her contrary views with sentimental truisms. She brushed aside Charles B. Loomis and John Kendricks Bangs, two popular writers, by labelling their respective outputs as "nickel-in-the-slot" literature and "potted fiction." In a staged controversy on the American home she charged that Charlotte Perkins Gilman, a formidable feminist, was advocating marriage only as an orderly expedient for human breeding. Ida Husted Harper hesitated to argue woman's suffrage with Mrs. Harris contending that when one's opponent keeps saying "Home, Children and Motherhood" there was really no "use of the other side saying anything."[19]

She enjoyed it all immensely. Not only was she meeting famous people on equal terms, but she was seeing something of the country—at the *Independent's* expense. In 1904 the magazine sent her to St. Louis to do a series of articles on the World's Fair. On trips to New York she met the editors she had come to know so intimately through correspondence. Holt insisted she stay at "Number 3, Fifth Avenue," a hotel which attracted such radicals as Gorky, the Russian novelist, and his wife. The atmosphere there she found quite different from Dr. Ward's old-fashioned home in which he and his two sisters still held family prayer. It was there that small Faith, encouraged to ask a blessing before her Yankee hosts, responded with, "He prepareth a table before me in the presence of mine enemies." [20]

She loved both Ward and Holt, wrote them chatty letters, and prized the autographed pictures wheedled from them. Her relations with Ward became those of an unpredictable daughter and an indulgent, amused father. Holt's cheerful faith and interest, both in her and her work, made it easy for her to live with his unquenchable liberalism. The one flaw in her connection with the *Independent* was Literary Editor Edwin E. Slosson. When he joined the magazine in 1903 he made it evident immediately that she would be doing business with a meticulous, impersonal executive. If that was not shock enough, after Ward's and Holt's easy ways, Mrs. Harris must also suffer Mrs. Slosson, a feminist addicted to journalism and "a female Ph D!" The advent of that lady was, she decided, like "turning a literary anaconda into the office." Inevitably the two clashed. When Mrs. Slosson wrote an *Independent* editorial labelling Confederate veterans "tainted heroes," Mrs. Harris sent word, via Mr. Slosson, that she was proud to be descended from two generations of such heroes. Soon she was complaining to Holt that Slosson was deliberately holding up her book reviews. When Slosson rebuked her for "back-biting one editor to another," she retorted, rather weakly, that he was "mighty self-righteous to take over something that was God's business." In time she disciplined herself to work with him and even to consider him human. There is no evidence, however, that she and Mrs. Slosson ever became intimate.[21]

Mrs. Harris respected Ward and Holt, but she revered Paul Elmer More, Maurice Thompson's successor. She had never known anyone like him, and certainly not anyone more unlike herself. More was a scholarly recluse, concerned with such bygone matters as Manichaeanism, Hindu epigrams, and the Greek Church Fathers. It was perhaps this very difference in their temperaments and interests that brought them into an unlikely friendship and, later, into an even more unlikely literary collaboration.[22]

When More wrote introducing himself, she promptly acquainted him not only with herself but with her family and literary peculiarities. She wanted to know more about him. What did he look like? Was he hard to get along with? What were his literary standards? It was the first of many long, intimate letters he would receive. Mrs. Harris kept him posted on the doings of the Harris family: Lundy had been grouchy because breakfast was late; Faith had turned a somersault from a high haystack; a boring preacher had called expecting to get another free meal. In turn she wanted news about More's "women folks" and the baby girl he must be so proud of. But especially she wanted his picture to hang beside those of Ward and Holt. In his replies More seemed more inclined to discuss pseudo-Celticism and the structure of the modern novel, but he continued to write.[23]

He became her literary oracle. When he disapproved of a book, she declared she could "no longer stay in the same room with it." As much as she hated to revise her writing, she begged him to criticize everything she sent him. If he happened to mention an author, she would scurry to get hold of his works. At times, however, she let More know she had opinions of her own. While continuing to admire his chaste style she warned him she was about to describe a novel as "a graceful, pretty story in pink tights that kicked its pretty heels at the reader." Nor did she propose to accept entirely his harsh evaluation of Frank Norris's *The Octopus.*[24]

In 1902 More revealed that he had not found their correspondence distasteful. He suggested they do a novel of letters which would reveal the intellectual viewpoints of their respective sections. He would be a Northern newspaper editor, and she a Southern girl who had written a critical letter to his paper. The love element, he added, would be underplayed. Mrs. Harris thought it a splendid idea.[25]

Mrs. Harris's letters to More during the writing of the book are more entertaining than those she contributed to it. At one point she complained of the difficult position More had put her in. It was embarrassing to ask a married man questions about love, but what else could she do when he wouldn't make himself clear? She was going to put the questions bluntly. Did Phillip Towers, the hero, chase Jessica Doane, the heroine, around the dining-room table or "tote her off to the woods"? Also, what was Jessica wearing on her feet the night Phillip called up to her bedroom for her to come for a walk in the woods? It was a point, she said, that needed some thought. Country girls didn't own bedroom slippers, and if More wanted Jessica in shoes and stockings, then Mrs. Harris would have to describe the putting on of those articles, a detail she considered rather intimate. On the other hand, if nothing was said about Jessica's shoes and stockings, the reader would assume she went barefooted to the woods. Mrs. Harris served notice on her collaborator that she didn't propose to write anything she wouldn't want Faith to read.[26]

These delicate questions were finally resolved, and "The Jessica Letters" appeared anonymously in *The Critic* during the fall and winter of 1903, and in book form, with the authors' names, the following spring. It was at best an uneven collaboration. Jessica's sprightly observations keep the narrative alive while Phillip is discoursing on the wisdom of Thomas à Kempis and the iniquities of Jane Addams's Hull House. Phillip's one concession was to carry a volume of Catullus's poems on an afternoon walk with Jessica. Even Lundy, while reading the manuscript, muttered, "Any fool could see he isn't in love with her." Paradoxically, the characters do not express the prevalent economic and social views of their sections. Phillip's attacks on social humanitarianism would have found no favor with Northern intellectuals, and Jessica's defense of this trend would not have been echoed in the South. In reality More and Mrs. Harris saw eye to eye on such questions.[27]

Mrs. Harris's pride in her first book surmounted a malicious hint by Slosson in his *Independent* review of the *Letters*. After polite praise he slyly expressed some doubt that "the passions and tenderness in some of the letters are fictitious." Mrs. Harris pretended to believe that Slosson was praising the romance for being so convincing, and thanked him kindly.[28]

Slosson's insinuation was off the mark. Mrs. Harris did admire More, but her admiration was nothing more than another example of the friendly, personal relationship she always sought with editors. She could do her best work only under that condition, and she was aware of the practical value of these friendships. When More left the *Independent* for the New York *Post* in late 1903, she appeared brokenhearted, but her grief was not so great that she forgot to ask him for free-lance work on his newspaper.[29]

From 1899 to 1909 Mrs. Harris would consider herself a member of the *Independent* "family." The magazine would continue during that decade to be the main source of her slowly-increasing income, and the medium in which most of her writing was published. Towards the end of that period her name would appear more and more in the *Critic, American,* and, finally, the *Saturday Evening Post;* but she would never find elsewhere the excitement and satisfaction she had known in the small, dingy offices on Fulton Street when Ward, Holt, and More had supervised her literary apprenticeship.

5

· · · · ·
· · ·
·

Lending Providence a Hand

CORRA HARRIS was an incorrigible optimist. When problems came
—as they would throughout her life—she put complete confidence
in the solutions she devised. She once wrote Faith that "to believe
in the future with invincible courage is to believe in God." It was
fortunate that she could believe this.[1]

Since Lundy's return from Texas, she had never considered him
completely normal. For several years after leaving Rockmart he
had kept himself rather well in hand. In 1900 the family moved to
Young Harris, where, through Candler's help, Lundy had secured
a teaching position at the Methodist college there. It was not long
before rumors began to spread that Dr. Harris was not behaving
well. Perhaps they were prompted by stories that had drifted in
from Oxford, but Mrs. Harris decided to move from the dormitory to the local hotel. It was discouraging, after the good things
she had been hearing about his teaching and Sunday night sermons. Dr. Sharp, president of Young Harris College, seemed nervous about having his old Emory professor on the faculty. Perhaps
the worsening situation reconciled Mrs. Harris to Lundy's return
to the ministry at the end of the year. She never cared for Dr.
Sharp after their stay at Young Harris.[2]

Mr. Harris first served as supply preacher for the small town of
Groveton, near Augusta, and next for a church at College Park,
an Atlanta suburb. Although Mrs. Harris later satirized College
Park in *A Circuit Rider's Wife*, she and Lundy enjoyed his kind,
rather worldly congregation. But supply pastorates offer short-
term security. In 1902 Mrs. Harris took charge of the situation,
ingratiated herself with Methodist leaders, and Lundy was appointed assistant secretary of the church's Board of Education in
Nashville, Tennessee.[3]

For several years the move seemed a reasonably happy one.
John D. Hammond, secretary of the Board, valued Lundy's

knowledge of educational matters and gave him regular raises. The Harrises entered the social and intellectual life of Vanderbilt University, although Lundy, to his wife's annoyance, always sought out the most unimportant guests at parties. He was stubborn, too, about Mrs. Harris's efforts to interest the *Independent* in his literary ability. At her instigation, he did a few book reviews, but refused to take advantage of her friendship with Holt and Ward. He seemed, however, content enough with life in Nashville, preaching occasionally at some small churches, reading his Greek books, and fitting up a rather expensive study in their attractive little house.[4]

Some time in 1907, however, Mrs. Harris saw danger signals. Lundy began to brood and to drink surreptitiously. She placed the blame for his returning melancholia upon Bishop E. E. Hoss, who, she said, bullied Lundy unmercifully at the Board. From all accounts, Hoss did enjoy having his own way, but Mrs. Harris had become prone to hold the Methodist clergy responsible for Lundy's lapses: Haygood for giving him whiskey when he broke down in 1884; Candler for retarding his recovery in 1898 by blocking a student petition that he be re-hired on the Emory faculty; and James Sharp for his hostility while they were at Young Harris. Hoss probably deserved, more than the rest, the role of whipping boy.[5]

In January 1908 Mrs. Harris persuaded her husband to get leave from the Board and visit his brother Henry in Deland, Florida. Lundy's letters home must have disturbed her. He lost his overcoat and ring—fortunately recovering both. He and Henry set out for the coast on a walk through thirty miles of swamps alive with snakes and alligators. In his account of the trip he told proudly how he had dispersed a herd of wild cows by singing "Annie Laurie" at the top of his voice. The tone of his letters swung back and forth between exuberance and gloom. After describing Henry's eccentricities he concluded that "every male Harris ought to be strangled at birth." The Florida jungle, he wrote, was a thing of beauty, but "the trees mimic death rather than life." Mrs. Harris was probably relieved to get him back under her eye.[6]

Her abiding fear that Lundy would eventually attempt suicide was justified. Among the Harris Papers is an undated note of his saying that he was about to take a large quantity of morphine he had gradually collected. He may have attempted or threatened suicide several times. In 1931 Charles Dobbins of Columbia University stated in his master's thesis on Corra Harris that her husband tried six times to take his life. Mrs. Harris made Dobbins cut out this passage before he published the thesis as a newspaper serial.[7]

It is certain, however, that Harris almost killed himself shortly after his return from Florida in 1908, not by morphine but by a self-inflicted wound. A little over a year after Dobbins's serial appeared Mrs. Harris admitted in a newspaper article that while they lived in Nashville, Lundy had decided "to put out his light and go forward with awful courage into the dark." In a letter to a friend, written just before her article was published, she was more explicit about the tragedy. Her husband, she said, had "twice stabbed himself in the neck aiming to cut the jugular vein and nearly hemorrhaged to death." Another note of Lundy's sets the date of this attempt as March 2, 1908. He explained in it that he was "taking his life because he could not overcome the drink habit." He went on to praise Mrs. Harris as "the best of wives" and to ask that she give Little Lundy his love, "if you meet him in another world." After a long stay in the hospital and several weeks at home, Harris returned to work apparently in good spirits. But in her long vigil by his bed Mrs. Harris must have recalled, more than once, her warning to Candler that one day she might find her husband "dead and bloody by his own hands." How close she had come to prophecy! [8]

Mrs. Harris must have tried to keep the reason for Lundy's confinement a secret. It is impossible to say how well she succeeded. Faith was away at school, and their correspondence during the spring of 1908 contains no mention of the sad affair. Certainly after Lundy's recovery Mrs. Harris maintained a brave front. In a letter to Faith the following March she declared that the past year had been the happiest of her married life, and in one to Candler, a month later, she said that Lundy had found God again. Obviously she had not given up the struggle.[9]

If Mrs. Harris had been asked about her daughter in 1909 she would have replied spontaneously that Faith could not be a greater joy to her. Everything about the girl seemed radiant with life—her mind, body, and especially her lovely face. She had done well in every school she attended: at Young Harris, where she had joined her parents, at Cox College in LaGrange, and now at the Woman's College in Baltimore. To her mother's pride she had become editor of *Kalends,* the Woman's College monthly publication, and had developed a haughty little style of her own. Mrs. Harris had been promoting her to Holt, sending him samples of Faith's journalism, suggesting that the daughter, not the mother, make a tour of female colleges for a series of articles which he wanted. Faith, she would have said, was not only going to be a wonderful woman, she might well become a successful writer, even more successful than her mother.[10]

Behind all Faith's charm and accomplishments, Mrs. Harris saw a danger: Faith was Lundy's daughter. She had the same aristocratic good looks, the same precise, honest way of thinking. But she had inherited other traits from her father which troubled Mrs. Harris. The child was outspoken, sensitive, and painstaking with everything she did. When a sorority sister explained that she had prayed over a decision, Faith commented "Your God tells you some strange things." She meticulously apologized to a dean for what he *thought* a *Kalends* editorial meant—not for what it really meant. The strain of school was becoming evident in her face and in her letters. Deeply worried, Mrs. Harris suggested that she spend her vacation at a rest sanitarium. Faith became almost hysterical at the idea, and declared she would "go raving crazy" there. Her mother said no more on the subject, but continued to worry.[11]

Mrs. Harris was strangely drawn to the daughter so unlike her in appearance and temperament. As she put it, "There is an element of manly coarseness in me; she is just fine and feminine with pretty, thin young wings." A protective feeling for Faith seemed to grow with the years. Once she explained this feeling to a friend.

Did you ever notice how young people are sometimes happy without cause? Well, to me it is the most anguishing spectacle when it comes to my own child. I am afraid the illusion will pass, that she will find out what a terrible, exacting cruel thing life is for most of us.[12]

She decided that Faith was too frail for marriage. Experience and observation had convinced her that the adventure exacted considerable endurance. Picturing her own grandchildren she felt a surge of abhorrence: they seemed to "stand and threaten Faith." So far the daughter had apparently not resented this interference. She had made no protest when her mother insisted she was not strong enough even to consider marrying a young man in 1908. In fact, as Mrs. Harris grew more protective, Faith became more dependent upon her. In a letter from college she wrote that hearing from her mother was a "blessing" that brought their hearts closer together.[13]

Physically Mrs. Harris was probably in poorer health than Faith at this time. Worrying over family problems, writing far into the nights, and resuming work at daylight, she was undermining a robust constitution. In 1905 she underwent several operations for an abscess in her side, and she was back at her desk before her wound had healed. Now she was suffering periodically from stomach trouble and nervous exhaustion. Apparently she never considered a vacation.[14]

In March 1909 Faith, instead of Lundy, became Mrs. Harris's most immediate problem. The girl wrote that after graduation in June she was going to apply for a teaching position in some girls' college. Faith had presumably entered the Woman's College to train for that profession, but by now Mrs. Harris had other ideas in mind.[15]

Her reply to Faith's letter was a masterpiece of persuasion. She began with the sad admission that she had been "living for the time you would be with me." In a more practical vein, she then described a career far more promising than teaching; Faith could live at home and write. With her mother's connections she could earn well over three hundred dollars a year. Also, she could work only when she felt strong enough, but, Mrs. Harris emphasized, "if you contract to teach, you've got to teach sick or well." Good food and rest would build up her depleted body. Finally came the irresistible appeal: Mrs. Harris needed her. For years she had wanted to write the novel she had never had time to write. The family's financial needs had tied her to hack work. If Faith took over the easy household duties, her mother would have the needed time. With a successful novel behind her, Mrs. Harris would never again have to grind out article after article. The novel was bound to make money; Marie Davis, a local writer, was said to be certain of a fortune from hers. "If you will come home," she concluded, "and give me a chance, I think I can do it." [16]

The idea of a novel was not thought up by Mrs. Harris to bring Faith home. For some time she had been composing a collection of autobiographical letters, and had submitted several, first to the *American,* which was not interested, and then to the *Independent,* which had accepted them. Later, however, she had asked Holt to return them; she was still dubious about allowing her "tragedy" to be "written . . . out in public print"—or, so she later told More. But the temptation to publish "Letters of a Minister's Wife" was still strong. She was convinced that the novel would accomplish "a vengeance" she longed to wreak, that it would make her rich, and that it would contain "some of the best literary work" she had ever done.[17]

The "vengeance" which Mrs. Harris sought was against the

Methodist hierarchy which, she remained convinced, had willfully thwarted Lundy's advancement in the Church. She made no apology for considering the money she might get from her novel—either to Faith or More. Besides the expenses of her immediate family, her father and her brother Albert were a constant drain upon her and she was also generous to other members of her family.[18]

Mrs. Harris had reason to believe that she might do an "eloquent" novel. In her "Brasstown" stories, which she published from time to time in the *Independent* and *American,* she had shown a talent for lively local-color fiction. Pappy Corn, the narrator in most of these stories, tells in one how he broke a young preacher from corn liquor, but admits that afterwards the delinquent's sermons fell off sadly. In another, Tom Purcell, impersonating Jesse James, solicits funds for Preacher Milam's new church, and in a third, Buck Simmons borrows a circus monkey to illustrate a preacher's sermon on the Devil. Some of the stories reflect the darker side of mountain life. Loyal little Billy Merriweather, a village incorrigible, dodges a rampant revivalist and sleeps with the mountain-side sheep until Preacher Milam returns to take him into the church. When hatred for his unfaithful wife unhinges Billy Stark's mind, the wife takes him tenderly to her lonely mountain cabin. With the experience gained from writing these stories, a natural gift for letter writing, and an eventful life to draw on for material, Mrs. Harris had reasons to believe she could succeed with a novel of autobiographical letters.[19]

But she had better go to New York and talk the novel over with More. Although she had not kept in touch with him recently, she could still count on his kindness. She had already planned to be at Faith's Commencement in June, so she could go on from there to New York. She wrote More who replied he would be delighted to see her. Then the expected letter from Faith came. Of course she would give up teaching and do everything she could to make the novel possible. Mrs. Harris was all set now—except for one more step in her plans.[20]

She had decided that her novel must be serialized first in the most widely-read magazine in the country—the *Saturday Evening Post*. On March 18 Churchill Williams, one of its editors, had given her an opening. In turning down a story of hers he expressed the hope she would send in something else. Back came her immediate answer that she was afraid Mr. Williams was merely making his rejection less disappointing. When Williams wrote assuring her that "we at the *Post* are very definitely interested in your work," she proposed that he come to Baltimore in June, where she would be attending her daughter's graduation, and look over a longer piece of fiction she had done. Perhaps she had decided that rejections by mail could be made too easily. Williams agreed to meet her.[21]

On June 1 Williams wrote that he could not get to Baltimore, but invited Mrs. Harris to stop off in Philadelphia on her way to New York. The *Post* would pay her fare from Baltimore and she would be able to meet Mr. Lorimer, the magazine's editor. That was inducement enough for her. She readily agreed and even forwarded her manuscript to Williams knowing that in a few days she would follow it into the *Post* offices.[22]

6

. . . . .
. . .
.

Greener Pastures

AT THE Woman's College Commencement Mrs. Harris accepted the "glorified distinction of being Faith's mother." The attention of faculty and students she knew was a tribute to her daughter's popularity. Her pride rose higher with each event in the program. With dimmed eyes she watched Faith march off the platform with her diploma. At the Senior Reception she saw her daughter in evening dress for the first time and thought of how many book reviews had gone into the dressmaker's bill. But it was worth it all to watch Faith at ease among those brilliant girls from all over the country—a college graduate.[1]

When Mrs. Harris had got Faith off to visit a classmate in Michigan, she turned to the business at hand. Things were shaping up well. On June 8 she had received a letter from Lorimer himself. He had written that the manuscript in its present form would not do, but that it did have possibilities provided she was willing to rewrite it "along rather different lines." He would like to talk to her if she would run down from New York on either June 15 or 16. So, on the morning of June 16 Churchill Williams ushered her into Lorimer's office.[2]

George Horace Lorimer had single-handedly brought the *Saturday Evening Post* into its era of greatness and was pushing it into a dominant place among American magazines. The son of a strong-willed clergyman, he had inherited the ability to devote an abounding energy to one abiding purpose. When the younger Lorimer had joined the *Post* as literary editor in 1898, it had a circulation of ten thousand and had just been sold to Cyrus Curtis for the same number of dollars. Within a year he had become its editor-in-chief and within a decade had upped its circulation past the one million mark. Lorimer's genius lay in an almost infallible instinct for what his readers would read. He needed no research department or "listening post"—and little advice from his editors

43

—to tell him what to run. Intent on a mass circulation he keyed the magazine's editorial level to the tastes of the middle class, while running just enough sophisticated matter to satisfy their literary pretensions.[3]

When Mrs. Harris entered the palatial office, a stocky, square-jawed man rose from behind a heavy desk. She took note immediately of his candid blue eyes and sensitive mouth which, she decided, could turn up at the corners "either agreeably or disagreeably." Lorimer wasted no time on pleasantries. Instead of asking her to sit or seating himself, he revolved his chair, placed a knee on it and began to talk. Now and then he thumped a bundle of papers to emphasize a point. It was her manuscript, and she soon realized he remembered as clearly as she did what was in it. He spoke of her characters and their actions as if they were real people and incidents. With no apologies he told her what she must take out and put in. If she could satisfy him with the revision he had outlined, he would publish the "Letters." Later she could not remember the little she had said.[4]

Still in a daze she walked the short distance to the south-bound train carrying an imposing bouquet Lorimer had extended when they said goodbye. Why did the people on the street and later the passengers on the train keep staring at her? They couldn't possibly know she was going to do a serial for the *Post*. Gradually she became aware of the flowers still clutched in her hand. Not until later did she learn they were orchids, not lilies.[5]

In her autobiography Mrs. Harris says nothing about seeing More on this trip. It is doubtful that she did. Once she began pushing on the *Post's* door she probably forgot all else. There are no further letters from her in More's papers. He would scarcely have shared her excitement over the favorable meeting with Lorimer. On reaching Nashville she wrote Holt and Slosson of her good fortune with the *Post*. They sent appropriate congratulations and hoped she would still spare time for their needs. Holt could not refrain from adding, "Lorimer won't print your best stuff, whereas I will." Of course she would do an occasional piece for him; she would not forget how much she owed him. Besides she must make the *Independent* receptive to Faith.[6]

On July 30 Mrs. Harris, with her mind and desk cleared of lesser matters, began her revision of the "Letters." Without applying pressure Lorimer kept her aware he was interested in her progress. He wrote that she must take all the time she needed, but he would like to use the serial for a fall feature. She should work with the idea of satisfying herself; in that way she would most likely satisfy him. He was confident that after their talk, she could hardly go wrong. As always, Lorimer knew how to get what he wanted.[7]

She mailed her manuscript about August 1, and two weeks later received a letter which she must have opened with unsure hands. Lorimer would run it! He even said she had done a piece of work he was proud to publish in the *Post*. Casually he mentioned that he was going to pay two hundred dollars for each of the six installments. Twelve hundred dollars! Almost exactly what she was making for a year of reviews, articles, and stories.[8]

Lorimer went on to say, however, that her manuscript still wasn't ready for the printer. She must let him use the blue pencil as he saw fit. Throughout the rest of the month she received more of those brief, incisive notes reporting his pruning. He would not allow such anti-clerical slurs as "a sleepy, two hundred and fifty pound, corn-fed bishop." Nor could she sprinkle "damns" throughout her story like a housewife mixing raisins in cake batter. And she need not bother to remind him she was a preacher's wife. He was a preacher's son and knew what his readers would say about a preacher's wife who was also "a fluent cusser." Exasperated with chapter three he dumped it back upon her with orders to rewrite the whole thing, cutting out all digressions and sticking to the story. Also, he did not like the title; she must find a new one and cut out the word "Letters" since the story would not be written in that form. Such sharp instructions would have irritated her coming from Slosson and hurt her from More. But Lorimer was so different.[9]

It was well into the fall before a check came for twelve hundred dollars—a notice that Lorimer was finally satisfied. He always paid upon acceptance of a manuscript. A fall feature was out of the question by then, and the Christmas season was a bad time to launch a first serial. Thus it was January 22 before Mrs. Harris read on a *Post* cover, "A Circuit Rider's Wife, The Story of Two Itinerants." She and Lorimer had agreed to publish it anonymously. Perhaps she still drew back from acknowledging whatever secrets she was revealing; undoubtedly he knew that readers became interested in unnamed authors.[10]

From letters that began pouring into the *Post* it was evident its readers took the serial for genuine autobiography. Thus began the legend of "the Circuit Rider's Wife," which has faded over the years but remains largely unquestioned. An analysis of the story will show on what shaky foundations the legend rests.

The early fortunes of Circuit Rider William Thompson and his wife Mary parallel the beginnings of the Harrises' married life, but before long the narrative gradually slips from autobiography to pure fiction. Mary, reared in a carefree, worldly home, marries earnest William and goes with him to the Redwine Circuit. Although unprepared by background and temperament for a rural religious life Mary copes admirably with its problems. She stretches William's salary to their modest needs, protects him from hardhearted bishops and presiding elders, and rescues him humorously from his periodic losing of "the witness of the spirit." In a remote mountain cabin Mary's only child dies at birth. Submissively William plods from circuit to circuit, pathetic and slightly bewildered, never rising in the church but always living the simple Christian doctrine he preaches, finally giving up the ghost on the old Redwine Circuit where he began. After she has buried him, Mary goes to live with a rich New York sister, glad to breathe again in a freer, more worldly atmosphere. Before long, however, she rebels at big-city ways and returns to Redwine where she can feel close to William's spirit.

A Circuit Rider's Wife reads like the meandering fireside tale of a lady who is rather self-conscious of her part in the events she is relating. The story is built with lively anecdotes separated from each other by the teller's leisurely observations. She has amusing stories to tell: of the small boy assuring William that the two Biblical bears couldn't possibly have eaten forty-two people; of William, a nightshirt trailing under his coat, marrying a hard-pressed runaway couple; of the village reprobate tempting William into a wild buggy race one Sunday afternoon. The narrator recalls pathetic incidents, too, such as the dying of a grandmother convinced she had lost salvation by switching from the Baptist to the Methodist Church, and the suicide of a man who had tried to hear a call from God at every Redwine revival. Mrs. Harris's penchant for moralizing keeps a brake on her narrative; once warmed to a subject she finds much to say before returning to the doings of her characters. After the first chapter of the story a reader might as well resign himself to the absence of dates, locations, and chronology. At one point Mrs. Harris says, "I do not know if I have made you understand that all this time the years were passing." But she wanders on, reminding her readers that St. Paul never dated his enduring epistles. Perhaps she felt that, like her, the readers had become so absorbed in her story they no longer cared when or where the events took place.[11]

Mrs. Harris would continue to insist that William Thompson was Lundy, even though her husband and blind George Stone, probably his closest friend, could find no resemblance. In later years she even declared that she wrote *A Circuit Rider's Wife* to give a true picture of him to the public. The plot of her story would have made that a difficult task: William spent most of his life plodding from circuit to circuit while Lundy after a year on a single circuit went on to a college faculty for ten years, and from there to an administrative job in a sizable city. But even without that obstacle, Mrs. Harris could not have depicted her husband's character, first because she could not comprehend him, and next because she could not have borne to expose those tragic incidents so necessary to reveal him. In her hands William becomes a kindly, rather bewildered eccentric, content to depend upon his sturdy wife and untroubled by intellectualism or religious speculations. One cannot imagine him tramping the Texas desert in search of God.[12]

As a matter of fact, Mrs. Harris wrote the story not to show Lundy's character, but her own. The title is accurate, and the contents prove the title. The sorrows of William are related so that his wife can display her strength and resourcefulness by coping with them. Mary is, however, only a likeness of Mrs. Harris; not a finished picture. She lacks her prototype's masculinity, driving ambition and, to a degree, her robust self-centeredness. The omission is understandable. Like many people Mrs. Harris was more conscious of her admirable traits than of her dubious ones.

Readers of the serial took for granted that the anonymous author was telling her life's story. The *Post's* mail grew heavier with letters addressed to "Mary Thompson," "The Circuit Rider's Wife," and "Mrs. Circuit Rider." The writers discussed the serial as autobiography. A woman said it was so "genuine it must be true," and a man hoped that William had not "really died." A young preacher wrote the author he would like to marry "such a girl as you must have been in your youth." Only a few writers bordered on skepticism, like the man who wondered if the story was partly fiction. The single question asked was for "the wife's" name. One man promised to keep it a solemn secret. Even when the book was published, bearing the author's name, reviewers referred to it as an "autobiography" and to Mrs. Harris as the "biographer wife." One publication declared that "the story is not fiction; it is, on the contrary, grim truth." The serial had obviously left the impression Mrs. Harris hoped for.[13]

Better still, the picture presented of the author-heroine received wide applause. Many readers thanked her as if she had written exclusively for them. More than one husband and wife reported they had read the story aloud and discussed it afterwards. They labored to explain how deeply she had moved them. A man could not find words in the dictionary to express his admiration, and another admitted that at one point he had "cried like a baby." [14]

These letter-writers came from an American middle class reared in an agrarian Protestant society. Those who had moved to cities or done some reading seemed troubled by the new ideas they were encountering. They welcomed Mrs. Harris's conservative views on divorce, radical thought, and urban immorality, caring not a whit when she stopped her story to sermonize on such subjects. She was a "refreshing contrast," one said, to the growing output of "questionable and exciting novels." Others predicted she would hearten people still trying to follow "the lessons taught by hill-billy parents," and that her writing would be read by millions in spite of the influx of foreigners into this country. The less pretentious said that her story brought to mind their parents, one-room schoolhouses, and small white churches. The more literate compared her serial favorably with George Eliot's novels and Joel Chandler Harris's stories.

Strangely enough, Mrs. Harris's handling of religion produced little comment and even less antagonism. One man thought she was a little hard on the Methodists, but he went on to declare that she had done a real service to religion. The rest seemed pleased to find such an intelligent woman still holding to the basic beliefs of Christianity while denouncing bishops, presiding elders, and city preachers. She had taken care to create that view of her religion. In a prayer to William after his death, Mary had said: "There is something wrong with the church, the church system, something wrong with the institutional religion the church is propagating, but there is nothing wrong with the truth of God for which you stood and made me stand for thirty years." [15]

American Protestants would not ask for a fuller confession of faith; they liked to elevate their religion above their church.

When the serial became a book bearing the author's name, the press received it kindly. The *New York Herald* dwelt upon its gentle humor, and the *New York Times* placed William and Mary among "the true heroes of religion in this country today." The church magazines followed the same line. The *Methodist Quarterly Review* thought that Mrs. Harris's story merited respect and admiration, and the *Methodist Advocate,* published in Nashville, found her account of circuit riding life truthful and pathetic. By 1910 both secular and clerical journalists had confronted too much skepticism on higher intellectual levels to dwell upon a criticism of ecclesiastical authorities by a country preacher's wife.[16]

Throughout the rest of her life Mrs. Harris loved to tell how the press had hounded both her and *A Circuit Rider's Wife.* Feeling the need to specify her detractors, she declared that Bishop Hoss had subsidized the weekly newspapers of the Southeast to attack not only her book but her character. Since she failed to name the corrupted papers, it has been impossible to quote their attacks.[17]

She could, however, always point back to the unfavorable notice two Atlanta clergymen gave to her story and how roughly she handled one of them. From their respective pulpits, Dr. A. A. Little of Westminster Presbyterian Church called the serial, then running in the *Post,* "a travesty on true religion," and Dr. J. W. Lee of the Park Street Methodist Church observed that William Thompson could have borne more easily the hardships of this world if he had kept his mind on the world to come. Mrs. Harris brushed aside the Presbyterian as if he had no business in a Methodist quarrel; she doubted that he had enough sense to understand what she had written. Then she went for her Methodist brother. She agreed with Dr. Lee that preachers should ignore worldly discomforts, but she wondered if his words might not have carried more weight if they had not come from the incumbent of a plush city parsonage. Perhaps her rejoinder decided other clergymen to suffer with Christian forgiveness her derogatory story. At any rate no others spoke up.[18]

Mrs. Harris would have preferred more evidence that her book had disturbed the Methodist clergy, but this minor disappointment faded in the glowing future she could now contemplate. She had discovered her gift for intimate, chatty fiction and a national audience eager to hear her views and know her better. Also, she must remember the larger checks she could now expect and demand for her writing. The twelve hundred dollars from "A Circuit Rider's Wife" seemed enormous when it arrived, but she knew the *Post* paid more to recognized writers—and she could see no reason why she was not headed for their company. Other magazines would soon be soliciting her work, and book publishers always gave consideration to serials Lorimer accepted.

She was moving into another literary world. Behind her was the *Independent* with its high-minded editors, bent on informing and stimulating a few hundred suffragettes, college professors, and social reformers. Ahead loomed the great *Saturday Evening Post* dominated by a single editor who would make her reputation and fortune if she could entertain and hearten his vast circulation.

She was prepared to satisfy Lorimer, but she did hope that Lundy and Faith were going to be less troublesome in the future. She needed to have her mind free for writing. Surely they could live more happily in the security and comfort she would soon be able to give them.

7

. . . . .
. . .
.

The Circuit Rider Returns
to Oxford

MRS. HARRIS's tendency to look ahead was evident early in her writing career. Before she had put the finishing touches to "A Circuit Rider's Wife," she was planning two articles, two stories and another serial for the *Post*. Lorimer approved her idea for the serial; his women readers always liked to hear how a resourceful wife handled a problem husband—a theme Mrs. Harris felt competent to explore. He suggested, however, she first get "A Circuit Rider's Wife" ready for print. She agreed, but kept on planning. She must make sure her name appeared again in the *Post* as soon as possible.[1]

She had to take time off, of course, to get her first serial published as a book. Lorimer became hugely amused at her shrewd bargaining with staid publishers, telling her that if he could write business letters like hers, he would be a partner of J. Pierpont Morgan. Her demand for a guaranteed royalty lost her Appleton and Bobbs Merrill; and, in spite of Lorimer's efforts, neither Harper nor Macmillan found her serial sufficiently promising. Finally she signed with Henry Altemus of Philadelphia, but only after he had upped his standard payment of ten per cent to twenty on the first thousand copies. In February 1910 she travelled to Philadelphia to iron out details with him. The book came out in August, but by then she was so busy with "Eve's Second Husband," her forthcoming serial, that she had time only to leaf through it.[2]

She got the articles and stories written before she started on the second serial. Lorimer accepted them, but only after he demanded and received some revising. In the articles he pointed out where she had put in "too much personal opinion unsupported by fact" —a flaw he would see more of in her future writing. From one of the stories he cut out a section which proved to be her favorite scene. Still he would have no part of it. Aware of her disappointment, he promised she would find "the operation" on her story painless after he had administered anesthesia "in the shape of a check for $250." In consenting, she could not refrain from suggesting he also remove the cow from her copy and have the baby fed on Horlick's Malted Milk. He was properly amused, and she responded well to the anesthesia. There would be many such tilts in the years ahead, with Lorimer always the victor.[3]

The writing of "Eve's Second Husband" was an uphill fight all the way. She began it in late March, but within a few days severe abdominal pains forced her first into a medical examination and afterwards into a hospital for a gallstone operation. Before the end of the month she insisted on being taken home; within a few days she was back in the hospital for a second operation, probably for adhesions. It was May 21 before she could sit at her desk with a drain in her side that made writing painful. Lorimer was surprisingly kind. In brief, humorous notes he reminded her it was unladylike to talk about her "insides" and suggested sending her doctors a case of champagne to enliven their visits. The nearest he came to mentioning the serial was urging her to get well so she could again enjoy the pleasure of work. She was anxious enough to resume that pleasure.[4]

Worries undoubtedly retarded her recuperation. During her stay in bed she brooded constantly about Faith. The girl had brightened the Harrises' home, but she had not fallen in with her mother's grand plans. With all her fine prospects Faith had become more and more indifferent about her writing. She did not seem too concerned when Slosson refused her a by-line for her *Independent* reviews, or when Lorimer turned down her "debutante story" with the impudent comment that it had "too much of her mother in it." And very likely it had. Now Faith had gotten behind in her book reviews. Peeping into a notebook kept by her daughter, Mrs. Harris found a witty observation: "I live in a house where everything is used for copy." She was not amused.[5]

Faith, her mother decided, had her mind on other things. She was seeing far too much of Harry Leech. Harry came from a good, but impoverished, Nashville family. He was handsome, educated, and personable, but, in Mrs. Harris's opinion, completely unfitted for the ruthless world of modern business where only strong people, like herself, could succeed. Besides, Harry had those very same weaknesses which had handicapped Lundy; he was high-strung, inordinately proud, and far from robust. He could never give Faith the security and comforts she deserved and must have. Also, her daughter was not the type who could combine marriage with a literary career, and it would be a shame for her to waste her talents and education on household drudgery.

One evening Mrs. Harris asked Faith to sit down by her bedside for a little talk. She began innocently enough. Faith must try to get her reviews to the *Independent* on time. Its editors were old family friends who would like to help her get started as a writer. She was neglecting a wonderful opportunity and giving her time to unimportant things, doing housework the cook was supposed to do, running about to silly parties. Certainly she ought not to go out every night with Harry Leech. And incidentally Mrs. Harris did not approve of those "low shows" they were going to. Warming to her subject, she added that Harry was a clean, honorable young man, but she couldn't help wishing "if you are going to care for him . . . that he had a stronger physique and that he seemed more suited for the emergencies of our exacting times." [6]

Faith left in tears, sobbing that she had been a failure. The next morning Mrs. Harris wrote her daughter a conciliatory note, insisting she had not reflected upon Harry's character, but had only tried to make Faith put her remarkable gifts to some use. But she retracted nothing. All the carefully contrived sermon accomplished was to lose Mrs. Harris her daughter's confidence, and, perhaps, hasten an engagement. Within a few weeks Faith was writing Harry about wedding plans, and that same day, writing her mother without any mention of the coming event.[7]

If Mrs. Harris discussed Harry Leech with Lundy, her problem apparently failed to arouse his concern. Since the first of the year he had been sinking again into religious despondency. He had chosen to oppose pugnacious Bishop Hoss in the battle between Vanderbilt's Trustees and the Methodist Church for control of the University. Hoss had ordered the Board of Education to assist the Church's attorneys, and Lundy had refused. With his mind troubled by secular problems, he began to entertain his old religious doubts.[8]

Reading these signs Mrs. Harris persuaded Lundy to get a leave of absence and visit his brother Henry again. Her apprehension was not lessened by his letters from Florida; they indicated he was brooding over the new scientific concept of the universe. With a pathetic attempt at whimsy he wrote her that in a prehistoric existence he must have been "a tadpole big enough to swallow a bishop or a whale." He had become so frightened of a catfish he could no longer read the Book of Jonah. Had she seen then a notebook he was filling, she would have been even more alarmed. In it were such questions as: "Does God wonder about anyone's solar system or solar plexus?" "Can an ant see God?" "Is God a grin, a tear, or Christ?" Then there was the question so fearfully reminiscent of "the Austin debauch": "What would happen if I took Christ to a sporting house?" Desperately he tried to believe in a naturalistic God. On the train home he ran into Warren Candler and urged him to give up his worn-out orthodoxy and turn to "the true religion." He considered again his life of Christ: he would put Him in modern life and thought. His last letter warned Mrs. Harris that he, she, and Faith were going to find a home in the country where they could live close to God. His words echoed a letter written Candler from Texas: "If you two won't, I will—yes, though it mean breaking asunder the very cells of life and reason." Perhaps it was then, waiting anxiously for his return, that Mrs. Harris decided she would buy a quiet place in the country with the money from her second serial.[9]

In whatever mental state Lundy arrived home, he rose to the ordeal of his wife's two operations and long recuperation. She never forgot his affectionate attention, sitting by her bed for hours, sometimes singing to her the old hymns of their circuit riding days. But all the while she watched that faraway look in his eyes which meant his thoughts were on that other world. Once she tried to divert those thoughts by telling him she was going to buy that house in the country with the money from her serial. Lundy seemed hardly to hear her. When she returned home, she would wait fearfully for him to come back in the evening from the stormy offices of the Education Board. A letter from Faith to her mother in early July tells of a worsening situation.

You poor, dear lady. I don't see how you are going to keep up the fight. I hope you won't. I am sorry for Daddy but I am sorrier for you. He *hates* life [italics Faith's]—you love it. You ought to have the chance that has been denied you for twenty-odd years. Oh it's horrible! [10]

Mrs. Harris, however, had no notion of giving up either her chance of authorship or the hope of saving Lundy. The two objectives had become for her synonymous.

In spite of the nagging pain in her side she worked desperately at the serial. Aware of the pressures upon her, Lorimer encouraged her at every turn. When she warned him that she might fail to finish the serial, he replied sharply, "your sort of people don't fail." It was exactly what she wanted him to say. As soon as her copy started to come in, he suggested she send along each installment when it was finished. In that way he built up a backlog of confidence for her to fall back upon. As she entered the home stretch, he waved her on with the prediction she was "going to reach our pocket-book" with the finished product. Perhaps he knew how she planned to spend the money, for he offered to break his rule and allow her an advance on the serial. She refused; she would earn it first. By early September the entire manuscript had been accepted—even though she must do some revising. "I wish I dared write you," Lorimer said, "how good I think 'Eve's Second Husband' is." [11]

Everything seemed to brighten all at once. In late July Lundy followed the lead of Dr. John Hammond, his immediate superior, and resigned from the Board. Mrs. Harris had been urging him all summer to do this. He stayed on a while, however, against her protest, to help the Reverend Stonewall Jackson Anderson, Hammond's successor, learn his duties. When he finally left a month later, Mrs. Harris arranged, with the help of W. P. Lovejoy, for him to take a vacation at the farm of Clarence Anthony in Pine Log near Cartersville, Georgia. She assured him she would join him just as soon as she finished the revisions Lorimer wanted. Lundy left Nashville alone on September 9.[12]

Lundy's letters from Pine Log must have convinced Mrs. Harris that the change was doing even more for him than she had hoped. He wrote with all the excitement of a city boy visiting a farm for the first time; in fact, he called himself a boy when he told of swims with Anthony's small adopted son in the creek, of their long conversation on evil spirits, of their races with a neighbor's daughter to see who could pull the most fodder. When he was allowed to drive a team of mules to the corn mill, he seemed as proud as if he had received an honorary degree. Anthony's mother and four spinster sisters were as kind to him as they could be. He was sleeping well and eating so much that the pigs grunted recognition when he passed their pen. No, he didn't want the William James book; he would not have time to read it.[13]

Fortunately Mrs. Harris could put Lundy out of her mind for a while; by September 17 she knew that Faith and Harry were to be married. Harry left that same evening for Dallas, Texas, where, with the help of John Craig, a college friend, he expected to find a job. At Christmas Craig was going to lend him $150 so that he could return to Nashville, marry Faith, and bring her back to Dallas. There is no need to conjecture what Mrs. Harris thought of such plans.[14]

On Monday morning September 19 Faith walked downtown to

the postoffice hoping Harry had mailed a letter along the way to Dallas. Returning about noon she was terrified to see the front porch filled with people. It must be her mother! Silent friends moved to make way as she hurried up the steps. No, Mrs. Harris was seated in the front room paying no attention to the people hovering over her. With an expressionless face she told Faith. A wire had come from Pine Log. Lundy had died early that morning. There were no details.[15]

There was not much time for grief. Packing must be done, many wires sent, arrangements made for the funeral at Oxford. Fortunately Hope Harris was visiting them and could help. The three ladies caught the early evening train for Atlanta. They were undoubtedly awake when Dr. Lovejoy and Dr. Hammond joined them at Cartersville while a coffin was loaded in the baggage car. In the dim light of dawn mother and daughter listened to what they must have expected to hear.

Fifty years later Mrs. Linnie Anthony Crowe, youngest of the Anthony sisters, told the story one autumn evening in a Cartersville rest home. Mrs. Crowe's unemotional face and steady voice gave her account the inevitability of Greek tragedy. Dr. Harris was a good man, she said. Made himself a member of the family. Worked in the field with the help and joined in family prayer. That Sunday morning when he didn't come to breakfast, Clarence went to wake him up. Dr. Harris wasn't in his bed, and it hadn't been slept in. Clarence went down the road looking for him and found him in a ditch about two hundred yards from the house. His eyes were open and he began to talk as soon as he saw Clarence. He said he didn't need a doctor. He'd had these spells before, and this one was over now. All he needed was some sleep. Clarence helped him home and put him to bed.

While they were eating breakfast, they could hear Dr. Harris snoring through two closed doors. It didn't sound natural, but they figured he was just tired out. She went on to church and after the preaching told Mr. Reid, the minister, about Dr. Harris's spell. He must have known something about Dr. Harris, for he got worried. He sent a man for the doctor and came back with her. They went in Dr. Harris's room and found the letters he'd written to Mrs. Harris, Clarence, the coroner, and the undertaker. In each of them he said he'd taken an overdose of morphine.

The doctor came, but he couldn't do anything. They walked Dr. Harris up and down and gave him black coffee, but he got weaker and weaker, and kept saying, "I'm tired; let me sleep."

Finally the doctor saw it wasn't any use and laid him back on the bed. He died before day.[16]

As the train travelled towards Atlanta, Mrs. Harris read Lundy's letter to her.

Dear Corrie:
The end has at last come. Goodbye, my darling. My last thoughts are of you and Faith. I shall love you both eternally if love is hereafter permitted. You have been unutterably good to me all our days together.

Ever,
Lundy

September 17, 1910
10:30 P.M.[17]

When Mrs. Harris had read the brief telegram from Pine Log, she had no hope that Lundy had died a natural death. As she wrote Candler while waiting at Rockmart years ago, her life would be foreshadowed by the fear of her husband's suicide. But why had Lundy taken his life in the happy atmosphere of the Anthony farm where he had seemed to shed so completely his official worries and religious doubts? An observation by Thomas Hardy suggests an answer. In *The Return of the Native* he says that "men have oftener suffered from the mockery of a place too smiling for their reason than from the oppression of surroundings sadly overtinged." In the dark quiet of that country night Lundy Harris may well have realized that the peace of those few brief days was not for him.

They buried him in the late afternoon in the old Oxford Cemetery, by the small graves of his sons and against a background of tombstones raised to bishops and clergymen who had found greater comfort in the Methodist faith. Faith wrote Harry of the burial.

The funeral at Oxford demonstrated that hundreds of people loved him with a depth of devotion I did not realize. Everything was simple and beautiful. They all knew he had done wrong sometimes, but that did not deter them from paying him every honor that love and friendship can pay. We buried him with his family on that quiet hill under the cedars. It had just rained and it was cool and sweet and I knew that he was happy for the first time since he was a boy.[18]

Throughout the funeral and the first days back in Nashville Mrs. Harris maintained her stern composure. On September 24 she took advantage of an opportunity to loose her feelings. A polite note of condolence arrived from the Reverend Stonewall

Anderson, Dr. Hammond's successor on the Education Board. He received immediately an unusual acknowledgement. Mrs. Harris explained what a shock it had been to get a letter from "a man largely responsible for my husband's death." After elaborating on the impropriety of his note she begged him never to communicate with her again. "My sanity," she wrote, "depends upon forgetting the men instrumental in my husband's death." [19]

One can hardly believe that Anderson earned such a denunciation during the short time in which Lundy was acquainting him with his new position. Perhaps he received the tongue-lashing Mrs. Harris was saving for Hoss. The Bishop was too wise to extend his sympathy.

Sensibly Mrs. Harris refused to rake the past for omissions and mistakes of hers that might have aggravated Lundy's melancholia. She did regret not accompanying him to Pine Log, but, after all, she had stayed at work so that she could give him a more extended rest. Hoss, Anderson, and, to a lesser extent, Candler were responsible for her husband's final breakdown. She would continue to believe she had "never failed Lundy." [20]

To the end of her life she would defend him. She made Faith understand that his infidelities had been "not of the spirit but of the body," and, near the height of her literary fame, she declared, "My chief distinction is in having been married to such a man." In her last years she loved to recall Lundy's courage in defying an infuriated Bishop Hoss, and his charm which drew his Emory colleagues and simple people like the Anthonys to him. His religious mania had thrown up a barrier between them, but she remained proud of her husband. [21]

When quiet returned to the Nashville home she turned resolutely to her immediate problems. She would not brood over her loss. In less than three weeks after Lundy's funeral she had the revision of "Eve's Second Husband" in Lorimer's hands, and he pronounced it "splendid." Now she must prepare for the ordeal of Faith's wedding. [22]

8

. . . . .
 . . .
  .

Mother and Daughter

DURING the fall of 1910 Mrs. Harris began to plan a future without
Faith. Once she fell to making plans, her recuperation was under
way. She was going to buy a house. So far her married life had
been passed in country parsonages, college dormitories, city flats,
and rented cottages. She was going to move from Nashville; it had
become unbearable. The gossip about Lundy that reached her
was, she knew, only a part of what was being said behind her
back. Tradesmen were appearing with bills. She believed she had
already paid some of them, but she could not afford to have it said
she was refusing to settle Lundy's debts. She would have to wait
until her mind became less crowded before she decided where she
would live.[1]

Since she had consented to the wedding, she must see that it
went off properly. She rented another Nashville house so that the
ceremony would not be performed in surroundings charged with
sad memories. Then she took Faith to Philadelphia in October to
buy her a trousseau. While there she talked over a third serial
with Lorimer.

During the three months before the wedding Mrs. Harris was
not the only one to suffer. Harry knew she was not welcoming him
into the family. Faith had relayed her mother's consent: "All she
asks is that you be sure of yourself financially." Harry had been
pondering the same question. He could hardly bring himself to
tell Faith that his salary at the Dallas Telephone Company would
be only $55 a month. But he poured out his other worries to her.
Perhaps Craig would not be able to lend him the money to come
for the wedding. He warned Faith he would not permit Mrs.
Harris to support them. Next he began to brood over the possibility he was unsuited for marriage. In a moment of despair he
offered Faith the chance to break off the engagement, then wrote

59

hurriedly that without her "life would be one long terror for me." [2]

Faith also tortured herself with probing questions. She could not help but wonder if she had inherited "tragic potentialities" from her father. Was it right to leave her sick mother alone after their common loss? Then, Mrs. Harris, very illogically, became angry at Harry's hesitancy and suggested perhaps he did not want to marry. The marriage was saved by Faith's capacity to love abundantly both her mother and Harry, and by his own love and desperate need for the courageous, affectionate girl. Harry and John Craig arrived in Nashville on December 23.[3]

Until the evening of the wedding on December 24, Mrs. Harris controlled her throbbing emotions. Unfortunately Craig chose just that time to call her aside for a talk. With the best intentions he told her that the young couple was going to find it hard to live in Dallas on Harry's salary. Happily they were behind closed doors when Mrs. Harris's tirade broke loose. She would not give Harry Leech any money! Not one cent! That was just what he expected when he "inveigled Faith into marriage." If Craig attempted to defend himself, she was in no state to hear him.[4]

Perhaps the burst of temper enabled Mrs. Harris to watch quietly during the ceremony. Harry and Faith left immediately for Dallas unaware of Craig's mistake and subsequent punishment. Mrs. Harris spent Christmas Day before the living room fire, writing a loving letter to Faith and wishing Frankie McCrory, her daughter's friend, had left with the other guests. She didn't need people to be good to her.[5]

It was Faith that found the separation intolerable. She took an instant dislike to Texas people and food. The Leeches shared a house with Craig, his wife, baby, and mother-in-law. Almost daily Faith wrote home of her problems and drudgery: Harry's office hours were long and his salary inadequate; she had to do all the cooking and housekeeping; the Craig baby got sick one day at the dining table. Her letters gradually became appeals for help. She was tired and "so homesick"; something was "going to snap" in her any day. During college days, Faith had periodically written home in that same tone. The truth was that she could not be happy for long away from her mother.[6]

For a while Mrs. Harris restrained herself to giving encouragement and advice on how Faith might cope with the Dallas situation. Her daughter and Harry, she said, must learn to expect hardships. It wouldn't hurt them to see a sick baby; she had mopped up after two of them. But for all her restraint, Mrs.

Harris could not conceal her delight when Faith wrote on January 27 that they were coming back to Nashville. Eagerly she began to lend a hand. She would expect the Leeches to come straight to her house and stay there until they found one of their own. Then she got busy about a job for Harry. Soon she was writing that she and Mr. Smith, president of the Nashville Telephone Company, had been putting their heads together, and something good would be forthcoming. Also, she had just written her old friend banker Woods White in Atlanta.[7]

Inadvertently she had set up one of those misunderstandings that were to dog her relations with Harry Leech. He had been in communication with Smith, for whom he had once worked. Faith wrote her mother that she must stop interfering in their life. Harry, she said, had "enough wires of his own to pull." Stung by this rebuff, Mrs. Harris divulged her one-sided talk with Craig at the wedding as proof that Harry had married with the expectation of her help. Faith, in turn, lost her temper and replied that they could not now stay at her mother's when they came to Nashville. She would often visit her mother, of course, but without Harry. Mrs. Harris became alarmed. With the Leeches passing up her ample house for a cheap apartment, and with Harry refusing to see her, Nashville gossip would flow again. Gaily she wrote Harry to "come along home and give up your hurt feelings and notions." Her appeal was supported by a letter from Harry's mother telling of Mrs. Harris's emotional and physical condition, and urging him to forget his pride and do as she asked. So, like his mother-in-law, he repressed his resentment.[8]

A happy Faith reached Nashville late in February to be welcomed by an equally happy mother. Mrs. Harris, however, wisely left for Horne Springs, Tennessee, before Harry arrived the following month. She was quite excited by the new serial she was working on. Lorimer had heartily approved of its outline the past fall, and she would have a new publisher for it. She had bargained so outrageously with Doubleday Page that Lorimer feared she was going to end up without a publisher. Triumphantly, however, she obtained a five-thousand-dollar guarantee on each of her next three novels. In late April she sent Lorimer the manuscript for "The Recording Angel" and followed it in person to be present when he set the amount of her check. On the way up, she stopped in Atlanta to send Faith a linen suit and Harry two silk shirts. The Leeches seemed content in Nashville, still living in her house, and she wanted to keep them contented. Harry had gone to work for the Telephone Company, and Faith was enjoying old friends.

Mrs. Harris could concentrate now on her own promising business.[9]

On May 10 Faith received an excited letter from her mother. Lorimer was paying four thousand dollars for the serial and asking for no revisions. But that was not the half of it. He had offered her the most wonderful assignment! He wanted her to travel in several European countries and write articles on the progress of woman's suffrage in each of them. She would have a generous expense account and be well paid for the articles if they were as good as he expected.[10]

Meanwhile, a shrewd plan was taking shape in Mrs. Harris's mind. She hurried down to Johns Hopkins Hospital for a physical check-up. Returning to Philadelphia she reported to Lorimer— and, by letter, to Faith—that the doctors found she had recovered completely from her operation, but was alarmingly nervous and still rather weak. She suggested to Lorimer that, in view of the full report, perhaps she ought to take Faith along. According to her, he thought it an excellent idea. Wasn't that wonderful? Faith must begin buying a wardrobe which, of course, her mother would pay for. In the same mail Harry got a letter from Mrs. Harris asking him if "he could lend Faith to her" for a couple of months. Harry must stay on in the house, and perhaps he would like to have his mother come to visit him.[11]

With marked unenthusiasm Harry told Faith she could go, but reminded her that he had "given in on every point" to her mother since his marriage. That was enough for Faith, even though the thought of her mother in Europe alone filled her with terror. She wrote that she could not leave her husband for that long. Promptly Mrs. Harris came up with a new suggestion. Why couldn't Harry get a leave of absence and come too? Harry settled the argument. He could not possibly ask the Telephone Company for leave after just starting to work, but Faith must go. He would be all right. Mrs. Harris wrote back praising Harry for sticking to his job. She promised that Faith could come back when the trip was half finished.[12]

Mrs. Harris spent June in Nashville and went back north in July to make final arrangements with Lorimer. Before following her, Faith arranged with Harry a wireless code calculated to cover all emergencies at home and abroad. On July 22 the two ladies sailed on the S. S. *Cedric*.[13]

Neither Mrs. Harris nor Faith seems to have left America with a cosmopolitan point of view, or to have attained one during the trip. On shipboard Faith became irritated by the British sailors' clipped accent, and Mrs. Harris was alarmed by the brandy consumption of an Englishman at their table. Mother and daughter maintained a parochial antagonism towards the nations they visited and, keeping largely to themselves, apparently made no European friends during their trip. Mrs. Harris decided the French were "natural liars," especially customs officials and taxi-drivers. Faith was horrified to hear that 20 per cent of Berlin's children were illegitimate; she could hardly believe it of those "stolid and solid" women she saw drinking beer in the cafés. Almost certainly she echoed her mother when she described Europe's attitude to America as "that assumed by a room full of well-dressed women towards a beautifully-dressed woman whose youth and assurance galls the others because they have only dignity." [14]

Cut off from other people, living together in hotel rooms and train compartments, mother and daughter began to get on each other's nerves. Harry's letters kept Faith upset; he was lonely; he criticized Mrs. Harris for letting Faith visit Edinburgh by herself; he was getting "tired of the whole silly episode." Her worries about Harry annoyed Mrs. Harris; Faith was making herself ill and getting nothing out of their wonderful trip.[15]

One evening in a Paris hotel Faith began to lament that a pending maritime strike was bound to make Harry fear she would not get home on schedule. Mrs. Harris's famous temper blazed. In the harshest terms she declared that her daughter was injuring her health with worries and ruining what should have been a happy experience for them both. Cowed and frightened Faith went weeping to bed.[16]

Before going out the following morning Mrs. Harris left a pathetically honest note for her daughter. It was terrible, she wrote, that two people who loved each other as they did could so cruelly hurt one another. They must realize the differences in their nature; she was "a rough woman" made unfit by her suffering for living with anyone but strangers; Faith was sensitive, delicate and ready to sacrifice herself for anyone she loved. She had forced the trip upon the girl who had endured it until her strength broke. Mrs. Harris went on to say that Faith's terrified face had haunted her all night. She would take care that there would be no more such scenes. They must never again live together for so long. When she got home she was going to buy a place close to Nashville so that they could visit conveniently but not for any length of time. As anxious as her mother for a reconciliation, Faith happily agreed.[17]

Bravely Mrs. Harris was resigning herself to the conviction that

Faith was placing her marriage above all else. She could not see a deeper, tragic truth; Faith could never remain happy away from either her husband or mother.

On October 5 Faith sailed from Le Havre. At the dock she and Mrs. Harris embraced tenderly: the daughter already beginning to worry about her mother travelling alone in Spain and Italy; and the mother excited by the adventuresome prospect of visiting two countries without knowing the language of either.

Mrs. Harris got along famously without Faith and the help of foreign languages. Hearing before she left Paris that the city was flooded with counterfeit francs, she quietly passed off any du-bious-looking bills on the rude cab-drivers. In Madrid she went to a bullfight with two young Englishmen, an adventure Faith would have denied her. Convinced that all interpreters were cheats, she called alone on a Spanish countess, and the two sat silent smiling at each other until a more bilingual guest joined them. On the way to Rome she stopped off at Monte Carlo and might have taken a whirl at the roulette wheel if someone had explained the game. She became alarmed when a newly-married Italian couple seemed on the point of forgetting they were in a railroad car, not in a bridal chamber. She had become puzzled about European men. Libbie Morrow, a Nashville friend, had warned her they would pinch you to attract your attention, yet not one had pinched her. She wondered if she had a forbidding face, but finally decided such stories probably came from women who are always imagining "men are after them." Her health and spirits seemed to improve as the trip progressed. She arrived home just in time for Christmas, "her sides bulging with things for Faith and Harry." [18]

"An Old Woman and a New One in the Old World" appeared in the *Post* the following January. The serial reads like autobiography but is obviously fiction. Pretty young Peg, chaperoned by wise, comfortable Aunt Peggy, visits Europe to collect material for a book on woman's suffrage. The two ladies easily handle such European problems as rude government officials, predatory young English aristocrats, and French stocking salesmen who take a personal interest in their customers' legs. In the closing install-ment, Aunt Peggy summed up patly the views of European women on suffrage. English women want the vote because their nation cannot produce enough marriageable males; German women want it because their husbands, formerly close by at their farm work, are now absent for many hours in factories. On the other hand, French women are too bent on love and Italian women too primitive to concern themselves with voting. Or, as Aunt Peggy concludes, "the women will get the vote in the country where the men make the least love to them." It is, certainly, an entertaining theory.[19]

During the first two months of 1912 Mrs. Harris relaxed from her writing. According to her, the time passed pleasantly. In the evenings she would stretch out on a couch before the living-room fire and listen to Faith or Harry read aloud from Dickens, Scott, and Wilkie Collins. But in late February she felt "a fit of blackness" coming on. Perhaps she had been idle too long, or, more likely she realized that the time had come when she and Faith must separate for a while. She went back to Horne Springs in early March where she began work on "Arden," a new serial designed for the *Post.* Her writing, however, did not go too well; she had other things on her mind.[20]

In April Mrs. Harris went down to Elbert County to visit her kin. Her arrival there created a stir. Her serial "The Recording Angel," running then in the *Post,* had its setting in Ruckersville, and several of its characters bore the names of either Rucker or White. Warmed by home-town popularity Mrs. Harris let her imagination run wild in talking with a young lady who later turned out to be an Atlanta reporter. The newspaper story resulting from this pleasant chat was hardly factual; Mrs. Harris was said to have visited the Lorimers at their Newport villa and to be considering an invitation from the Montague Glasses on the Riviera. Mrs. Harris maintained that the lady reporter had misquoted her, but she resolved to be more wary of the press in the future.[21]

After her stay in Elbert County Mrs. Harris visited friends in College Park. From there she went on to Pine Log where she had engaged a room at Clarence Anthony's in the house where Lundy had died. As she explained to the horrified Faith, she went there to feel near to her husband in "the place where he had last been." Later she defended her visit by declaring she had gone as "women go to the cemetery and sit awhile by the dust of their beloveds." [22]

While in Pine Log Mrs. Harris declared that she felt her husband's presence one evening. Also, she claimed to have found, without any instructions, the ditch where Lundy spent his last night. But whatever mystical communication she established there with her husband, her mind was, for at least a part of the time, on a more earthly matter.[23]

Mrs. Harris was thinking of building a house in Pine Log. She found there the peace and solitude which Lundy had described in his letters. Perhaps she was not unmindful of that possibility when she decided a month after his death that she would some day visit the place where he had briefly been so content.[24]

The confusion of Faith's return to Nashville and the European trip had delayed Mrs. Harris's plans for a house of her own. But the idea had grown, and its appeal had become more compelling. The loss of her husband by death and her daughter by marriage had left her defeated and lonely, but the loss had made her free to choose how she would now live. Her immediate revision of one serial and the trip to Philadelphia to discuss another one reveal that her thoughts were again on the future. The focal point of her planning had become a home with roots and security.

From Pine Log she wrote Faith what she had in mind. She could never live for long in Nashville or any other city where gossip was always a threat and living too frantic for her work and health. First, however, she was going to make Faith secure. Unlike her, the Leeches loved Nashville, so she proposed either to buy a house for her daughter or give her an income sufficient for an apartment in a "good neighborhood." Then she would build a house for herself, near enough to Nashville for them to visit each other. She and Faith had learned they could never share a house. "We are continuously getting on each other's nerves," she wrote, "when we live together." [25]

She admitted to Faith a preference for settling in Georgia. Twice recently she had given evidence of this inclination. *The Recording Angel* was dedicated to her native state, and in a newspaper interview in Elberton she had called Georgia her "good and patient mother whose face always shines in the sun." The rolling country around Farmhill had left an indelible imprint upon her mind.[26]

In her letters to Faith she tells of finding everything at Pine Log to her liking: the wooded hills and lushly-cultivated valleys, the open fire in the clear, still evenings, the mockingbird outside her window which put an opera orchestra to shame. The people in the neighborhood lived the pastoral poetry of the Scriptures, even though the maiden Anthony sisters ate with their knives, and after prayers she must get rapidly from the living room before Clarence proceeded to wash his feet. As Lundy had done, she joined in the household chores and farm work. In the late afternoons she went for long walks. She had not felt so well for years.[27]

During one of her rambles she came unexpectedly upon a clearing and the ruins of an Indian cabin. A strange feeling came over her that the little house had been waiting in the wilderness for her coming.

The hidden hill upon which this cabin stood was covered with a dense growth of trees, brambles, bushes and weeds. Still I recognized it as my house. You do see things at times which belong to other people, but are by nature yours.[28]

The search for the site of her house was over.

9

. . . . .
. . .
.

Building for the Future

NOTHING brightened Mrs. Harris's life more than an idea for solving some problem. Once it had taken hold of her she forgot everything else in the pleasure of planning each detail and anticipating the happy change in her affairs. She did not, however, spend her enthusiasm in daydreaming. A period of strenuous activity immediately followed the conception of her solution. The three years following her decision to build at Pine Log were probably the busiest and most satisfying she would ever enjoy. From the spring of 1912 until Christmas of 1914 she led an exhausting, nomadic life: supervising construction at Pine Log, retiring to some Tennessee resort for writing, travelling to New York and Philadelphia to sell her manuscripts and obtain additional assignments.

There would be time enough to rest in her country place when it was finished. In those peaceful hills she could write without distractions between visits to friends in Atlanta and Nashville and business trips north. Better still, she could entertain there the people she wanted to see. She always felt more comfortable at social affairs in her own house than at those given by her friends. Once she was settled she planned to farm her rich valley land; she might well make the place pay for its upkeep. Faith figured prominently in her plans. If things failed to go well for Harry in the business world—and they probably would, sooner or later— her daughter could live with her until he got back on his feet. Of course she could not mention that possibility to Faith, but they all ought to feel more secure when she bought the land. There was nothing like land to give you a sense of security.[1]

The little cabin, hill and land around it were exactly what she wanted, but she was not going to let it get around that she wanted to buy. The owner would immediately raise his price, especially to an outsider with money. She would get Paul Akin, a Cartersville lawyer and son-in-law of W. P. Lovejoy, to make the inquiries. Meanwhile she must get some writing done; she was going to need plenty of money for the house she had in mind.[2]

About the middle of June she left Pine Log and spent several weeks with Harry and Faith in Nashville getting her affairs in shape for the move to Georgia. The last of July she went up to Red Boiling Springs in the Tennessee mountains. She must get "In Search of a Husband" finished up for Lorimer. He had liked her outline for the serial; in fact, had suggested that she put aside all else till she finished writing it. If he bought it, she would buy the Pine Log land with the money. She always preferred to earn money for immediate needs, no matter how large her current bank account. On trips north she usually wrote a story to pay her expenses.[3]

For a month she worked steadily. Living in a hotel with people she did not want to know got awfully dull at times and became even harder to bear when Faith was late in sending some cigarettes. She simply had to smoke while she was writing. After considerable coaxing she got her daughter to come up for a short visit on August 10. Revived by the visit, she put the final touches to the serial and returned to Nashville the last of the month.[4]

The lease on her house there had expired and the Leeches were living in an apartment, so she spent a month at the Tulane Hotel. In October she went back to Pine Log to stroll happily over "my piney hill," which she still had not bought, and visualize all she planned to do there. While at the Anthonys' she took care of an irritating piece of literary business. When Lorimer turned down her serial "The Co-Citizens," a satire on the Suffragette Movement, she asked Wallace Steger of Doubleday Page to sell it to another magazine. Nothing in her contract with those book publishers obligated them to that task, but amiable Steger tried to place the manuscript and failed. He wrote Mrs. Harris suggesting that they wait a while before bringing out the serial in book form. Convinced that Steger wanted to defraud her of the five-thousand-dollar advance called for in her contract, she accused him of attempting "a fiendish, canny trick." Alarmed he wired he would come at once to Pine Log bringing the money. Mrs. Harris, however, arranged to meet him at Lawyer Akins's office in Cartersville "to see that he does not go back with that check." Everything went well, she reported to Faith. She even consented to revise the unwanted serial, "after I finish the work for Lorimer."[5]

The last of November she set out for Philadelphia with the manuscript of "In Search of a Husband." To her disappointment

Lorimer wanted quite a bit of revising done. It was too bad. After all, she had explained she could not buy her farm until she sold the serial. But she went dutifully to an Atlantic City hotel to do her re-writing. From there she wrote Faith that the serial was as good as sold and that Lorimer had predicted it would earn a hundred thousand dollars as a book. And, oh yes, Libbie Morrow of the Nashville *Banner* might be pleased to know how well she had done.[6]

In early January Mrs. Harris felt confident enough of her revision to buy an ample site for her country house: two hundred acres of valley and hill land. She let Isma Dooley of the Atlanta *Constitution* know of the purchase, and that newspaper shared the news with its readers under the caption "Corra Harris Establishes Eden among Georgia Hills." Significantly the article said that Mrs. Harris was building "a home for herself and daughter."[7]

Atlantic City was much to Mrs. Harris's liking: the crowded Boardwalk, the brisk winter air, the attentive Negro waiters at her hotel who assured her they preferred Southern guests to Yankees. Lorimer came for a visit with his wife, with whom Mrs. Harris did not feel at ease. She was flattered when Lorimer ordered two rolling chairs for a Boardwalk promenade and put Mrs. Lorimer in the second chair alone. On January 6 Mrs. Harris was distressed by a wire bringing the news that Wallace Steger had died. But she admitted to Faith that she was glad she had got the five thousand dollar advance out of him. Russell Doubleday took over her account and came down to talk business. She was not impressed with his appearance: "a long, lank, Jew-nosed, thin-faced man as devoid of magnetism as a reed." He proved, however, quite amiable. Yes, he would be glad to peddle "The Co-Citizens" to magazine editors, and he would consider publishing "An Old Woman and a New One in the Old World" if Mrs. Harris would lower her royalty demands. She let him know she was not satisfied with the sale of her novels and brushed aside his explanation that many people who had read her *Post* serials did not want to re-read them in book form.[8]

Even after getting the revised serial to the *Post* Mrs. Harris did not start for home. She had other business on her mind. Back in 1909 she had warned Lorimer that she might have to do an occasional piece for the *Independent,* and he had understood—a bit too readily. But if he was going to turn down her serials, she had better enlarge her literary market further than just the *Independent.* Now was the time, while she was so close to New York. Perhaps she derived some pleasure from realizing that she could pay for this additional expense from "The Autobiography of a Mother-in-Law," a story he had asked her to write. Before beginning it, however, she made sure—through Faith—that Harry would not take offense, and, in addition, she took the added precaution of writing it under the pen name of Mary Bain Wright.[9]

During her stay in Atlantic City she made two trips to New York and sent Faith glowing accounts of her business and social success in that city. W. F. Bigelow of *Good Housekeeping* begged for stories, and Colonel George Harvey of *Harper's* bought one, with a down payment, sight unseen. She found Harvey something of "an ass," but she liked the way he did business. Hearst Publications wanted to see some of her work, and she decided to hire a literary agent, Paul Reynolds. She spent March in Nashville, but returned north in April to be present when Lorimer set the price for "In Search of a Husband." She sent Faith the glorious news: he was paying five thousand dollars. Faith must release the news, so that it would appear first in the Atlanta *Constitution* and the next day in the Nashville *Tennesseean*. And make sure to tell the Nashville *Banner* it would get her next "scoop." [10]

She left for home in May. How exciting it had been: bargaining with famous editors, dining at Delmonico's and the Waldorf, visiting a naughty night club. Perhaps she did like big cities.

But back at the Anthonys she decided there was nothing like the country. She enjoyed hugely Miss Linnie's suspicion that their guest wanted to marry Clarence. All she wanted from Clarence was his consent to manage her farm. Unhappily she soon learned that her house would not go up over night. Local labor was unskilled, and ordered material slow to arrive. Also, she wasn't sure she should hire the architect she had in mind after hearing that he had been divorced. Growing restless, she joined the Anthonys in farm work long enough to acquire blistered hands and a sun-burned face. Fortunately she hit upon the idea of a serial about a worldly lady who found contentment in a mountain valley. When Lorimer showed mild interest in her theme, she left for Roan Springs, Tennessee, to put it into writing.[11]

From August 4 to early in September she labored at the new serial. The small mountain town was not without excitement. The local Holiness preacher threatened to denounce Mrs. Harris from the pulpit if she mentioned him or his congregation in her ungodly writing. The arrival of a peroxide blonde created a stir among the other hotel guests. These, however, were minor disturbances compared to the night when mountain desperadoes shot up the hotel. But in spite of such interruptions Mrs. Harris sent her serial to the *Post* before September 9 and returned to Pine Log.[12]

She spent the fall on the move: Nashville, Atlanta—where a new job of Harry's had taken the Leeches—and Pine Log. At least the workmen were getting the grounds in shape, and she could approve the divorced architect's plan. In her enthusiasm she helped clear a road until a fall from an embankment left her with a pain in her side. Then she became impatient to get at some writing. Lorimer had turned down "The Worldly Pioneeress" serial. Now he was on a European trip, probably trying to "get himself together," Mrs. Harris confided to Faith, after "drinking too hard." Bigelow had also refused the serial, and Doubleday had not sold "The Co-Citizens." She had better get back to New York after Christmas.[13]

A proposition from Holt would pay expenses for the trip. He wanted her to do a series for the *Independent* giving her views of New York. Besides a modest fee for the articles he would get her a hotel due bill. She would have plenty of time to do other work.[14]

While carrying out Holt's assignment—and finding no end of uncomplimentary things to say about New York—Mrs. Harris stirred herself to make new literary connections. Miss Sonya Levine of *Metropolitan Magazine* agreed to meet her price for short stories, and young Norman Hapgood of *Harper's Weekly* called, disconcerting his hostess by continuing their conversation from the bathroom where he had gone to "wash-up." But perhaps she expected him to be unconventional. They had become acquainted the past summer when she wrote attacking a defense of prostitution in his magazine. Her most advantageous connection, however, was made with Arthur Vance of *Pictorial Review*. He immediately contracted for a story "suitable for a family magazine" and was to prove a depository for material rejected by Lorimer.[15]

Still miffed with Lorimer for returning her serial, she did not stop in Philadelphia on the way up and wrote him some excuse from New York. Cheerfully indifferent to her intended snub, he replied that she was really a big-city lover and that the "white lights are beginning to look pretty good to you." She decided to slip an anonymous story by him only to have it recognized and returned. When she warned she would prove her literary worth by publishing elsewhere, he said she would be going to unnecessary trouble. The *Post* judged each piece submitted on its merit. However, he added, "I think you ought to make good with all those editors you've been flirting with." She would never learn she could make nothing off of Lorimer.[16]

Lorimer had diagnosed Mrs. Harris accurately: she was having a gay time in New York. Her letters to Faith read like a debutante's diary. Russell Doubleday took her to lunch, Holt escorted her to the theatre, and Dorothy Dix came for tea. At a literary party, given by a Miss Tutwiler, she met among others Ellen Glasgow, "a little, round, fat, pleasant-looking lady who was quite deaf." She felt less comfortable at one of Mabel Dodge's famous salons where she encountered "Socialists, Anarchists, artists and mad men of every description" dressed in the most outrageous costumes. At one point in the evening she feared the guests were going to start cutting each other's throats. She enjoyed a banquet of the Authors' League until she spotted a Negro at the table. The next day she felt compelled to send in her resignation from the League. In between such social engagements she went to the opera and to concerts. She decided she must be a person of importance, otherwise "so many people would not be so astonishingly nice to me." [17]

She returned to Nashville in late March highly pleased with herself. Of course all her literary efforts had not turned out well. Lorimer had again proved difficult, and Edward Bok of *Ladies Home Journal* had not seemed interested in her work. In time she would come to believe that Bok was prejudiced against her. But she had still done all right on the trip. Besides the *Independent* articles, she had sold five stories: two to *Metropolitan,* and one each to *Harper's, Good Housekeeping,* and *Pictorial Review.* Best of all, nice Mr. Vance was considering that eternal "Co-Citizens." [18]

As she wrote Faith, she had never "been so interested in anything as my Valley home." By then she had decided to name her place "In the Valley," and had ordered engraved stationery with that address. Faith met her there. Another small cabin had been built, since she could not go on living at Anthony's. It was delightfully cool, with doves cooing in the nearby bushes. The two ladies had an exciting time unpacking all the things Mrs. Harris had bought in New York for her house and planning where they would go. After Faith returned to Atlanta, Mrs. Harris stayed on till June, her work interrupted only once by Al Harris's funeral at which she took charge of all details.[19]

As summer came on, Mrs. Harris discovered that "In the Valley" could get quite warm—a fact that was to trouble her in the years ahead. Also, she was worried because Vance had not written his decision on "The Co-Citizens," and Lorimer had been silent since she returned. In the middle of June she left for New York to arouse some interest in her affairs.[20]

Again she went straight to New York and was overjoyed to find that *Pictorial Review* would publish "The Co-Citizens," even though Vance would pay only $2,500 for it and asked for considerable revising. "The strain is lifted," she wrote Faith. Now Doubleday could delay no longer bringing it out as a book.[21]

She took rooms at the Seymour Hotel and settled down to work in the depressing city heat. In her letter to Faith she made no mention of the great war about to break out in Europe. Nor did she apparently connect it with a note from Lorimer who had written her asking that she let him know when she finished her work in New York. On August 3, however, a wire explained what he had in mind.

How would you like to spend a few weeks in London for us doing woman's side of the war.[22]

Mrs. Harris knew from the first that she would go. But she restrained her excitement and wired back that she would first have to see if her family was willing. She would come down for a talk as soon as she finished the serial for Vance. What she did not tell Lorimer was she wanted to find out what he was going to pay for her articles. They ought to bring a good price.[23]

Then she wrote Harry to find out if Faith could refrain from worrying too much while her mother took such a trip. She enclosed a letter to her daughter which Harry could give her after reading the one to him. In her letter to Faith she minimized the danger of her assignment and told how delighted and amazed all the hotel guests were at "my chance to go to England." She made the last revisions on the serial and went down to see Lorimer on September 14. He was planning to pay her $750 an article and set no limit on the number she wrote. The expense account would cover all her needs. He would arrange for her to sail on September 23.[24]

From then on Mrs. Harris took a firm stand with Faith. Her daughter must remember they were both descendents of Confederate soldiers and she must show some confidence in her mother's wisdom and strength. If Faith could not rise to the occasion, Mrs. Harris would go anyway. "I cannot allow your anxiety to interfere with my war plans," she wrote. Her daughter could come to New York for the sailing.[25]

So, on September 23 Mrs. Harris waved goodbye to Hamilton Holt, Russell Doubleday, and a tearful Faith. Lorimer was in Philadelphia reading the first war copy from Irvin S. Cobb and Sam Blythe, already on the scene.[26]

On reaching London Mrs. Harris's anti-British feelings came alive. Reared in the Civil War tradition she expected to see weeping women, marching soldiers, flags waving, and bands playing. Instead her taxi passed an occasional group of boys, drilling in a holiday mood, and a few people standing before a small bulletin in the London *Times*'s window. She decided the British were not taking the war very seriously.[27]

She was surprised not to receive a warmer welcome and greater cooperation. In a letter to Faith she said that members of the Woman's Emergency Corps were so aloof she found it difficult to report their patriotic activities "without malice and ill feeling." Horatio Kitchener, Britain's despotic Secretary of War earned her displeasure by refusing to let the Emergency Corps serve in France. She was not amused by his explanation that the two pests he had suffered during the Boer War were "flies and British women." The casualty lists depressed her so deeply that she called at Kitchener's office to learn how many men had been killed so far. Stopped at the door by two sentinels she said she had come to ask the Secretary the number of war widows in the country. When the amused Tommies refused her admittance, she informed them she was an American reporter and that she would never visit that office again. Perhaps she never submitted to Lorimer the angry article based on this incident. If she did, he decided not to publish it.[28]

With two publishable articles on England completed, Mrs. Harris left for France on October 16. She took with her as interpreter Mrs. L. M. Grove, daughter of James Fraser, the anthropologist. The arrangement proved unhappy. In a letter from France Mrs. Harris complained to Faith that "every day or two I have to jump on the lady I have with me as interpreter and mash the guts out of her for her insolence." [29]

In Paris she found that the war had ebbed from the city gates leaving behind "a large and personal silence." Everything was so different from England: "The English believe their country cannot be invaded; the French have suffered too many past invasions to be startled by the current one." In the Paris hospitals Mrs. Harris was moved by the sight of Catholic nuns attending kilted Scots, turbanned Moroccans, and even hated Germans. She was vastly impressed by the number of prominent French women doing menial war work. But in the slums of Paris she saw wild-eyed, unkempt women like those who had stormed the Bastille. Would these also march if the war dragged on? [30]

Before leaving America Mrs. Harris had decided that somehow she was going to get into the fighting zone. She considered herself a war correspondent, and war correspondents did not report in safety miles behind the fighting lines. Lorimer had warned Faith that her mother was "jealous of Irvin Cobb [who had come through Belgium with the German Army] and . . . determined to dash around herself a bit." Rather cautiously she edged north out of Paris. She and Mrs. Grove visited Senlis, demolished by the Germans in their sweep to the Marne, by mixing with a train-load of French women returning to their demolished homes. She did a moving description of that war-torn city in her second French article. Then she decided to visit Soissons, well within the range of enemy cannon. French officials finally gave her a pass, but only to Compiegne, a few miles from Soissons. In Compiegne she persuaded the mayor to issue a permit for her and Mrs. Grove to drive a little way on the Soissons road. The driver of their ancient carriage refused, however, to take them on into Soissons even though she offered to double his fare. Bitterly disappointed she returned to spend the night in Compiegne and hear at intervals the faint sound of cannon to the north.[31]

Perhaps Mrs. Harris might have tried again, but her two attempts to get closer to the fighting had intensified her abiding fear of being arrested for a German spy. She would have welcomed the danger of the trenches, but she shrank from the prospect of arrest, search, and imprisonment. In London she had been shaken when a porter in her hotel was arrested as a German agent just after she had given him a letter to mail. On the ride back from Senlis she became convinced that a French officer in her railroad car would take her into custody when they reached Paris. But her greatest moment of terror came on the abortive trip towards Soissons. Riding back that night through the dark Compiegne Forest, she became aware of a French soldier keeping his bicycle abreast of their rickety carriage. In answer to Mrs. Grove's question he said he was "looking for German spies." Even after he disappeared silently in the darkness, the two ladies remained apprehensive.[32]

Strangely enough, when Mrs. Harris returned to London she amplified her *Post* account of the Compiegne adventure in a letter home. "Faith, I did get on the firing line," she wrote, ". . . I saw shells flying over my head. I can now die satisfied." She goes on to say that "from the 11th of November to the Fifteenth I was within the sound of cannon day and night." Obviously she had forgotten that on November 12, 13, and 15 she wrote Faith from Paris. Her mind was, perhaps, too intent on returning home a heroine—at least to her daughter.[33]

In London she wrote two more articles. In "A Communiqué" she took a final dig at Britain's blasé attitude towards the war, and in "War and Hallucinations" she denounced war as a method of settling international disputes. The second article could have been written without a trip abroad.

After separating rather acrimoniously from Mrs. Grove, Mrs. Harris sailed for home on December 5. Near the coast of North Ireland she was in greater danger than at any time in her trip when two mines exploded within twenty-five feet of the S. S. *Transylvania*. In the Valley she received the welcome of a soldier returning from the wars. Faith had the new house in splendid order and had assembled Tinsley White, Harry, Hope Harris, and her four boys to hear what was going on in Europe.[34]

Mrs. Harris was forced to realize, in time, that she had made no mark as a war correspondent. The *Post* serial brought in few letters from readers and most of those were from German-Americans denouncing her reports of war atrocities by the Kaiser's armies. Mrs. Harris was not fitted by training or temperament to be a European correspondent. She was handicapped by a lack of the foreign languages and her stubborn insular prejudices; and she could never overcome a tendency to editorialize freely on the little information she had troubled to collect. She wanted desperately to be given another chance. But in January of 1915 Lorimer sent over Mary Roberts Rinehart in her place. Miss Rinehart obtained interviews with Allied Generals and Kings. When she returned she was wearing an expensive mink coat, bought with expense money, which, she admitted to an amused Lorimer, had kept the knees of several Generals warm.[35]

Years later in her autobiography Mrs. Harris admitted that on her assignment in the World War, she "did not go so far or do so well as those who went over later." [36]

10

. . . . .
. . .
.

A Noble Experiment

THE Christmas reunion was not a complete success. Mrs. Harris swore she would never be a party to a second one, and when her father announced finally that he was leaving on December 30, she did not urge him to stay longer. Perhaps Tinsley had been too vivacious for the younger generation. Harry, already back in Nashville, wrote Faith he could not understand why anyone would willfully assemble his kin. Unfortunately Faith repeated his comment as a joke to her mother. Mrs. Harris preferred to do the criticizing of her family.[1]

Harry had not been in a frame of mind to enjoy the holidays. He was worried by the situation at the Nashville branch of the Morris Bank where he was cashier—the most important position he had ever held. He had not so far enjoyed much success in the business world. Since leaving Dallas he had held for short periods five small-salaried jobs. In the summer of 1912 he had moved from the Nashville Telephone Company to the Union Bank and Trust Company; the following year he was with the Maryland Casualty Company as local representative, and then with the Atlanta Savings and Loan Company; and in the summer of 1914 he had joined the Morris Bank. Harry was apparently capable, but a compelling desire to prove himself made him impatient with the small pay, slow promotion, and dictatorial management of large corporations.

Mrs. Harris had helped Harry get four of these five positions. She had spoken or written in his behalf to Smith of the Telephone Company, Hail of the Union Bank, and White of the Atlanta Savings and Loan. When Harry's application to the Morris Bank hung fire, she obtained a letter of introduction from Hamilton Holt and had a talk with top officials in the bank's New York headquarters. To bolster his standing she authorized him to buy two thousand dollars' worth of Morris stock in his name. Mindful of Harry's pride she had always got his consent before giving help. He dutifully expressed gratitude, but could hardly have forgotten her prediction that he would never be able to support her daughter.[2]

Harry began his work with the Morris Bank in high hopes. As an officer, director, and stockholder he would have a hand in its management and share in its success. Unfortunately he was forced to take sides in a controversy that threatened the bank's progress. The directors and stockholders had split on the question of President H. L. Sperry's competence. Intense in all things, Harry became the most vocal of Sperry's critics. The issue would be decided at a stockholders' meeting in January, and Harry had assured Faith that the bank would get a new president shortly afterwards.[3]

From Nashville Faith kept her mother informed of developments. The crucial meeting was postponed till February because President Clark Williams could not leave New York until then, but Harry remained confident the home office was going to "dislodge Sperry." When Williams came, he showed his confidence in Harry by consulting him on bank matters. But then the President began meeting with different groups of Nashville financiers, and a rumor spread that a few wealthy men were about to buy a controlling block of stock. Harry became worried. These new stockholders would have their own protégés to push, and, worse still, there was no more talk of displacing Sperry. Nervous and despondent Faith began to suffer from neuralgic headaches.[4]

Back in the Valley Mrs. Harris was chafing to get into the fight, but she moved cautiously, still mindful of Harry's pride. She suggested inviting Williams and Richard Plater, a large holder of Morris stock, to the Valley for a week-end, but Faith said Williams would not have time. Next she announced she might run up to Nashville "in case things don't go well for Harry," and getting no objections, she came up for a few days. While there she got one of the prospective stock-buyers to talk with her son-in-law, reviving his hopes for a while. Later she offered to furnish the money for Harry to buy more stock, but by then he knew his battle was lost. The new stockholders announced that Sperry would be retained with even greater powers, and he stipulated that Harry must go when his contract expired in August. Furious at what he considered a betrayal by Williams and Plater, Harry threatened to file suit to liquidate the bank unless the stock he had bought was redeemed. Sperry was only too glad to buy these shares, and Harry resigned with a month's pay.[5]

All the while, however, Mrs. Harris was quietly planting an idea in the Leeches' minds. As early as February 11 she reminded Faith that if things went wrong in Nashville "there is a land of pure delight here with thirty years of health and labor" for her and Harry. A week later, when defeat seemed certain, she made them a definite and a most generous offer. If they wanted to try life in the Valley, she would give them the $1200 she had paid on the Morris stock and with that money Harry could "improve" a part of her land for his own cultivation. On the other hand, if Harry wanted to try another banking job, she would gladly take care of Faith until he got relocated. Her advice would be to "stay in the world if you can win," but to bear in mind "you can win here." [6]

Faith was only too ready to come; she always wanted her mother in times of trouble. But they must wait, she said, until Harry exhausted the possibilities of a steady, salaried job in Nashville. Harry had no success; probably he had no hope. Faith told her mother that when Plater and Williams "went back on Harry, it well nigh broke the boy's heart." In March he joined his wife and mother-in-law in the Valley. He had nowhere else to go. [7]

Mrs. Harris gave the Leeches a warm welcome. Her plan had blossomed into a glowing prospect. First, and above all, she could now restore Faith's health. As she later wrote Harry, her daughter was "in the right place for peace." But it was a wonderful opportunity for him too. She did not intend for him to be a dirt farmer; he could raise riding horses, pedigreed cattle, and Berkshire pigs. The Leeches were not to think she was doing them a favor. She needed them as much as they needed her; she was already overdue in New York and Philadelphia for conferences with her editors. Trying to bolster Harry's confidence, she explained that she had ample means to safeguard their project. Over the years she had constantly referred to her earning power as a reason for the Leeches to feel secure, even when he was employed. On her second European trip she had written Faith that she would make enough from her articles "to support all of us till the end of the war." [8]

Concerned primarily with Faith's welfare, Mrs. Harris gave no thought to the problems ahead for Harry. He had been reared in the city and knew nothing of farming. Necessity, and not a greater opportunity, had forced him to put Nashville and the banking world behind him. If she and he ever drew up a contract, it has not been found in her papers or referred to in her correspondence. In a letter from Nashville Faith had written of her husband's willingness to try "farming on a small scale," yet he was to find himself placed in charge of getting a barn built, making a contract with a tenant and, in fact, the management of the entire farm during Mrs. Harris's absence. Undoubtedly she made this shift in arrangement to show her trust in him; and she departed in a few weeks for the north to show that he and Faith would not be hampered by her interference. She apparently had no misgivings. In early June she set out for New York leaving him "with the bag to hold and Faith the turkeys and chickens." [9]

Mrs. Harris's letters home were filled with accounts of literary successes and praise for the Leeches' management of her farm and home. She had sold a story each to *Good Housekeeping* and *Pictorial Review,* but her exciting news had to do with Lorimer. He had been wonderful to her, bought an article, and got her started on a sequel to *A Circuit Rider's Wife.* If the serial pleased him, she would be able to "get that herd of Aberdeen Angus as soon as Harry gets ready for them." They must go ahead with all their plans, for she was "thoroughly satisfied with yours and Harry's managing." [10]

Meanwhile, back in the Valley, the Leeches had begun their venture in farming. Mrs. Harris had put ample labor and money at their disposal. Five Negroes, three men and two women, were on her payroll, and Smith, the Cartersville contractor, would provide carpenters for work on the barn and some smaller buildings. She had deposited in her bank what Faith called "a generous supply of money" for farm and household expenses. Harry received fifty dollars a month as salary, and he and Faith could use the twelve hundred dollars from the Morris Bank stock in any way they chose. Never before had the Leeches commanded such large sums. [11]

For a time Faith's letters to her mother carried enthusiastic reports of cheerful, bustling activities: crops were planted, clover curing, the barn beginning to rise, the garden producing and the hens laying. In the evenings she and Harry pored over farm journals. Harry's industry and judgment had won the admiration of both Whites and Negroes. Always seeking to bridge the gap between her mother and husband, Faith emphasized his gratitude for the lovely presents coming to him from New York. "Everything," the girl wrote, "is proceeding with the utmost smoothness." [12]

In mid-July Mrs. Harris's happy complacency about things at home was suddenly dispelled. Nervously Faith wrote that the money allocated for expenses was almost gone. She had tried to economize, letting two Negroes go, and Harry had managed beautifully, but unexpected expenses had put a continuous drain on their finances. Smith, whom Harry "hated," had exceeded their budget for lumber, and farm equipment seemed always in need of repair. Anxious to absolve her husband of blame, Faith included in her next letter an itemized account, with explanations, of their expenditures. She made no mention of her weariness and discouragement, but the tone of her letter revealed she was worn out from long hours and summer heat.[13]

Mrs. Harris was deeply disturbed, not about the money spent, but about Faith's state of mind. She had been picturing the girl as happy and healthy in the Valley only to learn that she had worked and worried herself to exhaustion, just as Lundy had done. And all over money, while she was earning it hand over fist in New York. It just didn't make sense. Immediately she sent a letter with an eight-hundred-dollar check. She assured Faith that she and Harry "had done splendidly . . . and probably saved me hundreds of dollars." Generously she went on to say that the enclosed check was not expected to meet all forthcoming bills. She would send more as it was needed. There was nothing to worry about. She would clear five thousand dollars on her current trip. There would be plenty of money for all of them.[14]

The same tragic situation was emerging again. Mrs. Harris could only relieve Faith's anxiety by helping Harry.

Mrs. Harris continued to write cheery letters which evidently failed to heighten the spirits of the home front. She returned in late September to a despondent household. Faith was alarmed about Harry's physical condition. The labor and strain of the past months had aggravated a chronic stomach ailment, and he was going to Nashville for a medical examination. During the few days before he left Mrs. Harris lost her temper with one or both of the Leeches. Later a letter from Faith to her husband in Nashville indicates that Mrs. Harris had become upset about "the routine" established by the Leeches in her absence. Faith reported happily that the issue had now been smoothed over.

Mama is thoroughly straightened out as far as we are concerned. I went over her yesterday with a fine-tooth comb and settled many points and she recovered from her melodrama. . . . it is all right today.[15]

The roots of the altercation very likely went deeper than a question of household management. Mrs. Harris was troubled by Harry's failure at farming. In December she wrote Dr. Andrew Soule, president of the State Agricultural College, asking him to come for a visit and give Harry some pointers on labor and cultivation. She explained carefully that her son-in-law had performed "prodigious labors" and she did not want to "take the heart out of him by meddling." Dr. Soule could not come, but he "did write very kindly" to Harry about his problems. Unfortunately, Dr. Soule had to explain that Mrs. Harris had prompted his letter.[16]

The family tried to make the most of Christmas. Faith became as excited as a child, and Harry praised an expensive mandolin from his mother-in-law. But a small farm house is not the place for three sensitive people to pass the confining winter months. Harry, suffering from a nervous stomach and anticipating another unfruitful year, became critical of Mrs. Harris and her ways. Apprehensively Faith watched her mother bottle up her anger. It would be loosed somehow in the days ahead.[17]

While at home Mrs. Harris kept her temper, but in late March, on her way to New York, she wrote Harry a blunt letter. First, she explained that she wanted, above all things, to make the Valley into a place where she, he, and Faith could have happiness and security. Still bent on that hope she was going to build a house for the Leeches there. It would cost considerable, but she would not complain if it lessened the friction between her and him. She would not, however, go ahead with their house until she could believe his attitude towards her would be changed. If he stayed on in the Valley, she would assume that he would never again treat her as he had during the past winter. As she put it,

You may say what and to whom you please about me, but you must not speak to me as you have in the past. I refer particularly to your reflections upon my manners, my character, my family, my friends and my Christianity.[18]

No letter of Harry's giving this assurance has been located, but he remained in the Valley, and Mrs. Harris evidently took that as his answer. Soon she was writing Faith gaily about the future in store for the three of them. Harry, she said, must forget about the money and make the Valley something they could all be proud of. He should realize that he was developing a place which might some day belong to him. Everything she had would go to Faith, with no restrictions on her leaving it to him if she died first. Also, Mrs. Harris wanted him to realize he was in full charge of everything. She would never interfere with his management, "unless his health fails or he proves, as I do not expect, incompetent." Unfortunately she had suggested two possibilities which Harry also must have considered.[19]

Harry may, or may not, have been encouraged by Mrs. Harris's buoyant messages, but he and Faith persevered. There was plenty to occupy them: the building of new fences, cultivation of additional land, the urgency of getting their house started. Mrs. Harris insisted that Harry, and not her lawyer, should deal with her tenant and the contractor. Both he and Faith knew that her mother bought the best material, and she expected the best work. She insisted that there be no economizing on her children's house; it must not be shamed by hers higher on the hill. They wanted the new house finished as much as she did, but the workmen were indifferent and the lumber not delivered on time. Weather retarded their crops. A hot, dry spell was finally broken by a rain which continued till it flooded the fields. Bills mounted, and the money drained away. Faith had no choice but to let her mother know the sad condition of their finances and crops.[20]

Again Mrs. Harris came readily to the rescue with a substantial check and the promise of additional ones when needed. Lightly she brushed aside her daughter's story of droughts and floods: all farmers must learn to expect bad weather; it was an occupational risk. There was no reason for panic about the farm; she was getting all the literary orders she could handle.[21]

A few days later, however, Mrs. Harris got a letter which did alarm her. Mrs. Paul Akin of Cartersville wrote that Faith had fallen down the stairs and was still suffering severe stomach pains. Mrs. Harris's frantic wire to Harry produced a brusque unsatisfactory reply. "Faith has entirely recovered from the attack," he reported, "as to the cause of same I know nothing." A letter from Faith alleviated her mother's anxiety, but increased her irritation. The girl declared she was perfectly all right again and that without her knowledge Harry had asked Mrs. Akin to write. He had decided not to let Mrs. Harris know himself because she might think he was exaggerating Faith's condition so as to get a trip for himself to Nashville. Faith was angry with both Harry and Mrs. Akin. Mrs. Harris was angry with everyone. It seemed clear to her that neither Harry or Faith wanted her back home in her own house. She wrote Faith that she was leaving New York as soon as she could finish up her business there. "I hope and believe you will be glad to have me come," she added. "Anyway, I am coming." She left about the middle of June.[22]

The last of June Faith was stricken with spasms of stomach pains. Harry and Mrs. Harris rushed her to Nashville where Dr. Joseph Gains operated immediately. The cause of Faith's attack was kept a secret. She had begged her mother not to discuss her ailment, so Mrs. Harris told friends that Gains had performed a dangerous, but successful appendectomy. Whatever the operation, it was a major one, for the recovery was slow.[23]

On July 12 Harry went back to the Valley to salvage what he could of his crops. At night, in the silent, humid house, he could picture life without Faith and "came as near praying as it is possible for me to come." Once before when she was away he had decided the Valley was a "horrible" place. Now he must have seen it as something evil which had robbed him of self respect and wrecked Faith's health. And yet Mrs. Harris expected them to go on living there under her orders, supported by her success.[24]

Five days after his arrival he was startled by a wire from Mrs. Harris announcing happily that Faith could be brought home. Alarmed, he wrote his wife immediately that he would not permit her to be "marooned in the Valley in this heat with no way to get out." Hurrying to Nashville, he lost whatever argument took place there, for three days later Mrs. Harris came back ahead of them to get everything ready.[25]

From the Valley she wired Harry that the road from Cartersville had been a little rough, but the drive quite pleasant. The Leeches found her car and driver waiting for them at the Cartersville station. Ordering the driver to meet them at Pine Log, Harry helped Faith onto the branch line train.[26]

The three were together again, often in the close proximity of Faith's sick-room. It is a tragic picture: mother and husband on opposite sides of the girl's bed, self conscious of each other, careful to say nothing that might provoke a storm.

In the evenings, when Faith had dropped to sleep, the other two would come together in the living room. In a diary Mrs. Harris kept a running account of those midnight seances. She and Harry would keep their voices down. He warned her that if she lost her temper again within Faith's hearing—as she had done with the hospital nurse in Nashville—he would take his wife from her. The diary entries tell how she sat helpless while he belabored her with threats and accusations. Physically ill, tied to an impossible situation, Harry may well have lost all sense of proportion. But, on the other hand, when Mrs. Harris escaped to her bed room, was she capable of recording honestly what he had just said, and what she had been obliged to hear? [27]

It is certain, at least, that she shackled her rage—for a time. Around the middle of August the Leeches left suddenly for Atlanta. Shortly afterward Mrs. Harris had this to say in a letter to Faith:

I failed through no fault of mine, and I do not see how you could have acted differently as the situation developed. I regret that having kept silent so long under such provocation, I was at last provoked into speaking plainly. I regret it because, however true, what I said hurt Harry, and I am sorry for that. I am the more sorry because it makes life difficult for you as my daughter.[28]

She began packing Faith's furniture for shipment to an Atlanta apartment. She must tell the contractor she had decided not to go ahead with her daughter's house.

11

. . . . .
. . .
.

Interlude

FEW people fail as tragically as Mrs. Harris did with their domestic problems; and fewer still recover as quickly and completely from such failures. Back in the dark days when Lundy disappeared from Oxford, when disaster was a new experience, she had been obliged to fight for self-control. By the fall of 1917 she was a veteran to sorrow and had cultivated restraint until it had become an instinct. Later she explained to Faith the discipline she had imposed upon herself.

I fight every fight in my life to a finish. I do my best until I have not an ounce of endurance left. Then, if I cannot win, I give up the fight on these grounds and turn around and win it with my soul.[1]

It became a point of honor with her to rise above continuous defeats. Also, a sturdy self-interest steered her away from brooding. She would not permit herself to be shackled by the past. "Life," she once said, "is not slavery, but a beautiful adventure." She must shake loose from grief and resentment if she expected to reach for the opportunities that lay ahead. Convinced as she was that Harry Leech had ruined her Valley plans, she put him resolutely from her mind. Without mentioning his name, she let Faith know he was not to be a topic of conversation in the future. "When I clear my conscience of a person," she wrote her daughter, "I usually forget that one."[2]

Her resolution to put the family break-up behind her was made easier by her burst of temper which prompted Harry's departure. With the release of emotions she could view rationally the sad climax, express regrets to Faith for having spoken so plainly, and even commend her daughter for leaving with her husband. Fortunately for Mrs. Harris, although not for certain people, she invariably found occasions for such tirades both in her deep sorrows and more passing disappointments. After Lundy's death she had made the Reverend Anderson a target for her anger, and before Faith's wedding, John Craig. When her first European trip did not turn out a bright adventure, she upbraided her daughter, and on a visit to Philadelphia she and Lorimer had disturbed the Olympic calm of his office with a row over her rejected serial. Healthy-minded people can resort to this method of relief.

Throughout the fall she kept her letters to Faith chatty and cheerful. All her days, she wrote, were "desperately full," planting a late garden, whitewashing the chicken-houses, even helping with the milking and fodder pulling. She reported amusing happenings: how she broke Bosco, her Great Dane, from sucking eggs, made a Negro woman she was discharging do an onerous chore before leaving, settled a boundary-line dispute between Tenant Tilley and Clarence Anthony by making them appear as a couple of quarrelsome boys. Although she resolved to interfere no more with the Leeches' married life, she could not repress the urge to help her needy daughter. She insisted on refunding Harry three hundred dollars, which she calculated he had spent on the farm from the money given them when she sold the Morris Bank stock. She made Faith mail her soiled clothes to the Valley washwoman and sent back with them hampers of farm produce, taking care to explain they came from Lena, her cook. The mother's loneliness, however, could be discerned in her bright letters, as when she told how she had called in the Negro servants to toast her in wine at her solitary Thanksgiving dinner.[3]

Faith's replies were brave, but they brought news that disturbed Mrs. Harris. The Leeches had moved into an Atlanta boarding house, and Harry had returned to work for Woods White, undoubtedly because he could find nothing better. Neither Harry nor Faith liked Atlanta. They had no friends in the city, and, as Mrs. Harris knew, they could never be happy outside of Nashville. Faith admitted that neither of them was well: she could expect her days of wracking pains each month, and Harry usually returned in the evenings with a blinding headache.[4]

In late September Faith made the first of many solitary trips to the Valley, setting out under the cloud of Harry's disapproval. Mrs. Harris's wild denunciation still echoed in his memory, and he could only see his wife as going "into the camp of the enemy." At times he would insist that a proposed visit be shortened or even given up. Always fearful of aggravating his nervous state, Faith would sadly write her mother that their plans must be changed. Mrs. Harris kept down her resentment. "The fact that you love your husband," she replied, "does not, and never could, affect your relations to me." She would never issue an invitation, since it might well intensify Harry's opposition, but would only repeat that Faith was always welcome. She did, however, make it possible for her daughter to come without asking him for railroad fare. At regular intervals she commissioned Faith to make some purchases in Atlanta and sent more money than was needed. Fortunately for both, the brief visits continued; otherwise they might have found the separation unbearable.[5]

Neither mother nor daughter could look forward to Christmas, a day that had always meant so much in their family. Mrs. Harris decided to pack a Christmas dinner and spend the holidays in Rockmart with her ailing sister Hope. She sent Faith a small check with the explanation, "A little remembrance—not what my heart would send, but you know how things have been." Her daughter joined her after Christmas for a couple of days in a Rockmart boarding house. She found her mother preparing to take Hope to Nashville for an overdue operation. It might prove a sad trip and would certainly impose another strain upon Mrs. Harris. But she told Faith, "Never yet have I failed to do what I had to do." [6]

Happily Hope's operation revealed no malignancy. During her recuperation Dr. Joseph Gains became more concerned about the "well" sister. Mrs. Harris had written him the past fall that she was not feeling her best, and he could see that it was so. One day he found her asleep in a vacant hospital room and, in spite of her protests, kept her in bed several days. The past months had taken heavy toll of her strength and spirits.[7]

Once back in the Valley, around the first of February, she seemed to revive. Soon she was planning next year's crops, badgering her servants, worrying about investing a large amount of cash with the country obviously headed for war with Germany. An outburst of temper indicated the state of her nerves. On February 20 Faith wrote that Harry had forbidden her next trip to the Valley and, in the ensuing argument, had repeated those accusations of her mother's that had driven him to Atlanta. In her angry reply Mrs. Harris reaffirmed every word she had said and turned Harry over to God, "who," she said, "doubtless has better facilities for forgiving him than I have." [8]

With family relations at a stalemate and Valley affairs in order, Mrs. Harris prepared for another Northern trip. During the past two years she had come to concentrate her literary sights upon *Pictorial Review* and the *Post*. She had not, however, enjoyed uniform success with the two magazines: as Vance grew more receptive, Lorimer proved more difficult. In 1915 and 1916 Vance had published four stories and a serial, had accepted another serial and ordered a third. He was nice, too, about paying in advance. During that same period Lorimer had run three articles and one serial, but his interest in her fiction seemed confined now to the Circuit Rider saga.[9]

An incident in 1916 had pointed up the dissimilarity between the two editors. Mrs. Harris sent Lorimer a slight, romantic story, "The Windmills of Love," with the assurance she could get nine hundred dollars for it elsewhere. He returned the manuscript with the brisk suggestion that she let her agent, "Brother Reynolds try his hand at it." She decided to do just that. Reynolds was informed of her price and instructed to get an acceptance before he released the manuscript. A hitch arose. Gertrude Lowe of *Woman's Home Companion* was certain she wanted the story but refused to meet the price before she read it. Mrs. Harris suddenly remembered that Miss Lowe had supplanted Vance on the *Companion*. She was certain he would jump for the manuscript. Reluctantly Reynolds wrote Vance explaining that Miss Lowe would get the story unless *Pictorial* wanted it on Mrs. Harris's terms. Vance replied that he did want it, and Mrs. Harris triumphantly forwarded his letter to Lorimer. Lorimer congratulated her and offered to testify cheerfully to all interested parties that Mrs. Harris was "not a liar." [10]

On April 1, 1917, Mrs. Harris headed north to chat with these two editors. It was not a propitious time to sell either of them; war with Germany was declared shortly after she reached New York. Lorimer held up for several days her trip down to Philadelphia and then rejected her outline for a serial. The best she could do was to get a promise he would read another she had in mind. She was not so patient with Vance who also could not see her immediately. When she presented her revision on "The Solution" she included a bill of $150 for expenses incurred during her wait. After collecting in full, she decided to see no other editors during her trip. "I refuse to throw myself on the open market," she wrote Faith.[11]

Mrs. Harris's lofty attitude towards the literary market was not entirely a pose; she had become intent on her country's decision to enter the European War. On the way up she had stopped off in Washington to hear President Wilson deliver his declaration of war to Congress. Wheedling an admission ticket from her congressman she watched "a plain man in a black coat and grey trousers, very bald on top," mount the rostrum. His face, she decided, "looked like a national funeral." As his stately rhetoric dominated the silent chamber, she felt as if she were "listening to my own conscience." She was disappointed when Washington did not respond with an outburst of patriotism. "We are going to war on a cold collar," she warned Faith.[12]

Four nights later she heard New York newsboys crying war. Hurrying from her hotel to Times Square she found the usual number of people going leisurely and quietly about their business. For the next few days she pored over the newspapers; a German submarine had been seen off Montauk Point, and others were said to be laying mines along the east coast. Yet, New York remained unperturbed; people seemed concerned only with having a good time. Hoping to find some demonstration of patriotism she attended a war rally of women at the Hippodrome only to watch a program that reminded her of a church tableau in rural Georgia. It was London all over again and look what happened to the English. However, she ought to ease Faith's mind; the girl would be worrying already about Harry's going to war. Writing with the authority of a veteran war correspondent, she assured her daughter that America would never send over more than a small expeditionary force. Still avid for first-hand news she went back to Washington. The nearest she got to governmental activities was to hear a small group of congressmen in a hotel lobby discuss conscription as if they were already bored with the subject. She decided it was time to get back to the Valley.[13]

At home she set about putting her farm and household on a wartime basis, planting a large vegetable garden, digging a food cellar, and doling out monthly supplies to her cook. Throughout the war she remained intensely and vocally patriotic. She declared that if she had sons, she would "expect them to leave before sundown the day war was declared." When Hope's sons, who had also inherited Tinsley White's fighting blood, left for service, she became louder about draft-dodgers. As the war went on, she became convinced that her county was a "hot-bed of pro-Germans," and she reported her tenant to the Federal Food Administration for his failing to plant wheat. She spoke at Liberty Bond rallies and invested in government securities until 1918 when she began to wonder if their interest rate would be lowered when peace came.[14]

Secure in the peace and plenty of The Valley Mrs. Harris brooded about Faith in wartime Atlanta. Harry's salary could barely cover inflated food prices and the rent of a cheerless boarding house. The streets of the city were crowded with soldiers from

Fort McPherson and "uppity" Negroes. In May of 1917 eastern
Atlanta was swept by a fire which war-minded citizens immediately decided was the work of German agents. Frantic with anxiety Mrs. Harris packed her car and set out to rescue her daughter,
but at Pine Log she learned that the fire was under control.
Faith's letters sounded more and more depressed. Harry, over-
worked at Wood White's, often came home too exhausted to
appear at the dinner table. When Faith visited The Valley in
June she showed deep signs of strain. Mrs. Harris could barely
contain her bitterness against Harry. Was there any greater
cruelty than to deprive a wealthy mother of the right to help her
needy daughter? [15]

In late July the United States Mail delivered official-looking
letters throughout the country. One arrived at the Leeches' boarding house: Harry must report to the Nashville Draft Board for a
physical examination. Faith poured out her fears in a letter to her
mother. Harry was sure to be drafted . . . he wouldn't ask exemp-
tion as a married man for fear of appearing a coward . . . she
could not live on a private's pay . . . he would come out of the
army—if he came back—too old for a good job . . . the separation would break her heart—"if it could still be broken." [16]

Mrs. Harris refused to see the prospect as the end of the world.
She replied that if Harry was found physically fit, which was not
certain, he could enroll in an Officers' Training Camp. He would
make an excellent officer, would prove a "madman of courage."
Faith must learn to behave like a soldier's wife. She would not
have to live on a private's, or even an officer's pay. Her mother
would look after her until Harry returned. Mrs. Harris's encouragement could not, however, soothe Faith's real anxiety; Harry
might not return.[17]

The Leeches' situation grew more confused. Woods White
wanted to know what men he would lose to the services, and
Harry, troubled with the same question, had an Atlanta doctor
examine him. Although the doctor reported slight signs of tuber-
culosis, Harry, perhaps defiantly, resigned his unhappy job and
left for Nashville with Faith. There another civilian doctor pronounced him fit for service. The Army, however, has the last word
in such matters, and its medical board recommended that he be
given a temporary discharge on physical disability.[18]

Harry again made a tour of the Nashville banks. He and Faith
wanted above all things to move back to their old friends. But
again he found no opening. Fortunately before leaving Atlanta his
friend Ross Cheshire had offered him a job with the local branch

of Goodrich Tire Company. At least Harry could feel that this position had not been obtained through the help of his mother-in-law. In September the Leeches returned to Atlanta.[19]

Their fortunes seemed, at last, to be taking a turn for the better. Just before the frightening summons from the Army a more welcome letter had come to Faith. *Country Gentleman,* a farm journal of the Curtis Company, had accepted her humorous article on the raising of pigs. The enclosed cheque was larger than her year's earnings from book reviews and children's stories for church publications. She relayed the exciting news to her mother. Now she could buy Harry the things he had been denied. Better still, she might soon be able to divide the burden of household expenses. Mrs. Harris shared her daughter's joy and expectations. "You are at the beginning of a brilliant career," she wrote. Like her mother before her, Faith might become the main support of her family. How strangely alike their married lives had become. Each had been forced to take over responsibilities from a beloved but unstable husband.[20]

Unexpectedly Lorimer took a hand in Faith's career. He had taken over temporarily the management of *Country Gentleman* and was looking for new contributors. In August he wrote Faith that he was sure that she could do a type of article which he needed. That same day he let Mrs. Harris know he expected her "to do some little stunts" for his agricultural magazine.[21]

Both ladies hung back. Faith wanted desperately to continue publishing, but her mother had frightened her with tales of Lorimer's ruthless, exacting ways. Although Mrs. Harris was pleased with the invitation to Faith, she was not flattered by the opportunity to see her name in a farm journal. She confided to her daughter that her idea was "to do no more stunts than it is possible to avoid on his little Weekly." What she wanted from Lorimer was a more receptive attitude towards her serials for the *Post.*[22]

Lorimer made no mistakes. He would land both mother and daughter by using the daughter as bait. In a letter to Mrs. Harris he promised to let Faith take time to decide, but pointed out that "if she wants to make a more or less regular writing connection, she is missing a bet." A week later he warned Mrs. Harris not to high-hat the "little farm journal"; under his care it was going to be worthy of anything she could write. On September 25 he played his ace. "The great idea for *Country Gentleman,*" he wrote Mrs. Harris, "is a series of letters between you and Faith." Could they come to Philadelphia for a talk with all expenses paid?

12

·····
···
·

A Brief Reunion

GEORGE LORIMER usually managed to stay a step ahead of his friend Corra Harris. When she got an idea for a *Post* serial or story, he prepared for a lively discussion on either its acceptance or cost. So far he had enjoyed these verbal tilts more than she had, for the decisions lay with him. In the end Mrs. Harris always smothered her resentment with the hope that she could some day out-smart him. Once she explained to Faith that Lorimer was "a bully and the best editor in the country." [1]

When Lorimer suggested that Mrs. Harris do "some little things" for *Country Gentleman,* she decided to let *him* do the selling for a change. He needed her name in his farm journal. Casually she replied that she would try to oblige him. But the proposed series of letters set her to thinking. It might give the girl just the confidence she needed, and the money earned would be enough to make her realize that through her writing she could put her household on a secure, comfortable basis. But Mrs. Harris did not propose to drop everything, grab Faith, and hurry to Philadelphia. It would do Lorimer good to wait a little. She instructed Faith to write him that they could probably get up in a couple of months. [2]

Lorimer raised no objections over the delay, but named an approximate date in November for the two ladies to discuss with him their "sister act." Very likely he was amused by Mrs. Harris's studied indifference. More than once he had endured her sulkiness when he turned down something Faith submitted to the *Post*. [3]

As the time drew near for the Philadelphia trip, Mrs. Harris had to drop her nonchalant posing—at least before Faith. Her daughter offered a series of excuses for not going: she could never endure the strain of meeting deadlines; she could not please Lorimer; and, as Harry had told her, she did not know enough about farming to write about it. Mrs. Harris demolished each objection. When Faith had written a couple of letters, she would see how easy it was. She knew, from experience, more about farming than her mother knew about politics, religion, and high society, the subjects of her successful novels. Harry, she pointed out, ought to recall how his wife had stood by him and "show wisdom and kindness in the critical period of your life." Finally Mrs. Harris played her trump card: if Faith would not go, then she would go alone. Faith went.[4]

On November 23, Mrs. Harris, with her daughter in tow, walked into Lorimer's office. Evidently their "sister act" won his approval, for a week later he was writing Faith, "I am sure you are going to work up a fine series." In early January he found the first installment to be what he wanted.[5]

It was the most worrisome literary venture Mrs. Harris ever attempted. She found the actual writing easy enough, but, in addition, she must make sure Faith had also written acceptable copy, shield her from Lorimer's pressure and caustic wit, and keep her from breaking under the strain. Even Lorimer's praise could not convince Faith that her contributions were not crude and far inferior to her mother's. She begged Mrs. Harris not to pass her copy if it was bad; she would not feel hurt if she had to revise it. The pressure of deadlines began to frighten her. "I cannot write," she told her mother, "when they rush me so." During a visit to the Valley, she admitted she was "terribly broken." [6]

Mrs. Harris encouraged her daughter at every step. She declared that Faith's first installment was "splendid" and that the second showed she had attained "that marvellous thing called style." Practically no revisions had been necessary. Only occasionally had she "taken the liberty of correcting a few words." Of course Faith could "keep up the licks." Both of them were doing splendidly.[7]

Wisely Mrs. Harris took over the job of persuading Lorimer to run enough installments so that Doubleday could later publish them as a small book. They must make the most of this opportunity. She wrote Lorimer that they would probably have enough letters to run through the year. His reply settled that question. He did not believe that "a series of epistles from the best seller in the Bible would be good for a year in the *Country Gentleman*." She also volunteered to relay to him Faith's wish that the letters be published anonymously. Knowing his desire for her name in his journal, she was probably trying to needle him. For once she got a rise. "Of course she wants to sign them," he replied; "we all do, yourself and myself included." Lorimer could have turned the tables by agreeing, temporarily, to an anonymous publication. It was the last thing Mrs. Harris really wanted for a serial designed to establish Faith as an author. Perhaps Lorimer was too busy to play games.[8]

Even with Mrs. Harris bearing most of the burden, Faith almost dropped out of the collaboration. In January she suffered a severe colic attack while working at her copy. Her occasional trips to the Valley kept her going. "I feel that I will go mad," she wrote her mother, "if I am not there . . . with you." In April Harry persuaded her to undergo a physical examination by Dr. Gains in Nashville. Mrs. Harris seconded Harry's urging. She offered to finish up both sides of the serial correspondence, but Faith stubbornly refused. Fortunately Gains found nothing wrong with her except nervousness and digestive disturbances. Faith was able to get her two May letters to the press on time; she selected the serial's title, "From Sun-up to Sun-down." The two authors could enjoy a needed rest during the summer. Barton Currie had taken over *Country Gentleman* and decided to pick up the serial in the fall with five more installments.[9]

Apparently the fall installments went smoothly, but Mrs. Harris did not dispute Currie when he wrote in October that she must have found it a relief to get her last letter written.[10]

Lorimer had projected the serial as a dialogue on the relative merits of old fashioned and progressive farming. He and Mrs. Harris readily devised a simple plot and three main characters. John and Dora Waring inherit a farm from his aunt and, fortified with the most up-to-date agricultural journals, set about cultivating it. The young couple are plagued with sick pigs, rotting fences, bad weather, and unreliable help. Not far away Dora's widowed mother—none other than Mary Thompson—farms her own acres according to traditional methods. In the letters the daughter takes her problems to the mother who has not only plenty of advice and kindly criticism to give, but also comments to offer on such varied subjects as the lack of war-enthusiasm among her neighbors, the inadequate yield of Government securities, and the efficacy of castor oil for emotional and physical ills. Mary continues to deplore Dora's ideas on farming, but in the autumn loudly praises the Warings for their rich harvest and noble perseverance.[11]

Mrs. Harris and Faith unavoidably drew on their Valley experiences for technical information, but the authors seem to have gone out of their way to make the story autobiographical. John

Waring had a law degree and no knowledge of farming; Dora was graduated from "a sublimated woman's college." John has been declared physically unfit for military service. The Warings' cook and dog have the same names as Mrs. Harris's. Dora worries that her loneliness for her mother may be disloyal to her husband. One cannot ignore the possibility that both authors hoped the serial would be taken as a picture of the Leeches' stay in the Valley. They wanted desperately to conceal the sad outcome of that venture. In Nashville Faith explained that their ruined crops had discouraged them from any more farming, and Mrs. Harris in her autobiography said her son-in-law had been offered a job too promising to be refused. Apparently Harry raised no objections to the circulation of this subterfuge.[12]

The letters afforded more entertainment than help to the readers of *Country Gentleman*. Neither of the authors were successful farmers. They did, however, contrive a pleasant, convincing story. When Lorimer assured Faith she "was crowding Mother," it was not merely to bolster her confidence. Her style did betray some of her mother's mannerisms, but her contributions were lively and natural. Perhaps her anxiety to please Lorimer helped her maintain the anxious tone of Dora's letters. Mrs. Harris showed no such concern with her letters. More than once Lorimer complained about her digressions. He cut out her anecdotes about "a German spy" and "a flivver," and he warned that she was "getting away from the soil." She raised no protests. This was Faith's show.[13]

Mrs. Harris considered the serial the making of Faith. When the girl learned she would receive $150 for each letter, she became hysterical with joy and began planning all the things she would buy for Harry. Surely she would see now that her writing could be in time a major source of income for her family. Then, thanks to Currie, there would be enough installments for Doubleday to bring out the book. "I was not wrong," Mrs. Harris wrote her daughter, "to push you so harshly into that big pond; you can swim." [14]

During 1918 Mrs. Harris's output of her own literary work fell below normal for several reasons. It was late April before she felt sure that Faith could complete her half of the serial, but when she sounded out Lorimer about something for the *Post*, he thought she "had better clean up with Currie before coming back to the homestead." He showed little appreciation for the lift she gave his farm journal; he accepted only one story during the year and refused to send her back to Europe either as a war correspondent or, later, as a reporter at the Peace Conference. In the fall she stopped writing him and got an impish query as to whether she "had made an election bet that you wouldn't write to me or for the *Post*." [15]

Vance, as usual, did better by her. He not only praised her outline for a new serial, but made her a thousand dollar advance. She could have done several articles for *Good Housekeeping,* but William Randolph Hearst's unpopular stand on the war disinclined her to write for one of his magazines. Her own patriotic views had been expressed in her *Independent* article, "What Are We Fighting for"? which drew high praise from the War Department. [16]

As a matter of fact, she could not spare too much time for writing. She had to cope with food and fuel rationing and the rising cost of living. Her Negro servants caught the prevailing restlessness. Aunt Mary, the cook, started stealing things, and Lois, the maid, hid her mistress's spectacles and false teeth "just for meanness." Her chauffeur, the one servant she wanted to keep, announced he might leave her, but she broke that up by pretending she had thirty-nine applications for his job. In the fall of 1918 she became terrified by the influenza epidemic. She made herself "a 'flu mask" and on shopping trips to Cartersville sent a servant into the crowded stores. A steady increase in taxes annoyed her, especially after Vance sent in a report of her *Pictorial* income to the Internal Revenue Bureau. She asked Lorimer if she could claim her nephews as dependents and got a flippant reply: "In an Internal Revenue sense I do not believe you are the head of a family." In November she welcomed the Armistice, but feared the Allies were going to be too light on Germany. [17]

It was Faith, however, who gave Mrs. Harris more concern than all her other worries. Her daughter was obviously still not well. During the summer she ran a high fever and complained constantly of toothache. Her mother began to worry that the dentist might be giving her narcotics for the pain. The serial had not given her the confidence she needed; she wanted to keep writing, and Currie encouraged her, but she could think of no subjects. Harry became antagonistic to the credit manager at Goodrich and began to talk of getting another job. The state of his nerves showed in an unnecessary affront to his mother-in-law. In April she wrote him inquiring about Faith's health but got no answer. Mrs. Harris refused to take umbrage. "It is just water off a peaceful old duck's back," she wrote Faith. But now a troublesome thought haunted her. If Faith became really ill, would he let her know? [18]

A reconciliation between Mrs. Harris and Harry came about—somehow—just before Christmas of 1918. A factor may have been the more secure, better-paid job he obtained in September; Ross Cheshire opened his own tire agency and made Harry credit manager. But however the peace was effected, Mrs. Harris wrote Faith on Christmas Eve, "If only . . . I could have known, I might so easily have arranged for you and Harry to come out." She was going to save the turkey for the Leeches' visit to the Valley in early January. On Christmas Day Faith wrote her mother that the weather in Atlanta was bitterly cold, but "I have been warm in my heart that the shadow has passed from all of us." Mrs. Harris's new housekeeper recorded in her diary on January 10 that Mr. and Mrs. Leech had just left after "a happy visit." [19]

With her family re-united Mrs. Harris resolved to step up her literary output during the coming year. She must go north, and Faith must come with her. Her daughter would, of course, find plenty of excuses for staying at home. She was absorbed with her Atlanta apartment and, so far, had not been able to hire a cook. Also, she had been badly frightened by a violent stomach attack just before Christmas. But a change would do her good, and she really ought to talk with Currie about the serial he wanted and to call on *Cosmopolitan* Magazine which had asked to see some of her writing. And Faith did demur: she was too busy to go, and she ought not to attempt an assignment she might not be physically able to finish. Soothingly Mrs. Harris replied that the trip would be brief; that she had an excellent cook in mind for the Leeches; and that a young writer "must seize every opportunity at first." Again she got her way. [20]

Faith stayed only a day in Philadelphia and then returned home. Mrs. Harris went on to New York where she persuaded Addie, her old cook, to come south and work for the Leeches. After conferences with Vance and Slosson she also headed south. [21]

Apparently Mrs. Harris got more satisfaction from hiring Addie than from the modest amount of literary work she corralled. She directed Doubleday Page to turn over all the earnings of *From Sun-Up to Sun-Down* to Faith, so the girl could feel able to afford a cook. Now her daughter would have the chance to work with peace of mind. Mrs. Harris then turned to her own assignments. They were not imposing: the last part of Vance's serial, two articles for Lorimer and two for Slosson. She still felt inclined to kick herself for not offering Slosson's articles to the more generous Vance. But she realized she ought to do an occasional piece for the fading *Independent*. While north she decided to switch her book publishing from Doubleday to George Doran. Of course Doubleday had been nice to bring out *From Sun-Up to Sun-Down,* but he had not done too well with her novels.[22]

Through the rest of the winter things went pleasantly enough in the Valley except for one upheaval. The white couple Mrs. Harris had hired did not work out. One morning in March the housekeeper was badly frightened when Mrs. Harris yelled from the dining room, "What the hell is wrong with this coffee?" The husband also came in for a tongue lashing for letting the mules break out one night. By mutual consent she and the McClains terminated their contract.[23]

Things were going too well, however, to get upset about hired help. She would get some new Negroes who would not be so sensitive about her losing her temper. What a pleasure it was to be back on unrestricted relations with Faith. She decided not to invite Sister Hope and Addie for her birthday so that she and her daughter could be together alone. Faith was going right ahead with her writing; Currie had accepted an article and arranged a Tennessee trip to gather material for a series he outlined. It was true the girl still did not look well; writing always put her in a tension. But she could come for a good rest when she got back from Tennessee. The Valley was lovely now that April had come. "Everything is so peaceful here," she wrote Faith. "I do not allow my thoughts to dwell long on the future." Seldom had Mrs. Harris found the present that satisfying.[24]

In early April Faith left for Nashville fortified with her mother's instructions on the art of reporting. It proved an exhausting trip. During the days she drove over rutted roads in all sorts of weather, and in the evenings she attended Nashville parties given by her friends. Her spirits rose, however, as her material accumulated. On April 21 she left for Atlanta. She had planned to stop off at the Valley, but now she was eager to start her writing. "My mind is settled on work," she wrote her mother, "and I do not care to break into that rare privilege." Mrs. Harris applauded her industry; with her work behind her, the coming visit would be all the happier.[25]

On April 25 Harry telephoned Mrs. Harris. Faith had been stricken with a stomach attack and seemed in a critical condition. The following day Harry and Mrs. Harris took the sick girl to Nashville. Over the years Mrs. Harris had come to consider Dr.

Joseph Gains as almost infallible. After a brief look at Faith, Dr. Gains summoned the waiting husband and mother. The girl was beyond medical help. Faith lingered for over a week, dying Saturday morning, May 3.[26]

Mrs. Harris's correspondence reveals little about Faith's last illness. She knew her daughter's aversion to having her sicknesses discussed with outsiders. A friend spoke later of "a trouble the x-ray had not disclosed." On April 30 Mrs. Harris, without comment, warned Hope that she and Harry were waiting for the end.[27]

A condolence note furnishes a brief picture of the mother and husband together.

I knew nothing of the illness of Faith when I saw you and Harry standing on the Tulane corner, but I read tragedy in your faces, and the impression remains with me strongly.[28]

It was indeed a tragic picture.

Mrs. Harris once said to Faith, "I can adjust myself to anything, I think, even the loss of you." One year later she proved equal to that test—the severest she would ever face.[29]

Faith's death brought a deeper grief than the one she had endured after Lundy's suicide. He had wanted to die, had taken his life, and if he had refrained, his future would have been dark and uncertain. Mrs. Harris's reaction to the loss of her husband had been anger and resentment that it had to be. Faith's death, on the contrary, seemed to drain her of all emotions. She had lost more than a daughter: she had lost her only companion, the one person to whom she could give her confidence. As Minnie Porter, Mrs. Harris's half-sister, once said, "it was not easy to get close to Corra." Faith had died when her years ahead seemed most promising. Harry had found a good job . . . he and her mother had become reconciled . . . and she herself was coming into demand as a writer. Mrs. Harris believed, and would always believe, in her daughter's literary talent. Faith's career was to have been an extension of her own. Among the sad duties that fell to the mother was to store away the girl's notes taken on the Tennessee trip. She wrote on the package, "She passed away on May 3 without fulfilling the great promise of her life." [30]

It was the grief of loneliness that now burdened Mrs. Harris. When Lundy died, there had been Faith. Now she was alone. "Wherever I go," she wrote a friend, "there will be a terrible silence." She went on to say, it was "as if I stood at the end of a long, long road of the years to come and saw her passing, vanishing, growing dim to my sight." [31]

At the Nashville home of Effie Morgan, where Faith's coffin had been brought, tearful friends crowded around Mrs. Harris anxious to offer sympathy to a woman who had lost first a husband and now an only child. But almost fifty years later Miss Morgan still remembered Mrs. Harris's frightening composure. She did not weep at the grave-side in Mt. Olivet Cemetery. Later she told a friend that when she got to heaven, "I expect God to let me go around a corner somewhere, and cry like a woman till I have shed forty years of tears." She would not let Hope Harris or Isma Dooley come to Nashville, and after the funeral she left for the Valley alone. As Henry Harris was to write her, "You will do what you have always done, gather together the wreck of your life and go on." People expected courage from her, and she would not disappoint them.[32]

She was kind, even tender, to Harry Leech. Their common love for Faith, which had separated them during her life, brought them together in sorrow. She invited him to the Valley, but stipulated that they were not to talk of their loss. "We knew the grief and loveliness of Faith together," she wrote, "so there is nothing to say about that." He came, grateful for her acknowledgement of their mutual sorrow, perhaps anxious to be strengthened by her strength. Years later he wrote her that she and Faith had taught him "how life and death should be faced." She would remain convinced that Harry had hastened her daughter's death, but she continued to remember him more in pity than in resentment.[33]

Mrs. Harris found no end of things to do after the funeral, and once back home she set about doing them herself: answering condolence letters, discussing with Harry those possessions of Faith she would like to have, commissioning Ella Hergesheimer to do a portrait of her daughter. Soon she found time for more mundane matters. As early as May 6, three days after Faith's death, she instructed her banker to invest a sum of cash on hand. Next she was trying to interest a motion picture producer in *Making Her His Wife* and urging her literary agent to find a book publisher for "The Solution." By October she was planning a Philadelphia trip to discuss a new serial with Lorimer.[34]

Mrs. Harris claimed it was the Valley that restored purpose to her life. As she explained to Lorimer, "Faith is dead. Nothing I can do, or fail to do, will affect her immortal prosperity. All I want now is money to spend on this land which is the only dear and living interest I have."[35]

If there had been no Valley, however, Mrs. Harris would have found another reason for releasing her abounding energy from the shackles of grief. To put behind her this supreme sorrow and to persevere would throw an even brighter light upon her achievements. Like a character in one of C. P. Snow's novels she had always been motivated by "a healthy self-centeredness." She weathered the death of husband and daughter by never forgetting, even at the height of her suffering, that she was still alive.

13

· · · · ·

· · ·

·

The Uses of Fiction

IN 1912 Lorimer had explained to Mrs. Harris why he could not say whether her serials were "literature." A hundred years must elapse, he declared, leaving only "the dried bones" of her works, before an answer could be given. It seems reasonably safe to make such a judgment today—only fifty years later. Also, the novels must be considered for the light they throw upon their author.[1]

A grouping of the novels has been attempted to facilitate the purpose of this chapter: (1) The Circuit Rider Series, (2) The Satires, (3) The Premarital Group, and (4) The Marital Group. The five fictional serials written after Faith's death and later published as books will, of course, be included.[2]

THE CIRCUIT RIDER SERIES

Mrs. Harris followed up *A Circuit Rider's Wife* with *A Circuit Rider's Widow* and *My Son*. Lorimer brought out both as serials, the first in 1916 and the second in 1920. In *A Circuit Rider's Widow* Mary Thompson has moved to the small Georgia town of Berton where, from her pew in the local Methodist Church, she keeps a sharp eye on dull preachers and a dogmatic, gossiping congregation. Wise in the ways of rural religion she advises and champions Felix Wade, a new minister indifferent to his pre-scribed duties and bent on preaching and living the unadulter-ated gospel of Jesus. Frustrated by his hostile parishioners and threatened with censure from his bishop, Wade resigns the minis-try. Mary keeps her seat in church, but resolves to let the Berton Pharisees go their sinful way—a resolution not likely to be kept. In *My Son* she has better success in redeeming Peter Thompson, the only living child of her marriage to William, from the pitfalls of Modernism. Peter becomes a successful city preacher, but his sermons have more to do with modern psychology than with St. Paul. Mary brings him back to his father's faith by snubbing his radical friends, publishing an anonymous newspaper column on the good deeds of simple people, and encouraging his marriage to a girl who strongly resembles her future mother-in-law.

Mrs. Harris considered herself a highly successful critic of the Methodist Church. In a newspaper interview, four years after *A Circuit Rider's Wife* appeared, she boasted that the book had been condemned from a thousand pulpits. She declared also that the story of William Thompson stirred the Church to set up a fund of several million dollars for supporting its superannuated preachers. The three novels do present an unfavorable picture of the Methodist Church, but the agitation and reforms she claimed would be difficult to substantiate. It should be pointed out, however, that Mrs. Harris did not plan these books with the primary objective of exposing the sins of her denomination. As has been shown, she wrote *A Circuit Rider's Wife* mainly because she believed, quite rightly, that she could make it a creditable work that would bring her money. When the character of Mary Thompson took such a hold upon *Post* readers, both she and Lorimer saw the possibility in sequels. As a matter of fact, he suggested *A Circuit Rider's Widow* in which Mary Thompson would furnish "the talk and observations of an old church woman . . ." He may not have conceived the idea of *My Son,* but he did propose that in it Mrs. Harris, through Mary, should "tell a great deal about yourself and the development of your ideas and beliefs. . . ." Mrs. Harris undertook both serials mainly because they promised to increase her popularity and bank balance, and if Mary was to be the principal character, the stories must deal with religion, for that was Mary's field.[3]

The practices of the Methodist Church and liberal theology may not have impelled Mrs. Harris to write the Circuit Rider series, but she found both tempting targets. Her attacks against that particular church, however, lacked objectivity. As Walter Blackstock points out, she would have grown restive in any denomination, but her "life and experience were with the Methodists." Organizations, religious or secular, were not for her. On the other hand, she was basically too conservative to entertain religious Modernism. She had accepted traditional Christianity and, thereafter, studiously refrained from questioning her beliefs. It should be kept in mind that the convictions Mrs. Harris advanced in all her novels were her own. She might shape her stories to fit a magazine editor's policy, and she always tried to please her readers, but she remained consistent in her stoutly-held views.[4]

Fortunately for Mrs. Harris's popularity, her readers approved of the religious opinions expressed by Mary Thompson. They had been strictly reared in the church and were becoming aware of a spreading secularism throughout the nation. Anxious to retain their faith, they were pleased when intellectual Peter Thompson turned his back upon the new theology. Yet, many of them realized that their church meant less to them than it had to their fathers. Perhaps Felix Wade was right and its doctrines and rules were harmful to true religion. They were moved, therefore, to praise Mrs. Harris for opening "the possibility of a real, live Christianity," for writing novels that shone "with the ripening spirit of faith." Preachers, too, seemed to approve of her criticism. One wrote that he had preached better since reading *A Circuit Rider's Widow.*[5]

The religious issues Mrs. Harris presented in her novels are not so lively today. Even in small Georgia villages the church is less and less important in the lives of the people. The clergy has moved rapidly along the path of liberalism; the Modernists of the 1920's have been succeeded by the "God-Is-Dead" theologians of the present.

The few people today, apart from surviving friends and relatives, who have heard of Mrs. Harris inevitably refer to her as "the circuit rider's wife." In her day the novel was widely accepted as autobiographical. Gertrude Atherton found it classified as such in her hometown library. The faint echo of that notion has come down through the years, and the novel, with its character of Mary Thompson, does have importance for the author's biographer beyond its literary merit; it set the pattern for the rest of her fiction.

THE SATIRES

In *The Recording Angel* Mrs. Harris sits in judgment not upon a church but upon a small town—Ruckersville, Georgia. Her censor is blind Amy White who records in her unflattering diary the foibles of the local women's club, an institution especially distasteful to Mrs. Harris. Unknown to Amy, her bibulous husband augments his wife's chronicles with tales about the town's shiftless male citizens. Action is taken upon the state of affairs in Ruckersville when forthright, wealthy Jim Bone returns after an exile following his knife-fight with a drinking crony. Jim decides to put his hometown on the path of industrial progress and adapts the records of the two Whites to a stage play which he presents in town hall with a New York cast. In addition he

promotes a textile mill which will tower above the local Confederate monument. All turns out well. The citizens, men and women,
are shamed into civic pride; Jim finances a successful operation on
Amy's cataracts with the proceeds from his play, and Sylvia Story,
the town's beauty, accepts his offer of marriage.

The Co-Citizens is an unconvincing story of how politics were
cleaned up in Jordonville, another Georgia town, by the legaliz-
ing of woman's suffrage. Susan Walters, a shrewd, elderly widow,
and pretty Selah Adams rout the local political ring by intimidat-
ing tactics which border at times on blackmail, and obtain a local
option decision on women's right to vote. Mrs. Harris either did
not realize, or ignored, the necessity of getting state approval for
such an election. But, what is more important, the women win the
franchise, and Robert Sasnett, a personable young lawyer, the
hand of Selah.

It would be hasty to assume from these two novels that Mrs.
Harris was an advocate of either New South progressivism or the
Suffragette movement. Her correspondence with Lorimer reveals
that in the fall of 1910 she hit upon the idea of the blind secretary
of a woman's club who "jots down mentally all the members'
doings and failings." Later she enlarged her plot to include the
ladies' trifling husbands. But Mrs. Harris was too staunch a re-
gionalist to want Northern ways brought South. It should be
noted that Jim Bone's textile factory was to be financed by local
capital. In *The Co-Citizens* she dramatized the opinion she would
always hold on woman's suffrage. As she put it in a later article,
women should have the vote; but "gentlewomen should not run
for office except, perhaps the board of trustees of the local school."
Thus, she has Susan Walters refuse to stand for sheriff, and Selah
Adams to declare, after their victory, that she never wants to hear
the word "politics" again. Neither of the ladies was connected in
any way with the national Suffragettes Movement.[6]

Both novels can, therefore, be taken as an attack upon Mrs.
Harris's pet abomination—the feminist. She believed that women
should cultivate their literary talents—if, like her, they had talent
—and take full advantage of the right to vote, but they should
perform these activities as women, not as violent unsexed females.
"I dearly love to be a woman," she told Paul More. "If you star
in that role, no man . . . can hurt you."[7]

Amy White and Susan Walters were both promising characters,
but unfortunately the stories in which they appear are so improb-
able and contrived that neither character could be convincingly
developed.

THE PRE-MARITAL GROUP

All of Mrs. Harris's novels are essentially didactic. The Circuit Rider series exposes the shortcomings of Methodism; *The Recording Angel,* the backwardness of an entire community; and *The Co-Citizens,* the corruption in a small-town political ring. The eight remaining novels, all justly called "pot-boilers" by Blackstock, deal with the problems of marriage. Four tell how a headstrong modern girl was brought to a successful marriage, and the other four how a worthy wife coped with a weak or unfaithful husband.

In the first group Mrs. Harris follows strictly a plot popular in the movies and magazines of that day; a spirited girl, usually rich and socially prominent, is tamed for marriage by a stronger-willed man, who, like Horatio Alger's heroes, had risen without the benefit of family standing or inheritance. In *A Daughter of Adam* Nancy McPherson refuses, for a while, the advances of Black Manson, a self-made Northerner, because she knows he is also trying to buy her bankrupt father's Georgia farm. But Manson reveals he shares Nancy's love of the land and hopes to settle on it with her as his wife. He accomplishes both objectives. David Brock of *In Search of a Husband* works hard at his real estate business while courting Joy Marr, the fickle belle of a small Georgia town. Discouraged by Joy's refusal to give up her popularity, he gives her up and also his business, but returns, very timely, just as she comes back from a Northern resort where a New York capitalist, by suggesting love without marriage, has made her more appreciative of honorable David. In *Making Her His Wife,* John Ames, an enterprising rural storekeeper, has to accomplish that victory *after* he has married Olive Thurston of high Atlanta society, but he persists and succeeds. By winning madcap Ann Capers in *Flapper Ann,* Dr. Abel Fossdick, from the wrong side of the track, probably increased his professional prospects and social standing—although Mrs. Harris makes no such promise.

The outcome of these romances is never in doubt. The desirable suitor is bound to prevail over his wealthy, effete rival, either slowly, like stubborn Abel Fossdick, or suddenly like John Ames when he tosses roué Dickie Blake from a balcony onto the dance floor below. The young ladies are hardly wild, even by the standards of that day. Joy Marr refuses to stay another day at the resort hotel after an unwelcomed proposal, and Olive Thurston haughtily reminds Dickie Blake that she is a married lady even if she has left her husband. Even Flapper Ann Capers, the most unbridled of them, apparently smoked and drank in moderation—but not on the stage of the story.[8]

In these stereotyped plots Mrs. Harris makes clear a firm conviction about marriage. It was, she believed, the proper career for women. In a magazine symposium on "The Single Woman Problem" she offered a concise solution: "Don't stay single." Sprightly girls, like her four heroines, however, needed and got strong, decisive husbands. Mrs. Harris admired masterful men; she denied, not too convincingly, that she had patterned Jim Bone on George Lorimer. Her heroines would not be broken, however, by such husbands. She explained to Vance that Olive Thurston was to demonstrate that marriage was not "the whole existence for a woman," and she has Abel Fossdick say he will never completely trust his ex-flapper wife. Obviously these young ladies were not going to become docile and dull after marriage.[9]

THE MARITAL GROUP

In three of the four novels of this group, "the other woman" appears to disturb matrimonial peace. Two wives are equal to the challenge; the third rises above it. In *Eve's Second Husband* Eve West, back in Tennessee, hears that Adam, her second husband, is paying more attention to a Washington adventuress than to his Congressional duties. Eve has a noble portrait of herself hung in a Washington gallery—which Adam fortunately visits—and then runs up some huge bills on clothes and household expenses. Adam hurries home and promises reformation. Mary Madden, of *Happily Married* is content to dress plainly and bide at home until she hears that Pelham, her husband, is being seen with the red-haired wife of a friend. Mary buys a new wardrobe and plunges into civic work. Soon Pelham is again dividing his time between home and bank. *The House of Helen* at least offers a variation on this repeated theme. George Cutter is not only unfaithful but incurably dishonest. Helen is helpless. All she can do is refuse to follow him to the greater pitfalls of New York, adopt several children, and open the door of her orphanage to George when he finally returns broken by a well-deserved penitentiary sentence.

The Eyes of Love presents an even greater departure from the conventional marital problem. Betty Cutmore struggles bravely with the impossible task of restoring Windham to the health and sanity he had enjoyed before a shattering World War I experience. She remains steadfast even when he is unjustly suspected of murder. In the closing chapter the reader, but not Betty, is told that George has not long to live. Comforting assurance is given, however, that George's fine law partner will see that Betty does not stay a widow beyond the proper time.

The only comment required upon this group is to point out that it labors the second of Mrs. Harris's opinions about marriage: that patient loyalty, not divorce, is the solution for almost all marital problems. She had argued this belief in an early *Independent* article, and she had lived it, too. During her darkest days with Lundy she apparently never considered leaving him, and nowhere in her correspondence with Faith does she even intimate that her daughter might do well to separate from Harry Leech.

To reach a conclusion about Mrs. Harris's novels, the two primary motivations behind all her writing must be considered. She wrote for money and popularity. She would have preferred to write "literature"—as her question to Lorimer indicates. But she put aside that hope so as to give full attention to her more immediate ends.

She intended to earn from her novels all the traffic would bear. It became a game with her—a game with attractive stakes—to play editor against editor, and publisher against publisher; to browbeat or cajole them, as the situation required; and, in extremities, to invent special needs for more money. Lorimer remained impervious to her longings for a new piano, but Vance contributed to a new cow-barn, with the request it bear the following plaque: "Arthur T. Vance, *Pictorial Review* Foundation." [10]

She concentrated upon her serials, rather than upon her novels, for they brought in immediately larger checks. Up to a point, her editors found her more cooperative than did her book publishers. She welcomed their suggestions for plots, slanted her narratives towards their magazines' policies, and even undertook limited revisions—although she once made Vance pay for that imposition. Russell Doubleday and Walter Steger warned that a *Post* serial cut the sales of a book in half, and that Lorimer was making a journalist of her, but she was not one to pass up ready money, and, as she told Faith, she prized "the sweet comfort of keeping my name in the *Post*." [11]

She wrote at top speed and became fretful when she had nothing scheduled for her magazines. Between 1921 and 1926 she published eight serials: five novels, two autobiographies and a travelogue. Lorimer had to warn her against attempting two serials simultaneously, and in 1920 Doran faced the question of whether to publish first *Happily Married* or *My Son*. She could always, however, find a reason for her feverish output; she needed money to secure her family, to improve the Valley, to meet her outrageous taxes. Her unbroken writing becomes all the more amazing when one recalls that she usually found it a chore. Once she admitted to Faith that her latest publication was "the first I've done in three years that I really enjoyed." [12]

Fortunately for Mrs. Harris's aims, the type of fiction she wrote, almost instinctively, not only met her financial needs—real and imaginary—but won her devoted friends throughout the nation and beyond. Like *A Circuit Rider's Wife,* the rest of her novels were all highly personalized. Once she explained to Paul More, "about all I can do is interpret myself and everything else by myself." Later she admitted to Lorimer, "I cannot write a real story, but I can follow the trail of humor and the human heart close enough to touch a lot of people so that they are not reading a story but themselves." In all of her fiction she kept, not the narrative and characters, but Corra Harris—that is, her image of Corra Harris—in the forefront of her mind and story.[13]

Mrs. Harris did not depend upon fictional conflict to reveal her feelings and ideas. She sought a more direct contact with her readers. Each of her novels includes a character designed to bring to mind, through her words and actions, the author who created her. Mary Thompson, of course, served Mrs. Harris best; Eve West proved adequate; but Joy Marr would not do. (Mrs. Harris was, perhaps, helped to this conclusion about Joy because after *In Search of a Husband,* Lorimer accepted no more of her romances.) She, herself, admitted she had proved a failure as "a younger, livelier, more attractive woman in fiction." For that reason, she went on to say, "I always put in that dearer wiser old woman as a neighbor to the girl so that I may rest and dwell in her for a scene or two." This older woman appears and performs in most of the later novels: Susan Walters, Mary Madden's mother, Olive Thurston's aunt, Mrs. Broderick of *A Daughter of Adam,* and Ann Capers's grandmother.[14]

But no matter who tells the story for Mrs. Harris—Mary Thompson, Eve West or an impersonal narrator—she cannot rely upon them to say all that she has to say. Long digressions block the pace of her narratives. Some of them have no relation to the story: in *The Recording Angel* she describes three citizens of Ruckersville, who, she admits, play no part in the novel. Even when using the impersonal narrator or Mary Thompson, she will suddenly break into the story with such introductions as, "If you ask me, I should point out . . ."; "I do not say it is not . . ."; "Sometimes I fear. . . ." [15]

Lorimer and Vance recognized and, sometimes, deplored Mrs.

Harris's fixed habit of wandering from her story. But, realizing that her readers welcomed such preachments, they gave her space for them. Lorimer promised her, "you can tell a great deal about yourself" in a forthcoming serial, and Vance urged her "not to leave out too much of that delicious philosophy of yours." Even George Doran recognized that in her novels it was "never the plot that counts, but the truth of your way of putting things." Not that she needed this encouragement.[16]

Mrs. Harris was more aware than publishers or editors that she was doing all right. She had literally boxes of letters, most of them unanswered, from readers praising her novels for being "true," "wholesome" and "decent." One woman called John Ames "my ideal of a husband," and another considered Joy Marr "a profoundly dear philosopher." They read everything she wrote because she had written it. A woman admitted she would have had no interest in *Flapper Ann* if she had not seen its author's name. And they felt warmly close to her. As one reader put it, when she read a book of Mrs. Harris's she felt that the writer was smiling and putting out her hand.[17]

In varying degrees they got the image of Mrs. Harris she wanted them to have. An Iowa woman, perhaps, caught the fullest picture.

You are a mature woman. You have lived a quiet life and been very observing. You have a sense of humor as keen as a razor. It is a grim sense tho. You have been observing those people you tell us about for years, quietly storing the memory of them. You have been and are soul hungry for companionship. You are broad minded and intellectual to a degree that enables you to look upon common folks and see and perhaps later betray all their vanities and weaknesses.[18]

The readers Mrs. Harris satisfied so well were a special, transitory group. They agreed with her ideas and sentiments, and they could not have enough of them. They did not ask—they could not have appreciated—intricate plots and complex characters. They wanted right to prevail over wrong, and the old verities to outlive newfangled notions. So did Mrs. Harris. She wrote for these people and not for posterity, and she found her writing appreciated and highly remunerative. It could be said with considerable truth, that the success of *A Circuit Rider's Wife* largely checked the promise of the Brasstown stories.

From the 1920's on, Mrs. Harris's novels faded steadily in popularity. Few children of her devoted readers have even heard of *A Circuit Rider's Wife*. Less than fifty years have proved that she did not write "literature."

14

. . . . .
. . .
.

To See Ourselves

SOONER or later Mrs. Harris was bound to write her autobiography. She had a healthy interest, shared by many, in that subject. *A Circuit Rider's Wife* had covered only her year on the itinerancy; the worthy accomplishments and worldly experiences of the older, wiser Corra Harris remained to be told. In the fall of 1921 she talked the matter over with Lorimer.

She had come to the decision slowly. Back in 1916 Hamilton Holt had insisted she could write "the great autobiography of an American woman." She was not one to forget such encouragement. After her conference with Lorimer in 1921 he wrote urging her to get started on "that personal story which you have had on your mind for a long time." It was January 1, 1923, however, before she began writing the autobiography.[1]

Mrs. Harris intended this to be her greatest work, "the masterpiece" friends had been telling her for years that she would write some day. If she could only reveal "the tenderness in my heart and the wit in my mind," she would set a new style in autobiographies. For the truth she proposed to tell in her life's story would be a higher truth: not a record of her deeds, but of her "emotions . . . from the experience of living." As she explained to Adelaide Neall, Lorimer's secretary, "What I am banking on is this: that times and civilizations and illusions of men change, but the human heart never does. It is the one country we all inhabit together." [2]

Never did Mrs. Harris work so hard at a book. She claimed to have finished *A Circuit Rider's Wife* in less than a month; it was four laborious, anxious months before she sent the last installment of her autobiography to Lorimer. At times her spirits soared to the belief she was "turning out a dear, good old thing"; then she would become convinced "the whole thing is a damnable mess." She begged Lorimer and Miss Neall to say something kind

113

about her installments, but if they had adverse criticism to make, they must let her know at once. Cutting and revising had always annoyed her, but for the first installment she wrote twenty thousand words and retained only three thousand. "I will kiss my stars," she wrote Lorimer, "if this thing goes through and you are satisfied." [3]

The book presented two over-all problems. First, could she hope to interest the public in the kindly story of an old country woman? The modern world seemed "to have torn up the past . . . as a scrap of paper," to chase after every crazy notion or diversion that came along. The second problem was more demanding. Many readers had come to think of her as Mary Thompson, as a sedentary widow versed only in church and small-town affairs. Now she must enrich that image and show a widely traveled woman conversant in business affairs, at home with the great of the literary and social world. She sought sympathy and—if possible—help from Adelaide Neall.

I have already written three other lives of myself in the Circuit Rider books, yet not one of my own personal life. This book must cover the same ground in a different light, with different material and a different truth. But the woman must be such a woman as could have figured in the three earlier volumes.[4]

Then Lundy must be presented in the best possible light. Certain tragic incidents must be mentioned, but could be partially cloaked. When she had finished the last installment in which he appeared, she still dreaded to see in print what she had written. This time she took her misgivings to Lorimer.

This is as nearly as I can write the real truth about myself and Lundy, but I feel now I should have kept him clothed with the name of William, not Lundy. Somehow the name pains me, but to use Faith's name does not. If you feel the same way about it, we will make the change. I could just keep his name once: "when I meet Lundy Howard Harris, hereafter called William Thompson." [5]

Lorimer vetoed such obtrusive subterfuge, but he did quiet her fears by cutting out one or two sentences in which she took "the public a little too far in your confidence about Lundy." [6]

Considerable discussion took place before a satisfactory title emerged. Mrs. Harris vetoed "Corra Harris by Corra Harris" as too daring, and "My Own Life" because she wanted something "more biblical, more complimentary to me." She herself suggested "Living Waters," taken from Christ's promise of the drink he would give the woman at the well. Then she remembered that the woman was not a very proper character. "My Book and Heart" seemed appropriate. After all, wasn't the book going to be written in the language of the heart? [7]

Lorimer and Miss Neall willingly provided the encouragement Mrs. Harris asked for. He immediately sent her his judgment on each installment: the first was so good he didn't believe she could keep it up; the second sagged a little, but the third soared again; he liked the fourth. When he returned the fifth he assured her "it's going to make a fine book." Miss Neall prophesied it would be Mrs. Harris's best work. Enthusiastic for early publication, they increased the pressure on her. Lorimer wanted the installments as soon as possible; he was pushing for September publication. Well read in Mrs. Harris's fiction, Miss Neall felt constrained to suggest she stick to the narrative "without too much side philosophy." [8]

As early as March the strain began to tell on Mrs. Harris. She complained of distractions that were hindering her progress: the weather turned hot; spring house-cleaning was overdue; people were trying to come for visits. She was beginning to tire. "It is not the writing of the thing that gets me," she wrote Lorimer, "but the writing and cutting out the next day." Late in the month she escaped to Florida and the quietness of a Jacksonville hotel. It was May before the long burden finally was lifted and Lorimer wired to ask, "What do you think your life is worth in terms of dollars and cents?" She agreed that twelve thousand dollars was a reasonable estimate. [9]

The *Post* of September 1 featured "My Book and Heart." With warm pride Mrs. Harris read each installment as it appeared—a tribute she did not pay her other serials. She decided it merited a more appreciative book publisher than George Doran and signed a contract with Houghton Mifflin. She let Miss Neall break the news to Doran and was amused when he wanted to know where he had failed. What a fuss to make just because an author decided to change publishers. [10]

The toilsome planning and writing of *My Book and Heart* paid off. It is the most closely organized of Mrs. Harris's books—one might even say her only book in which organization is maintained. Each of the eight chapters covers a definable period in her life. Mrs. Harris correctly gauged the importance of the first chapter dealing with her childhood; it was indeed "the boards on which the important part of the narrative was to be enacted." Throughout her life she looked eagerly to the future, but what she sought to find was the affection, excitement, and security of those

Farmhill days. As she planned, her picture of untroubled Oxford in the third chapter accentuates the striving and sorrows of the years that follow. A definite location and central event set the form and duration of each chapter. Quite properly the death of Faith in the beginning of the last chapter opens the way for the author's ruminations on her past life and present situation.

Mrs. Harris's bright, witty style serves her well here. She brings characters and incidents to life with a well-turned phrase. Warren Candler, she says, ruled Emory College "according to the wisdom of the Lord and his own digestion, which was not always good." An introduction to Ella Wheeler Wilcox left Mrs. Harris with the impression that "the pleasure was all mine." Moving into the old Allen House at Oxford made her feel she had "rented the Twenty-Third Psalm to live in." Humorous anecdotes keep the narrative moving: Faith telling God a joke in her prayers; Sinclair Lewis's inability to stop talking about himself long enough to interview her; the New York radical at Mabel Dodge's party so obviously comforted with his vision of that city's certain destruction. Commendation is also due the author for keeping her "delicious philosophy" in hand, as Miss Neall had urged. Only in the final chapter—written when she was almost exhausted—does she occasionally relax her grip on the narrative.[11]

She could not, of course, bring herself to tell all about Lundy; and if she had, Lorimer would undoubtedly have emasculated her account. Years later he would refuse to publish her revealing obituary of her father. In the autobiography she protects Lundy's good name in various ways. She announces she will pass over his early Oxford debauch because "no good end will be served by recording the tragic circumstances attendant upon that period of his life." Her account of his breakdown in 1898 makes no mention of the flight to Texas.

In the spring of 1898 my husband was obliged to assume the duties of the English Department in addition to his Greek work. He did it well, but before the end of the term he was a nervous wreck. . . . I sent Faith to spend the summer with relatives and found a refuge for Lundy and myself far up in the mountains.[12]

Lundy's attempted suicide is camouflaged as another emotional collapse. Mrs. Harris tells of his violent altercation with Bishop Hoss and then goes on to say, "Things went badly for Lundy after that, and his health failed under the strain, and he finally came down with an illness which lasted for four months."[13]

It would have been futile for Mrs. Harris even to imply that her husband died from natural causes. The story of his death had been covered fully in the newspapers of Georgia and Tennessee. Adroitly she composed for the autobiography an account that neither denied nor admitted the suicide. First she describes how she watched Lundy decline in 1910 until she realized something must be done.

Early in September when I was sure I could finish the serial ["Eve's Second Husband"] for the *Post,* I persuaded Lundy to resign and take a vacation. But I could not go with him. That was the trouble. No man or woman wants to die. But sometimes they do for the lack of a moment of comfort. Thus Lundy passed, far from home on the sixteenth day of September, 1910.[14]

Mrs. Harris could expurgate Faith's story more safely and, therefore, more completely. The unnecessary competition of mother and husband for her abundant love must have been well kept from the public, otherwise Mrs. Harris would hardly have dared to picture the girl's married life in such glowing terms.

But presently she [Faith] became engaged to a nice young man, not rich, but well-born and well-bred, with exactly the kind of mind to be companionable to such a woman as Faith would presently be. . . .

. . . .

Faith was married in December, after her father's death, and went away with her husband as happy a bride and groom as you could wish to see. That helped, seeing her go straight into love and marriage as a woman should.[15]

The same gloss is spread over the Leeches' ordeal in the Valley.

During the next two years Faith and Harry gained by joy, by hard work, by all manner of experiments, even by the very violence of their happy energies, those experiences upon which Dora's letters in "From Sun-up to Sun-down" are founded.

. . . .

After two years Harry was offered a position that he could not afford to refuse. So Faith and her husband went away to life in another place.[16]

Ironically and unintentionally Mrs. Harris made Lundy's and Faith's death more moving by altering the facts of her two tragedies. Her readers would surely have been more resigned to Lundy's end if they had known that an incurable melancholia, and not the hounding of wicked men, had long before lessened his desire to live. Also, they might not have considered the loss of Faith so unexpected and cruel if they had been told that pressure and anxiety had been steadily undermining her health. As it was, they hastened to send their belated condolences to Mrs. Harris. One praised her for "not flashing the martyr's crown," and another said when she read of Faith's death, "my tears fell thick and fast." Several others reported outbursts of weeping.[17]

The readers certainly believed that Mrs. Harris had held back nothing. They declared that the great feature of her writing was "frankness," that through her autobiography they had become "better acquainted with a great soul," that now they really knew "something about her." The additional knowledge made them love her all the more. One woman declared, "I don't believe you could ever have done a truly wicked thing." Evidently Mrs. Harris had successfully made the transition from "the Circuit Rider's Wife" to herself, for they ceased to address her as "Mary Thompson." [18]

When the serial appeared as a book, leading newspapers concurred. The Springfield *Republican* called the autobiography "a frank, buoyant, humorous and human record," and the New York *Times* thought it made Mrs. Harris "more real than most of the people you know at first hand." Even the far off London *Times* read and pronounced it "a faithful and sincere record." [19]

Strangely enough a dissenting vote came from one of Mrs. Harris's most devoted friends. Hamilton Holt maintained that she had not written "the great American, self-revealing, female autobiography" which he had expected, because she had "omitted half the record." He could not, of course, supply in his review what his friend had held back from her autobiography. It is impossible, therefore, to know whether that "half of the record" Holt referred to was the full truth about Lundy and Faith. Certainly those missing facts would have revealed more clearly the will power and self-interest that were her dominant characteristics. Apart from these family matters Mrs. Harris held back other information needed to fill out the true picture of herself. Nothing in the story suggests that driving ambition which, as she admitted to Paul Akin, made defeat unendurable for her. Unrecorded also are those temper explosions that relieved accumulated tension. In planning the book she decided her image might suffer if she told how she made "the fur fly" in her literary brawls with London, Sinclair, and Dixon. She does recount a single instance of her shameless tactics with recalcitrant editors, but hastens to add that her readers would not consider she had "snitched" her victim if she "named the figures." The image created by Mary Thompson remained undisturbed by the autobiography, and the readers' acclaim rose to new heights.[20]

At first Mrs. Harris bragged about the avalanche of mail that poured in after each *Post* installment. She estimated that by December 1 over twelve hundred women had written. Then she became irritated not only with the size but the content of this mail. Letter after letter came from women seeking to prove "they have had and expect to have a harder time than I had." And their impudent questions. They wanted to know what Faith died of; what had become of Mrs. Harris's son; what she thought Lundy was doing in heaven. Then there were requests for money; didn't she want to finance a memorial window for Lundy, or send a girl, so very like Faith, to college? In desperation Mrs. Harris forwarded the letters to Houghton Mifflin for answering, and assured Lorimer she would never again "excite so much sympathy or start so many tears in this country." [21]

Lorimer took a different view of the abundant response to the autobiography. Mrs. Harris must do a sequel and come to Philadelphia at once for a conference. Wearily she consented although complaining that she was "an old woman and ought to be given a breathing spell." She went up in October before "My Book and Heart" had run its successful course in the *Post*.[22]

She could not, however, bring the same enthusiasm and energy to "As a Woman Thinks." She began it on January 1, 1924, and did not get in the last installment until the following October. This time there were no appeals to Lorimer and Miss Neall for encouragement. Their unsolicited criticism was not the sort to raise her spirits. Lorimer wrote that the opening chapters needed recasting, and the next ones were "slow in taking off." In August she was warned to stay closer to the subject, and a month later she was advised that new material must be incorporated in the ninth chapter. When she had finished Lorimer predicted that the sequel might not have "as wide an appeal as 'My Book and Heart.' " He waited almost a year to publish it.[23]

Lorimer conceived *As a Woman Thinks* as a companion piece to *My Book and Heart*. It would satisfy the public curiosity "about the kind of mind the *Circuit Rider's Wife* really has." As Mrs. Harris explained in the book, she had showed "how the kind of mind I have determined my conduct, courage, cowardice, and literally created the life I have lived in spite of everything." [24]

Before the first installment appeared in the *Post*, Adelaide Neall tried to cushion its failure for Mrs. Harris by declaring that Lorimer had given her a most difficult subject. Certainly it was too difficult a subject for an author who had dealt largely with the interpretation of the heart in the language of that organ. In the opening chapter Mrs. Harris tries to differentiate between her two autobiographies. Each person's life, she says, can be told only in two books: first, "the book of the heart, where we keep memories, the hopes that fail, our loves and hates . . ."; the second must be a record of the mind, "the place where we keep the law or break it . . . ," the repository of "the motives that stimulate us." Instead of clarifying this dubious definition of the mental process, she goes on to explain the mind as "an instrument . . . controlled by spiritual forces that reach us through the medium of the emotions." Later in the book she starts to grapple with some of Freud's findings, but decides it is dangerous to dip into the roots of thought. "Some mysteries," she says, "are sacred so long as they are hidden, but shocking when they are exposed." [25]

The orderly progress of the first autobiography is not present in the second. Since the author's avowed purpose was to unfold the developing of her mind under the influence of certain people, she tells how first her parents and then her husband enlarged her thinking. But by then she has begun to wander up the side roads of irrelevant ideas until she finally deserts the main course of her narrative and makes chapters of her digressions. Her headings announce such topics as "Do You Want to Write?," "Why Worship Europe?," "The Lady Politician," and "Isn't Life Exciting Enough." The impression grows that she is groping for material to fill out her book.

But a far more curious shift becomes gradually evident in the second half of the book. A new title seems to emerge and, strangely enough, it takes the form of a question: "Has My Life Been Worth Living?" Something had shaken Mrs. Harris's granite optimism. She questions her long striving for a literary reputation that will not last, decides she has become an "autocratic, overbearing" old woman to her Valley neighbors, even wonders if the image of herself she created is a true one. Bitterly she resents the time she has "wasted . . . for others without asking that they pay it back." And she had not found happiness. But perhaps happiness was only "a sort of clucking, devised by Providence to keep us up and going on." It might be suggested that Mrs. Harris's sad misgivings were only a bid for sympathy such as the wish expressed in *My Book and Heart* that a kind reader would slip into her cabin and put a pillow under her tired feet. This time, however, Mrs. Harris seems, for once, to be talking to herself, not to her readers. [26]

An explanation for Mrs. Harris's gloomy meditations is not hard to find. In the fall of 1925 she was physically and emotionally exhausted. Since Faith's death in 1919 she had written four novels, two autobiographies, and a large block of articles and stories. She had labored to make *My Book and Heart* a great work and she had found *As a Woman Thinks* a heavy ordeal. Chest pains and spasms of breathlessness warned that her heart was not functioning properly, and she became nervous and irritable, even quarreling with kind Miss Neall about galley proofs. In such a mental state she could easily see her past as a failure and her future as an ever-shortening period of illness and inactivity. In short, Corra Harris, at fifty-six, was getting her first view of old age and did not like what she saw.[27]

Gradually, however, her courage and love of life prevailed. Even before she got to the end of *As a Woman Thinks* she was again making plans. "I doubt," she wrote, "that any man or woman, however old, is really ready to give up the ghost." As for herself, she would continue to seek happiness "even if the quest must sink into the defeat of mere peace." She needed a change of scenery; needed to meet new people and consider new ideas. Once she could put the worrisome manuscript aside, she began to clarify and expand her trip. It would be no journey to New York for a few weeks. She would take a world cruise to start at California, go on to the Far East and from there to Europe. She had plenty of money. Lorimer had also paid twelve thousand for the last serial. She would come home a new woman.[28]

Perhaps she could not quite down the fear that she might not be physically equal to her great adventure, for she had an Atlanta specialist examine her. He confirmed her heart trouble, but approved the trip provided she would do no writing on it "except the possible keeping of a diary." She felt reassured.[29]

The news of her world tour set Lorimer to thinking. He had not been disappointed in her last serial; it had interested the *Post* readers and that was all he asked. He got off a letter to Mrs. Harris containing a casual suggestion: "Why not, if you start on the hunt for happiness, make it the basis for your next serial in the *Saturday Evening Post*." [30]

Even without Lorimer's proposal, Mrs. Harris would probably have disregarded the doctor's orders.

15

· · · · ·
· · ·
·

Behind the Golden Gates

ONE evening in March of 1925 Mrs. Harris sat before her living room fire holding the paw of Bosco, her Great Dane, and explaining why she must leave him for a while. Bettie and Trannie Rains, she said, would look after him when she was gone.[1]

The Rains sisters had become fixtures in the Valley. In 1921 Mrs. Harris had loaned their widowed mother fifty dollars on the promise that some of the six Rains children would "work it out." It was her best investment. First Bettie and then Trannie had come and stayed, not as servants and not as adopted daughters (Mrs. Harris always explained that the girls adopted her), but as co-workers in the never-ending Valley enterprise. Reared to labor, the sisters, still in their middle teens, devoted themselves to Mrs. Harris's plans for the future and remained little perturbed by her bursts of temper or exacting demands. Before long she came to look on them as promising projects well worth her training. She believed them capable of taking over the Valley in her absence: Bettie to manage the farm, and Trannie the house.[2]

Around April 1 Mrs. Harris travelled westward, somewhat in the spirit of Joaquim Miller's "Columbus," a poem she loved to read aloud. Still not easy about her health, she stopped in Nashville to let Dr. Joseph Gains have a look at her. He did not like what he saw; her heart was enlarged and her physical resistance low. She must rest in the hospital for three weeks. Resting, however, never appealed to her, especially when she had something on her mind. She managed to cut short her confinement, for on April 18 she was writing Bettie from Santa Barbara, California.[3]

She arrived there "tired, but still in the ring." The trip across the desert had been wonderful, and she had fallen in love with the bright weather and lush growth of California. Her second letter was a bit subdued. A long automobile ride had brought on a heart attack. The severe spasms must have frightened her, for she remained in bed for well over three weeks and sadly cancelled her boat reservations for Honolulu.[4]

But she was not going back to Georgia. After a nice rest she could at least see California—by easy stages. She began to take an interest in the local scene. The Japanese bellhops and the Scotch maid fussed over her, and people, some quite important, began to call. She welcomed an English sea-captain, an ex-Attorney-General of Alaska, and the stepdaughter of Robert Louis Stevenson. Her mind began to jump ahead. Hoping to interest the motion picture companies in her novels, she hired Paul Bryan of Hollywood as her literary agent. Immediately he began to press upon her the superior comforts and services of a hotel in the movie capital. On June 6 she felt strong enough to move there.[5]

For a while Mrs. Harris did not feel up to touring Hollywood. From a chair in the hotel lobby, however, she saw much that amused her. The aging actresses, with lifted faces and dyed hair, reminded her of graduates of a girls' school who had stayed on after commencement. She couldn't decide whether they were more bent on impressing each other or the gullible guests from the outside world. After a few days she became bored with their daily performance and accepted a luncheon invitation at Universal Studios. During the meal she flustered a leading lady by asking if she provided financially for her several divorced husbands. Afterwards she watched the filming of a picture and was shocked by the artificiality of the sets. She consented to pose for a picture with Minnie, Universal's trained elephant, although she doubted that its release to the press would give her proper publicity. Back at her hotel she decided that the day reminded her of a visit she once made to an insane asylum.

Her limited view of Hollywood proved disappointing. She found it rather tame even though people rolled their eyes and intimated that "behind the scenes frightful and awful things were going on." The only scandal she picked up was a remark that Charlie Chaplin was taking too much interest in very young girls.[6]

An ominous experience about the middle of June hastened her departure from movie land. Back in Santa Barbara she had learned that patriotic Californians could suffer an earthquake and, at the same time, ignore it. One day at lunch in her Hollywood hotel she became aware that the silver and china had come to life on her table. Then the table took up a gentle rolling. Looking up Mrs. Harris gazed into the anxious face of a lady from the next table.

"Did you feel that earthquake?" the lady asked.

"No, madam," Mrs. Harris replied, "and you'd better not feel it."

The management and guests of the hotel went calmly on with their normal activities, but Mrs. Harris packed that afternoon and left for nearby Los Angeles. Later she would wish she had moved herself eight hundred instead of eight miles.[7]

At the Los Angeles Biltmore Mrs. Harris remained in bed for a few days and caught up with her correspondence. Her letters to Bettie carried more questions about things at home than about her doings abroad. She did admit, however, that she wasn't feeling well, but couldn't locate the Los Angeles doctor whom the one in Santa Barbara had recommended.[8]

Then, on June 29 Bettie received a startling wire: "Am writing to let you know that I am all right frightful earthquake here Santa Barbara almost destroyed."[9] Soon she was forced to admit that she was not all right. In a letter to Bettie on July 11 she declared that "that earthquake nearly killed me," and that same day she telephoned Paul Bryan asking him to recommend a Los Angeles doctor. Bryan and his wife came and put her in a sanitarium. Almost immediately he wired Bettie and the Harris nephews that she had suffered a heart attack as a result of the recent earthquake and would be in bed for several weeks. Mrs. Harris remained alert enough, however, to offer the *Post,* unsuccessfully, an article on her frightening experience and to wire Vance that she would answer Joseph Hergesheimer's article attacking marriage.[10]

She would have no part of the doctor's suggestion that a nephew come to take her home. A rest would set her right again. And she did improve, so rapidly that the doctor let her leave the sanitarium on July 24 provided she would rest a week at a local hotel before going on to San Francisco.

Settled at the Los Angeles Ambassador, Mrs. Harris announced her presence through a newspaper interview declaring her belief in Evolution—and also in Christianity. The Scopes "Monkey Trial" had recently usurped the headlines. She wired Lorimer about a possible article on that issue, but got a curt reply that she was "sixty days late even if evolution goes on for sixty million years." Fortunately Mrs. Harris could forget Lorimer's impudence in the rush of visitors that came. She had not realized how many Californians admired her. Her mail swelled with invitations and the hotel phone rang constantly. Fortunately for her love of attention, her health took a turn for the better, and on the rest of the trip there were no more heart attacks.[11]

San Francisco, she proudly reported, was more attentive than

Los Angeles: "reporters, photographers, Lion Hunters, callers of every description." Then onward to Oakland, Berkeley, and Santa Rosa. She lunched with Zane Grey, visited Luther Burbank, and received an autographed copy of "The End of a Perfect Day" from Carrie Jacobs, a popular songwriter. At Oakland she boarded with a kinswoman of British nobility—although invited to stay with several millionaires for the distinction she would give them. On a second visit to Hollywood she met Mary Pickford and Douglas Fairbanks and left with a more favorable impression of the movie colony. The last two months in California were what she had expected the entire trip to be.[12]

It was all very pleasant and satisfying, but it must end soon. She must get back home to a future that demanded considerable thought.

Her heart ailment, she knew, was certain to get worse. Whatever years were left her would be largely spent in the Valley, and her activities there must be curtailed. But she saw no reason why they could not be happy years. The Rains sisters would be a great help and comfort. They had managed things wonderfully during her absence. Trannie, industrious and barely literate, had written little, but Bettie's many letters had been a treat. An inviting picture began to take shape in her mind. When she got home, she was going "to lie around, talk, laugh and have company." And there would be times when she could get out; even take trips. Perhaps not to California, but there was Florida, and Trannie could learn to drive the car.[13]

Of course she would keep on writing. When poor little Bettie reported that the weather had damaged her crops, she reminded the child that her Mrs. Harris could "still swing a pen." She had been swinging one all through the trip. Up to the middle of August she had written six articles while "taking the rest cure." [14]

She could not, however, ignore the fact that she was returning home a sick woman. Just before leaving California in early October, Mrs. Harris sent the Rains sisters rigid instructions as to how they must care for her when she got back.

Don't treat me as if I were ill, don't notice me, don't stop me if I start somewhere you think I ought not to go . . . I am fierce about being noticed. My heart will warn me quick enough. I must walk slowly now or get a frightful pain. Just let me feel and act as normal as I can, but don't try to stop me. I cannot bear being treated like an invalid.[15]

In early October the Rains girls welcomed and took charge of a difficult patient. During the following year of confinement, the slightest provocation sent her "into a fit of vehemence that greatly resembled temper." Undoubtedly she imposed a stringent routine upon her household. As she wrote a friend, "this is a hell of a place if you are not disposed to neatness, diligence and old fashioned happiness." There is no indication, however, that Bettie and Trannie found their task beyond their resourcefulness.[16]

In spite of Lorimer's prodding, it was May of 1926 before she felt able to start the California serial, and October when she mailed him the final installment. She told Holt she wrote "every line of it . . . propped up in bed." After reading the first installment Lorimer seemed a bit worried about Mrs. Harris's critical attitude towards her subject, but he demonstrated amply his satisfaction with the completed manuscript. He informed "Aunt Shylock" she could expect a check for twenty thousand dollars. She took no offense at her new name.[17]

In the opening sentence of "The Happy Pilgrimage" Mrs. Harris says, "I have no idea what kind of story this will be." Her uncertainty is understandable. She must do a full-length serial of a journey on which she had spent half the time in bed. Eight months had elapsed since her return, and she was never one to keep notes during a trip. She solved her problem as one might expect: the serial is primarily about Corra Harris, not California. The story follows vaguely the chronology of her trip—as nearly as one can trace it through lengthy passages that could have been written before the author left Georgia. She comments fully on the books she read and the ideas that came to mind while she lay for weeks in bed. It is, in a sense, a faithful diary of her trip, but, except for the last two installments, not an informative travelogue.[18]

The serial contains some excellent descriptions of rural California and the streets of its old cities. Her most graphic picture, however, brings up an unanswerable question. She tells how on the trip out she was gazing from the train at an awesome desert sunset when she was stricken by her first heart attack and saved only by the providential appearance of a doctor. Yet, she made no mention of this near escape in her first letter to Bettie from Santa Barbara. Was she afraid of disturbing the child in the midst of her heavy responsibilities? She reported her later attacks. One cannot help but recall that Mary Heard, Mrs. Harris's old teacher, once said she had "known for some time that Mrs. Corra Harris is very careless about facts that get in her way." The ex-pupil, herself, admitted that here and there in her works "a fallacious incident is included for the sake of art or to pass the time more agreeably." Perhaps on the train Mrs. Harris did suffer heart spasms too slight to be recalled until she faced the problem of livening her serial.[19]

When Mrs. Harris reaches that point in her story where she leaves the Los Angeles hospital, she introduces individuals to her readers, and some are worth meeting. The respectable, well-known ones, such as Burbank, actor Joseph Jefferson, and Zane Grey, appear colorless by the side of several characters from California's fringe groups. On the whole, Mrs. Harris is tolerantly amused with their idiosyncrasies. A lady astrologist informed her that the earth was on bad moral relations with a certain planet, and a white-haired tramp introduced himself as Peter, a tent-maker who lived by the sea. When a second-hand book-seller learned his customer was Corra Harris, he declared that her mother had just been in asking for all her daughter's books. Mrs. Harris was fascinated by an effusive Hollywood reporter, the mother of several infant prodigies who acted in the movies and contributed freehand illustrations to their mother's personal correspondence.[20]

Mrs. Harris was drawn to the outgoing, optimistic people of California, but their ways were not hers and, even less, those of the society in which she had been reared. She was returning home "without one conviction changed." But these people of a younger world had made much of her, and she prophesied that in time "they will pass out of this Tristram Shandy stage of showing themselves bottom upwards in these childish antics." She felt called upon to point out—kindly and humorously, of course—their absurdities. The "dearer, wiser old woman" of her fiction always tried to set young people in the right ways.[21]

California's pride in the height of its "native sons" amused her. When she asked to see a specimen, a fairly tall young man was produced after considerable search. She noted how the people loved to parade their frontier heritage. Mayor James Rolph of San Francisco, she reported, always sported "Forty-niner" boots and a ten-gallon hat. Hollywood, she decided, was not immoral but *un*moral. The actors and actresses "slipped in and out of marriage" with the same childish impulse of ante-bellum Negro slaves. She was a bit more perturbed about a tendency of Californians to "try out any kind of religion." She warned them it was "dangerous to study heathen religions and prance around heathen gods." [22]

Nor could she take lightly the tacit understanding among public and press that earthquakes must not be mentioned. During her trip two such disturbances had frightened her, and she did not like to be frightened. In her serial she gives national publicity to the Los Angeles tremors which, according to her, shook her hotel room and terrified a large group of citizens.

A quarter before six in the morning Pershing Square in front of my hotel was filled with clad and half clad and practically unclad men and women engaged in old fashioned prayers of fear to the Lord. Before noon no native of Los Angeles would admit he had felt the early morning tremors.[23]

When the installments appeared in the *Post,* Mrs. Harris began to skim the usual letters from people who "always enjoyed and benefitted" by everything she wrote. But as the mail continued, she began to pause over letters bearing a California postmark, whose contents struck discordant notes in the steady hum of praise. Unwittingly she had raised a storm on the West Coast quite different from the ones that had disrupted her trip. A lady asked how Mrs. Harris learned so much about Hollywood's morals while sitting in a hotel lobby. A "Native Son" offered himself as a towering example of that species. Another lady declared that Mrs. Harris's description of Mayor Rolph made it obvious that she had never laid eyes on him. Others pointed out such trivial errors as the author's statement that Robert Louis Stevenson wrote *Treasure Island* in Santa Rosa. California had obviously not been entertained by Mrs. Harris's friendly lectures.[24]

The most disturbing letter went, not to her, but to Lorimer. President D. F. McGarry of the Los Angeles Chamber of Commerce called her report of an earthquake on June 29, 1925, and a subsequent panic in Pershing Square "a flagrant misstatement" containing "not one iota of truth." He was shocked that a reputable magazine like the *Post* would publish such willful slander. Several prominent business leaders wrote letters supporting McGarry's charge.[25]

Lorimer decided that he, and not Mrs. Harris, had better handle this problem. Complaints from scattered readers were one thing; an official protest from civic and business leaders in a large city could damage the *Post's* reputation and circulation. In his reply he pointed out that the Associated Press had reported tremors in Los Angeles on that date, and that Mrs. Harris was "a semi-invalid at that time" and might have "exaggerated the Pershing Square incident." He wrote to Mrs. Harris, enclosing a copy of his answer, and asked her for "a short, clear, business-like statement" of what had happened. In an eight-page reply Mrs. Harris stuck to her story. She had indeed been wakened that morning by "a sickening, undulating motion of the hotel"; its foundations were creaking like a ship on the high seas. She admitted she had not seen the panic in Pershing Square, but visiting friends had described it to her. McGarry, she said, was "a willful liar," as all

Californians were on the subject of earthquakes. When no further word came from Los Angeles, Lorimer gladly let the matter rest. He predicted, however, that on her next trip to California, Mrs. Harris would be made a "Doctor of Inhumane Letters." It was an unkind gibe; Oglethorpe University in Atlanta had recently awarded her an honorary degree. But she made no retort.[26]

Tremors, probably not very heavy, were felt in Los Angeles on June 29, 1925. Santa Barbara, only a hundred miles away, was badly shattered on that date. Also, the same day a lady in the Los Angeles suburbs wrote Mrs. Harris, "Did the earthquake waken you this morning?" Paul Bryan referred to it as the cause of her heart attack, and, as Lorimer said, the Associated Press gave it brief notice. But Mrs. Harris's picture of Pershing Square cannot be substantiated.[27]

Mrs. Harris had to be assured by Adelaide Neall that Lorimer had not lost confidence in her. She was also disturbed by the outburst from the cordial people of California. Readily she agreed with Houghton Mifflin that the scene in Pershing Square and the description of Mayor Rolph's accoutrements should not appear in the book, and she safeguarded the location of *Treasure Island*'s birthplace by the wording "is said to have written." When her expurgated book appeared, she sent an autographed copy to Mayor Rolph and got a nice note of thanks. In the dedication of *The Happy Pilgrimage* she put on a brave front: "To California, with a grin for my critics and a heartful of love and admiration for everybody else in the state."[28]

The reception of the book did nothing to raise her spirits. Few letters came; her readers had no doubt already expressed themselves fully enough on the serial. But the reviewers now had something to say about its demerits. The Boston *Transcript* dismissed the book as "a series of lay sermons," and the New York *Post* decided the author had "a great deal of the soap-box orator about her." *The Saturday Review of Literature* warned its readers that to get at the author's thoughts, they would have to "wade through a sea of words." But the unkindest cut came from the *Independent,* the magazine where she had once felt so at home. Its reviewer pronounced Corra Harris altogether prejudiced and frequently ignorant.[29]

In retrospect the pilgrimage could hardly be viewed as happy. But, then, Mrs. Harris had never spent much time considering the past. Before she had seen the unfavorable reviews—even before she had seen a copy of her book—she was embarked upon another journey.

16

. . . . .
. . .
.

A Narrowing Sphere

BEFORE leaving California Mrs. Harris had thought that her next trip might be to Florida. When she finished "A Happy Pilgrimage," Lorimer urged her to go ahead with that plan. In November of 1926 a letter from Holt decided her. Holt had accepted the presidency of Rollins College in Winter Park and was already exercising his publicity talents upon prospective students and endowers. At his inauguration in March he planned to give a number of honorary degrees and wanted Mrs. Harris to have one.[1]

Mrs. Harris decided to go. Not that the honorary degree meant a great deal; Oglethorpe University and the University of Georgia had given her such degrees, and Oglethorpe had asked her for money "before the laurels of the thing got cold upon my brow." Nor was her primary concern to escape the winter cold and management of the Valley. What she wanted and needed was to be among accomplished, worldly people again: to charm them with her witty conversation, to share their interests and activities. Such a change would do more for her than any doctor could, and Winter Park seemed just the place. Prominent figures from the literary, business, and social worlds gathered there every winter to enjoy a quieter, more cultured vacation than the seashore resorts offered. With the Holts to sponsor her, she could become immediately a part of the colony. She wrote Holt to expect her in early January, but not to expect a donation because of her honorary degree. A bit hurt, he assured her that he would not.[2]

Basil Bradford drove her down, and the Rains sisters came along for the ride and to cope with emergencies. After settling her comfortably at an inn, they returned home, and the Holts took over with a full social calendar in hand.[3]

Dr. Joseph Gains and the Atlanta specialist would have shaken their heads more than once if they could have watched their patient during the next six weeks. Immediately she sent out six dresses to be pressed for the engagements ahead. Her letters home told proudly of luncheons, teas, dinners, and lectures. And such prominent people, all so attentive: Irving Bacheller, the novelist, Dr. Albert Shaw, editor of *World's Work*, the Chancellor of the University of Pittsburg, and "a handsome man" who paid her marked attention. She had never enjoyed better conversation, filled "with ideas and ideals, no bitter topics or idle gossip." "Everybody is kind and good to me," she wrote Bettie, "and as usual I feel beloved." She had decided that social activities were good for her.[4]

By the time of Holt's inaugural she felt quite at home among the group chosen to be honored with her: Bacheller, Shaw, Rex Beech, Henry Goddard Leech of *Forum*, Ed Howe of the *Atchison* (Kansas) *Globe*, Ruth Bryan Owens, two clergymen, and a Miami real estate dealer.[5]

In her letters she never mentioned her heart, not even when she emphasized how upset she was by the news that Bettie must have a goiter removed. She declared that friends had to restrain her forcibly from catching the next train home, but she calmed herself sufficiently to instruct Bettie about the hospital and doctor's bills. The girl must give her own note for which Mrs. Harris would, of course, furnish the money when she got home. If the bills were sent direct to her, they would be much higher.[6]

She left for home shortly after the inauguration ceremony, assuring all her new friends they could expect her again next winter. But back in the Valley she soon became aware that her strenuous activities at Winter Park were beginning to take their toll. Three years would elapse before she could venture that far again in spite of the urgent invitations from Holt and a petition from several others for her return. There would, of course, be short trips to Atlanta and Nashville, but during most of that time she must endure the life of a semi-invalid which she had contemplated so sadly after the California attacks.[7]

Confinement was harder for her than for most people, but she endured it without ever losing the desire to live. As she explained later to a friend, "I really am in failing health. . . . If so I hope it will last as much longer in failing as it has already lasted. I so much prefer failing to dying." [8]

At times she could even take a humorous view of her condition and the tender, but strenuous care she suffered from her two small nurses. In 1928 she wrote Bettie, in Nashville for a check-up by Dr. Gains, an account of Trannie's ministrations.

Trannie has dealt as sternly as any doctor. First she decided I was billious and gave me a damnable CRC capsule followed by a still more damnable dose of castor oil. When this only cleared my complexion and did not steady my noble stride from here to the kitchen, she dosed me with those digitalis tablets. The effect was to turn me purple all over and black under the eyes. Saturday she decided I ought to go out in the car . . . But on the way home I grew very faint and had to be dosed with the little bottle of amonia she keeps in my bag.[9]

The fact that Mrs. Harris could insist she felt "relaxed" and "much better" the next day is a tribute to her constitution.

A friend once wrote Mrs. Harris, "a philosopher like you who lives in a world of thought is never bored." The compliment was a bit wide of the truth. Mrs. Harris was never content for long without an audience and stimulating activities.[10]

During her illness she maintained what contact she could with the outside world. She issued plentiful instructions about the farm based upon information brought in by Bettie and Trannie: the birth of lambs, the progress of stone-work, the health of Flapper Ann, her frisky cow. Her acres must stay cultivated even though the labor obtainable was hard to find and usually shiftless. Almost every year she tried out a new hired man. One showed too much interest in pretty Bettie and another eased most of the work on to the Rains sisters. Bill Rains, the girls' young brother, stayed for a while to be teased by the three females about his non-laying hens and embarrassed by discussions of Trannie's new panties. To Mrs. Harris's annoyance, he left for a better-paying job. Advertisements for replacements often ended with such refusals as, "I thought you wanted a sup. and a excelent chauefer [sic], but the pay doesn't read that way." Mrs. Harris agreed with Bettie that they would all be happier if they didn't have to bring a man into their snug matriarchy.[11]

Fortunately she did not have to depend upon the farm for an income, even after the Stock Market crash of 1929. A few months earlier she had sold her securities, over her broker's objections, and put the money in savings banks. Later she re-invested it at rock-bottom prices. She had no patience with people who thought money "an indecent subject" of conversation. "It is not even a vulgar thing to strive for," she declared, "if you get it honestly for a good purpose." She could be generous, even lavish, in helping those she loved or in improving her possessions, but she would haggle over small expenditures. Once she sent a neighboring farmer a board bill for his bull who had not performed his expected services in her cow pasture, and, at another time, she wrote on her check to a doctor who could not ease her pains, "for a social call."[12]

But farm and business affairs took little time, and an uncertain number of empty days still lay ahead. Denied the excitement of travel and intellectual companionship with her peers, she kept up her correspondence with far-off friends and brought near-by ones to the Valley. During May and June of 1928 she entertained more than sixty guests. She had acquired two additional friends and correspondents, both highly valued: Ed Howe and Marjorie McClain. Howe, whom she met in Winter Park, was an atheistical puritan who could not understand a friend who said grace before a meal which included wine. Mrs. Harris refused to take his infidelity seriously and argued humorously with him as to whether the soul or the stomach was the more important human organ. Marjorie McClain, a bright-faced, intelligent young Atlanta matron, must have recalled Faith. Marjorie's visits brought the entire household to life, and her letters contained wise comments on Mrs. Harris's current reading. She and the Rains sisters became indispensable in these last trying years.[13]

Fortunately there was still her writing. It must be done now, however, a little at a time; she could no longer maintain those drives that had produced *My Book and Heart* and *The Happy Pilgrimage*. Also, she was getting more rejections. *Good Housekeeping* still took an occasional article, and *Country Gentleman* welcomed almost everything she sent; but *Pictorial Review* seemed to have lost interest in her. Of course, she was not up to fiction any longer which was what Vance mainly wanted. Fortunately, Henry Goddard Leech, another Winter Park friend, accepted several pieces in 1928 and 1929 for his *Forum:* a defense of the South's racial attitude, an attack on British propaganda for cancellation of its war debt, and a debate with Dora Russell, wife of Bertrand, on the question, "Are We Happier than our Grandmothers?" Mrs. Harris's negative stand on the question brought disapproving letters from such prominent women as Julia Peterkin, the novelist, and Margaret Sanger, the birth control advocate, but she remained unperturbed by their criticism. Her rock-bound conservatism stood firm against the rising tide of liberalism. When Edwin Mims published his *The Advancing South* she disturbed the affable author by declaring he had written with "his eye on Northern criticism." [14]

She kept her name in the *Post,* but not as often as in the past. In 1927 she assured Lorimer that her illness had not incapacitated her for further writing. She boasted that she was still on her feet and "the very picture of health" although "the old motor is a trifle weaker or I am a trifle lazier." Then she tried one of her tricks on

him. Carolyn King, a *Country Gentleman* editor, was coming
down to talk over some articles that magazine wanted. She would
like to tell Miss King that she had "promised two short stories and
at least three articles to the *Post*" and could not take on any
additional work just then. Lorimer permitted her to say he was
"interested" in seeing what she had written.[15]

Lorimer did publish two of her articles in 1928, but after
reading the manuscript of "Letters of an Accomplished Lady," he
advised, rather curtly, that she send it "to a woman's magazine."
Deeply hurt—the serial must have cost quite an effort—she gave
little time to the *Post* when she and Trannie made a brief trip to
Philadelphia in the fall of 1928. Miss King and *Country Gentleman* saw more of the two visiting ladies. But Mrs. Harris always
acknowledged gladly what Lorimer had done for her. In February
1929 she contributed to a collection of *"Post* Letters" commemo-
rating his thirty years' editorship. In her letter she thanked Lorimer for preserving "the trail of my thoughts" in the dusty files of
the *Post*. Later in that year she felt more kindly towards him
when he accepted the last serial she would publish, "Last Leaves,"
a collection of reminiscences and observations.[16]

Having negotiated the Philadelphia trip, Mrs. Harris decided
to venture another Winter Park visit. Again, perhaps, a proposal
from Holt helped induce her. He had hit upon a new publicity
wrinkle: visiting professorships were being announced for subjects
never to appear before in college catalogues. Already he had
appointed Professors of Books, of Hunting and Fishing, and of
Things-in-General. Mrs. Harris must come as the first Professor
of Evil in the history of education—of course she would be teaching students how to avoid that practice. Always mindful of her
image, she only consented on the assurance that the Rollins news
bureau would release no publicity "subject to vulgar sex interpretation concerning the course." [17]

After seeing her father through a dangerous operation Mrs.
Harris left for Florida in January 1930, driven by her Negro
chauffeur. She decided on a short stay in an Orlando sanitarium
before taking over her professorial assignment. Immediately she
wished she had gone straight to Winter Park. The sanitarium
doctors took her off cigarettes and coffee, and on Sunday she had
to attend religious services with a congregation of "sinners, saints,
fanatics and people of various creeds." Next, the drastic medical
treatment brought on a heart attack. At the first chance, she
escaped to Winter Park where a flattering reception hastened her
recovery. Proudly she wrote home that she could not possibly

recount "all the kind compliments and attentions I have received." [18]

Around the middle of February Mrs. Harris began her lectures to an informal group on a Rollins patio. On February 22 she wrote the Rains sisters that there was "much excitement here about my course in Evil; publicity spreading North and South." Holt was highly pleased. Even the London *Times* had carried an editorial on his academic innovation. On March 5 Mrs. Harris wrote from Tampa that the students had been so enthusiastic, "I am slipping out of town without telling them the course is over to avoid their protests." But an unexpected comment concludes her account of the course: "How much better both of you girls would have understood the lectures than any of the young men and women in that class." [19]

Rough drafts of Mrs. Harris's lectures help to explain her students' lack of understanding. She began by stating categorically that "man was born with no sense of good or evil . . . Naturally the first thing he did was to discover and found evil." Yet, shortly afterwards she declares that "evil did not exist until man discovered goodness." She suggested that as an antidote for evil the students should study "the character and qualities" of such Winter Park visitors as William Lyon Phelps, Albert Shaw, and Irving Bacheller. Perhaps she dealt more decisively with sex than with any other related topic. Sex, she declared, was not nearly so significant in human life as some psychologists claimed. A horse might be as highly sexed as a man, but no horse had ever built a great city. The preserved notes of one student quote such colloquial statements as, "I am a great fan of God," "My life has been a bully experience," "I expect God to pull off another good stunt in the future." At least Mrs. Harris created in her lectures that informal atmosphere which Holt prized.[20]

Mrs. Harris can hardly be blamed for failing to get a grip on a subject which has baffled philosophers and theologians for centuries. As a matter of fact, the Winter Park intelligentsia had little better success. Henry Leech arranged a "Socratic Dialogue," later published in *Forum,* so that Mrs. Harris, Holt, Bacheller and other pundits might consider the question. When each had delivered himself, Holt observed, "As yet none of us has defined what evil is." [21]

Public and press reacted strongly to the course, but not in the fashion Holt had anticipated. Several wrote they were certain Mrs. Harris must be teaching "goodness," but wanted their assumption substantiated. Others decided the course's title meant what it said and proceeded to attack the professor; she should have realized young people already knew enough about evil. She obviously did not have Christ in her heart; she was undoubtedly teaching Communism. One of her few encouraging letters came from a militant Protestant offering to supply anti-Catholic literature. Newspapers, on the other hand, refused to take the professor or course seriously. Over a picture of the class in session appeared the caption, "They're Getting 'Evil' Instruction." One editor assured Mrs. Harris that her appointment to the professorship was no reflection upon her moral character. Holt's excitement about an editorial in the London *Times* must have been stirred by a report that the paper was running one. Its content could hardly have delighted him. The editor suggested that future courses in America on evil would probably be taught by Chicago gangsters. Hearst's *Sunday American* mounted a massive attack. It ran a full page, decorated with pictures of bathing beauties, primitive women, and medieval personifications of sin. With dubious erudition the editor traced the long history of evil and pronounced Mrs. Harris too innocent to teach the subject. Later, in explaining the course to an inquirer, Holt remarked that it "received more newspaper publicity than it deserved." Coming from him the complaint sounds strange.[22]

Mrs. Harris proceeded on to Miami where homespun Ed Howe proudly introduced her to his millionaire friends and escorted her to dinner on a mammoth yacht. She needed this diversion; the bad press she had received troubled her. What would her Winter Park friends be thinking? And Lorimer? Again Adelaide Neall had to insist that "the Boss" was not disturbed. One of Mrs. Harris's rare references to her unfortunate course was when she hesitated to appear on the program of Rollins's "Animated Magazine" the following year.[23]

She returned home in late March to find her father dying. The Old Confederate had never lost his rugged courage, complaining lustily to the end that the hospital should include whisky on his diet. When he died in April Mrs. Harris felt her loss. He had been a problem and a burden, but she had inherited her sturdiest traits from him. She wrote an admirable obituary which admitted his weaknesses, but extolled his defiant love of life. (Lorimer disapproved of its frankness and refused to publish it in the *Post*.)

He belonged to that breed of men who lacked the dreary patience necessary for the long siege of dutiful living, but who can lead the forlorn hope of themselves over the top of disaster to some kind of victory.[24]

Late in the spring she could keep going no longer and took to her bed. The thoughts that accompany old age had begun to haunt her. A year earlier she had pointed out to Bettie how fast the kin and friends of her generation were dying: Sister Hope, Henry Harris, Banker Calhoun, and Edwin Slosson. Now her father was gone, the last link with that earlier world. In June she wrote Medora Perkerson of the Atlanta *Journal* that it would be "an act of charity" to come for a visit and suggested she bring a friend, "any friend to help pass the tedious hours." Evidently she did not improve with the summer, for in September she admitted to Marjorie McClain, "my blood pressure and pulse have gone out of all bounds." [25]

However, when she returned to Winter Park in January of 1931, on her doctor's advice, she broke all past records for social activities. By her count, she accepted seventy-nine engagements, joined a Rollins sorority, and, to Ed Howe's disgust, became friendly with a deposed European princess. In a letter to Medora Perkerson she casually mentioned a dinner she had given and included a list of guests in case Medora might want to do a little story for the Atlanta *Journal*. With an eye still upon the *Post,* Mrs. Harris let Adelaide Neall know of her social activities and concluded that a woman so sought after "must be still in possession of her wits, and may be capable of doing better work from so many refreshing experiences." [26]

But back home in late April she had little success with whatever writing she was able to do. During the rest of that year all she published was a single article in the *Post.* Humorously she admitted to Mrs. Perkerson that the only publicity she was receiving was from a sprightly advertisement offering a mule for sale. There seemed little likelihood of her rectifying that situation.[27]

Suddenly, in June she became confronted with the problem not of maintaining, but of safeguarding her public image. The past December she had given Charles Dobbins, a Columbia University graduate student, permission to do a biography of her for his master's thesis. Innocently she had even allowed him to visit the Valley in her absence and examine her personal correspondence. Now, she learned to her horror that he was planning to sell it as a serial to some Atlanta newspaper. If Hearst's Atlanta *Georgian* got hold if it, they would ruin her. Fortunately the Atlanta *Journal* bought Dobbins's manuscript and, probably through the intercession of Mrs. Perkerson, agreed that Mrs. Harris would edit it for publication.[28]

One glance at Dobbins's scholarship and Mrs. Harris must have

blessed Medora and the *Journal*. What that young scoundrel
hadn't learned about her personal affairs! She read on, the blue
pencil working over time. Such passages as the following disappeared completely from view.

Never in Mrs. Harris's writing does she reveal the cloud of impending
doom that hung over their house for twenty-five years.
Professor Harris suffered an attack of asphasia [*sic*] and was found . . .
in Texas laboring under the hallucination of being damned and in hell.
Six times . . . Lundy Harris attempted his life. The seventh time, years
later, when away from home he succeeded.[29]

She could not, of course, obliterate the fact of Lundy's suicide,
but she could not allow Dobbins's report of it to stand.

There on the eighteenth day of September, 1910, the circuit rider ended
his own life, a virtual martyr to the church which had claimed his life
service. He left behind this note: "I am so tired and want to go where
rest is never broken." [30]

Even though no post-mortem had been performed on her husband, Mrs. Harris suggested a physical cause for his desperate
mental condition. Retaining Dobbins's opening sentence, she went
on to explain:

Aside from the strain of controversy in his relations with the church
which had claimed his life service, he had by this time developed an
ulcer at the base of his brain which was the direct cause of the tragedy.[31]

Undoubtedly she was pleased that Dobbins's references to Faith
and Harry were modeled upon *My Book and Heart*. But his
literary criticism called for considerable rectifying. He did not
think kindly of Mrs. Harris's fiction and, like a true scholar, had
not hesitated to say so. She deleted and altered a number of
phrases and sometimes removed entire sentences in that section of
the thesis. One passage stood no chance of survival.

But as for more books, it seems doubtful that she will try again. Her
store of autobiographical material is about drained, and there is little
demand for the hopeful undisillusioned sort of fiction she writes.[32]

When Mrs. Harris returned the manuscript, she urged the *Journal* to use "as much of it as your editors please." They proceeded
to do so. But Mrs. Harris wanted no further part of budding
scholars. When another Columbia student wrote asking if he
could see her Joel Chandler Harris letters, she either refused or
did not answer.[33]

Ironically enough, Mrs. Harris's nervous concern with the Dobbins thesis brought a literary connection she would need in the few years ahead. Through her work on the manuscript she met Angus Perkerson, Medora's husband and editor of the *Journal Sunday Magazine Section*. The Perkersons introduced her to John Paschall, the newspaper's managing editor, and soon the three were welcomed visitors to the Valley. Gradually it came out that Mrs. Harris had done some political articles for the *Post*, but Republican Lorimer had turned them down because of her Democratic leanings. Paschall became interested. Would Mrs. Harris like to try her hand at a tri-weekly column in the *Journal?* Mrs. Harris decided that she would.[34]

17

. . . . .

. . .

.

Before We Go to Paradise

SHORTLY before he died André Gide was asked if old age had any
compensation. "Yes," replied Gide, "it is harder to carry one's
glass to one's lips, but one feels less thirsty." It was not so with
Corra Harris. As age and sickness became a heavier burden, she
stirred herself all the more to live.

She continued to make light of her troublesome heart, declaring gaily that she would delay ordering her tomb. To judge from
her correspondence she enjoyed periodic respite from her ailment
during the next three years, and her seizures struck with less force.
But, as she told her uncle, Wootten Mathews, she did not like to
"bother people with my sickness." Brief reports in her letters,
however, indicate she grew steadily weaker: "Out today for the
first time"; "I have been ill since you were here"; "I cannot get to
Atlanta until I am stronger." Friends confirmed the worsening
state of her health. In 1932 Bettie wrote that Mrs. Harris had
"suffered another hemorrhage from the nose," and a year later a
Valley guest noted that she was walking with a cane. But the
terminal attack did not come, and Mrs. Harris made the most of
its delay.[1]

Fortunately she did not have to curtail expenditures for what
diversions she could still enjoy. She saw around her the effects of
the Great Depression and became alarmed when the Atlanta
banks were closed. But, within a few days, her banker wrote that
she could draw upon the five thousand dollars in her trust account. A statement of her holdings in 1933 shows securities to the
amount of $134,250 with an estimated income of six thousand
dollars. This, with her annual pay of twenty-five hundred dollars
for her *Journal* column, could maintain her comfortable standard
of living. She even felt able to launch a welfare program for her
less fortunate neighbors. Purchasing "five hundred pounds of oat-

meal and a lot of seedless raisins," she and Trannie fed twenty-five children on porridge during the winter of 1933. She reported that the children thrived mightily on this healthful diet.[2]

She could feel secure in her Valley home, and the Rains girls kept the house youthful and lively. Their bright homely remarks delighted her, and she repeated them to friends. When asked what she thought of the novel *Lamb in His Bosom,* Bettie declared that after reading about so many childbirths, she felt like a midwife. Trannie guarded her mistress like a fierce little sheep dog. She ordered a Bible salesman away on the grounds that "Mrs. Harris don't have time for such foolishness, and besides we're getting ready to go to a funeral." The return of Bill Rains to the farm might not have added to the gaiety of things, but Mrs. Harris could feel more comfortable about her crops and cow barn.[3]

In letters to friends Mrs. Harris loved to describe her happy household, but to one she admitted that "heart disease tends to violence of temper," and, years later, Bettie said that "Mrs. Harris was a fine woman, but not always easy to live with." Very likely her confinement, as well as her ailment, contributed to these bursts of irascibility. She urged friends to come as a favor to her. If John Paschall did not make a promised visit, then "we are headed for a lonely week-end." Most of the invited guests needed no urging; kinspeople, old friends from Oxford, and newer ones from Atlanta arrived in large groups. They came assured of a cordial welcome, bountiful meals, and lively, congenial company. During these last years she invited more young people to liven up these gatherings. Marjorie McClain was invaluable when a sedate group arrived. Mrs. Harris enjoyed bandying ideas with her young guests, but she would not listen to any nonsense. When William Tate and Edwin Everett, instructors at the University of Georgia, offered some liberal views on the Negro question, she set them right with a lecture they still remembered thirty years later.[4]

But no one was more welcomed than a contingent from the Atlanta *Journal:* Editor John Paschall, City Editor John Pope, Sportswriter O. B. Keeler, and Reporter Ernest Rogers. Their arrival set off high festivities in the Harris household. First came a huge dinner, sparked by such lively, humorous discussions as a critique of their hostess's latest columns. Then hours of good talk, either before a roaring fire or on the porch in the sweet-smelling Southern darkness. Rogers usually brought his banjo to render such favorites as "Willie the Weeper" or "The Mythological Blues." If no strangers were present, shy O. B. Keeler might be persuaded to recite "Casey at the Bat." "Warden" Paschall and his "Three Musketeers" maintained a top position on Mrs. Harris's guest list.[5]

There were, of course, long periods when the house was quieter in the evenings, especially during those months when winter rains made the Valley roads dangerous, even impassable. Governor Gene Talmadge wouldn't get them worked, in spite of Mrs. Harris's promise to tell local voters he "did it for their special benefit." She could pass a lot of time reading and, occasionally, answering letters. But she didn't get much pleasure from her mail now. Too many people wrote asking if she was still writing or begging for loans to tide them over the Depression. Just as irritating were those other requests like the circular from Carrie Chapman Catt asking for her signature on a mass protest against Adolf Hitler's Jewish pogroms, or the letter from Theodore Dreiser about an appeal to free those Negroes in Scottsboro, Alabama, who had raped a white girl. Of course she wanted to hear from Howe, Paschall, and Holt, but she had to sit down on Holt when he asked her to employ a "fallen" girl he was trying to restore. She wouldn't think of letting Bettie and Trannie associate with a girl so conversant with sin.[6]

The long hours spent at her serials and their appearance in print had helped her to endure the grief of Lundy's and Faith's deaths. Again she sought to absorb herself in writing, but now that labor proved unrewarding. Magazines had limited space to fill; reader taste had changed; and she could no longer sit for hours at her desk. Yet she continued to write—articles, stories, even one serial—without getting a single piece published after the fall of 1931. Ironically her one article accepted, by the *Post*, never appeared in print. Lorimer held her observations on Prohibition until Repeal robbed them of any significance. He insisted on paying for it, but refused her offer of a substitute article without charge. Some editors grew impatient with her manuscripts, returning them with such rejections as, "No, no. These pieces are not for us," or, "It didn't fill the bill with us." Others, usually old friends, told of large backlogs of material, or explained they could only use articles with strong news value. By 1934 Carolyn King of *Country Gentleman* could write Mrs. Harris for a pickle receipt with no mention of her writing. Still she persevered, still holding, no doubt, the conviction expressed to Adelaide Neall in 1931: "I have a notion that if this depression lasts, I may become stylish again as a writer and thinker."[7]

With no more published serials, she saw Dobbins's prediction that there would be no more books coming true. In 1933 she failed to interest Houghton Mifflin in bringing out "The Diary of a Country Lady," which had run in *Country Gentleman* back in 1923–25. Her careful book publisher, however, did suggest a new edition of *A Circuit Rider's Wife*, provided she would buy the plates from Henry Altemus. After some discussion she got them at half price. When the new edition appeared Rich's Department Store in Atlanta put on an autographing tea where quite a number of people said nice things to her. It was all very pleasing, like the George Fort Milton Award in 1932 for an outstanding Southern writer, but such honors had to do with books she had written and seemed to point up the question as to whether there would be even one more.[8]

Over the years she had tried to sell her books to the movies through a series of literary agents such as Paul Bryan, whom she fired before she left California. Back in 1919 one had succeeded in placing *Making Her His Wife* with Gaumont, who produced it, for a brief run, under the title "Husbands and Wives." As late as 1931 an agent tried to interest her in further efforts, but she had evidently given up hope. It would be after her death before 20th Century Fox brought out "I'd Climb the Highest Mountain," based on *A Circuit Rider's Wife*. At least Mrs. Harris would have had no apprehension that the screen adaptation revealed any of her hidden secrets. It was as unlike the book as the book was unlike the true story of her life with Lundy.[9]

Mrs. Harris might explain to Adelaide Neall that her *Journal* column was only "a diversion," but without it those long days in the Valley would have passed more slowly. In fact, as Angus Perkerson predicted, she got "a world of fun" out of the column. Those were troubled times, and she had plenty of blame and advice to give. Like others, she fastened the responsibility for the depression upon Herbert Hoover; he was no better than an "international welfare worker" trying to "fool the country." She thought Franklin D. Roosevelt would do better, and even when he began to spend more money than Hoover had, she pointed out he was spending it on people at home. As the New Deal emerged, however, she began to have her doubts. She warned against repealing prohibition; a nation couldn't drink itself into prosperity. Also, with all this poverty at home, we ought to make Europe pay its war debts, or take a mortgage on such assets as the British Museum and the French Louvre. In general she observed Paschall's suggestion that she go light on Georgia politics; she did, however, refer to Gene Talmadge's "whoop on the hayseed plat-

form" and wished for gubernatorial candidates with self-support-
ing relatives. In 1933 she offered Talmadge some advice. Robert
Burns, a convicted highway robber, had escaped from a Georgia
prison camp and fled to New Jersey's protection where he wrote
his highly-publicized *I Am a Fugitive from a Georgia Chain
Gang.* Mrs. Harris suggested the Governor let other confirmed
criminals escape to such "Northern altruistic centers" where they
could again take up their professions.[10]

She did not, of course, miss her opportunity to castigate several
current writers. Atlantan Frances Newman, author of *The Hard-
Boiled Virgin,* was skilled in saying "the worst things with the
greatest possible delicacy." Carl Carmer, William Faulkner, and
Erskine Caldwell, the "Peeping Toms of Literature," concentrated on "whatever is evil and scandalous in the South." (Mrs.
Harris held a grudge against Caldwell. She bought his *God's
Little Acre,* attracted by "the sweetness of its title," only to find it
"the worst, the most damnable book that ever came into this
house.") She praised Carolyn Miller's *Lamb in His Bosom* for
restoring "Godalmighty" to fiction, but when Paschall successfully
pushed Mrs. Miller for the Pulitzer Prize, Mrs. Harris recalled
sadly how little the Atlanta papers had publicized *A Circuit
Rider's Wife.* When Mrs. Miller asked that a dinner invitation to
the Valley be postponed, Mrs. Harris consented, but told a friend
that the "Pulitzer Prize Winner" was going to get turkey hash—
not roast turkey.[11]

At times Mrs. Harris, like all newspaper columnists, was probably hard put to find subjects and meet deadlines, but she never
complained. She could always fall back upon such ancient topics
as divorce, sex, birth control, and radicalism. Also, she could do
sketches on her colorful rural neighbors—if she took care not to
offend. As she wrote Paschall, "I like writing for the *Journal* as a
prisoner likes looking out upon the world from his narrow
window." [12]

In April of 1932 she could not turn down Paschall's offer of a
reporting trip to Washington, although she warned him she
would be embarrassed to drop dead in a crowded city. She sur-
vived a wonderful visit. Calling at the Vice-President's office, she
informed a startled secretary that she had come to look at Mr.
Garner's wonderful eyebrows. She decided that Senator Huey
Long of Louisiana was a "vulgarian" and that Senator Glass of
Virginia was "a militant thinker with an arsenal for a brain." She
sat in on several important gatherings: an investigation of Richard Whitney, President of the Stock Exchange, which convinced

her the Exchange ought to be closed down; a convention of the Red Cross, where the principal speaker "slighted the poor mountain whites, but emphasized the suffering of the colored people"; and a hearing on the Veterans' Bonus which she believed would make thrifty Grover Cleveland "turn over in his grave." In spite of mounting blood pressure and another nose hemorrhage, she returned in high spirits to spread the word that Washington was "in a blue funk." [13]

During 1933 she made two public appearances. In February she addressed the Georgia Press Association in Atlanta on the editors she had encountered in her career. She sent a copy to Miss Neall so that Lorimer would know she still thought well of him. He commissioned Miss Neall to relay his thanks; by that time she had taken over the *Post*'s correspondence with Mrs. Harris. In May she attended a reunion of Emory's Class of 1893. When Warren Candler failed to mention Lundy among the college's great teachers, she made good the omission when her turn came. Later she attended services in the old Oxford Methodist Church, but declined a suggestion that she sit in the pulpit with Candler. As she explained to a friend, "the old Bishop is perfectly capable of beaning me with a hymn book." After the ceremony when she and he posed for a newspaper picture, the photographer told them to look at each other. "Don't you do it," she said to the Bishop. "You look straight ahead as if you're looking at God, and I'll look at you. That will be more proper." Candler, she once said, always made her feel "like a small boy with a pocket full of rocks." [14]

Around Christmas of 1933 she decided to venture a Winter Park trip. In November she had learned of a rumor in Florida that she had died. Perhaps she wanted to prove that the report had been exaggerated. She went down, alone, by train in February. A welcoming committee of sorority sisters met her at the station, and she set out upon an unbroken series of teas, dinners, and balls. It was a reckless but gallant gesture, and how she enjoyed it. She could talk politics with Daniel Roper and Homer Cummings of Roosevelt's cabinet, or with Republican Frank Kellogg from Hoover's administration. She enjoyed Marjorie Kinnan Rawlings, author of *The Yearling*, and young Edwin Grandberry, "a better writer than William Faulkner and no Judas to the South." At a meeting of Holt's "Animated Magazine," she warned the audience against James Joyce's "snot-green literature." She had given him up after fifty pages of *Ulysses*. She admitted that "this décolleté business has given me a cold and a bad pulse." But what could she do? Hostesses just would not let her decline invitations "on account of my ability to start conversations and break inhibitions." She reached home in April, happy but completely exhausted.[15]

Whether Winter Park brought on her final decline, or how rapidly she failed during the rest of 1934, it is impossible to say. Her correspondence for that period reveals the same strenuous pattern of living. In late November she was still "having a stream of company," although during some of their visits, she could only stay up part of the time. She continued to submit manuscripts—to *Harper's, Ladies Home Journal* and the *Post*—and her mail brought more rejections. Writing taxed her more and more. In August she admitted to Paschall, "By a great effort I am getting off my usual three Candles." [16]

The previous May she had developed cardiac asthma which she humorously described as "my first intimation of immortality." In July a heart attack put her in Atlanta's Emory Hospital, and another in November brought Dr. Allen Bunce, a cardiac specialist, to the Valley. Dr. H. B. Bradford of Cartersville was finding her a difficult patient. On one visit he practically had to take away her pen and writing pad, and order her to bed. Later, he learned she went back to work when the sound of his car died away.[17]

Just before Christmas perceptive Bettie reported on her patient to Mrs. A. W. Mathews.

> Mrs. Harris seems better some of the time, but she had another attack tonight. These attacks don't last long, but they are pretty painful. . . . She is up and about the house for half the day; the other half she spends in bed. She still works, and I suppose she always will. Anyway, I know better than to try to stop her.[18]

During the past winter she had reconsidered the question of where she would be buried. The decision would depend upon the completion of a project she had in mind. Formerly she had expected to be placed beside Lundy, but in 1930 she announced that she might build a small chapel in the front yard to house her books, manuscripts, and pictures. In 1934, before leaving for Florida, she drew up a new will with instructions that she was to be buried in the proposed chapel if it had been finished by that time. Perhaps she decided that without her tomb, the Valley would seem emptied of her presence. It was October, however, before she had plans drawn for the chapel. She still preferred to put aside thoughts of death.[19]

She passed Christmas day quietly with the Rains and a few local callers. In the afternoon she added a couple of codicils to her will. That night she thought about the real meaning of the day. Perhaps for centuries men of all nations had longed, without understanding their longing, for "the way, the truth and the light." Afterwards she slept well.[20]

In spite of heart spasms on December 31, she wrote a brisk letter to Paschall outlining columns she wanted to write, and during the next four weeks she got off the manuscripts. Apparently the winter routine of the household went placidly on.[21]

On January 27 she crumpled under severe heart pains. Her suffering became so intense she consented to a morphine injection on Dr. Bradford's promise to stay the night. In the morning he and the three Rains rode in the ambulance with her to Emory hospital. The Atlanta doctors gave little hope, but within a few days she rallied enough to complain sharply of the hospital service. One evening Medora Perkerson and Frank Daniel, also of the *Journal,* called and found her alert and talkative.[22]

Saturday afternoon, February 7, Dr. Bradford and the Rains came down. They found Mrs. Harris in good spirits. She expected to leave in a few days; Marjorie McClain was going to reserve a room at the Biltmore for her. The visitors left at four, much encouraged. Soon Marjorie arrived. But by then a reversal was taking place in Mrs. Harris's clouding mind. She suggested they hold up on the Biltmore reservation. She began to talk about Bettie and Trannie. "Then it got dark," she said. Marjorie glanced at the window. When she looked back, Mrs. Harris was dead.[23]

She had left explicit instructions for her funeral: a simple service by the Reverend Robinson of the Cartersville Methodist Church: no music of any sort; and the reading of "Lead Kindly Light" by the minister. But one seldom has the final say about his funeral. The Reverend Robinson was leaving on a trip. Bettie thought Warren Candler should be called. She knew those two strong-minded characters had retained a respect and even an affection for each other. The chapel had not been begun, but the family agreed Mrs. Harris should be buried where it would stand.

On the misty afternoon of February 11, the Harris and Rains families gathered in front of a coffin in the small north room of Mrs. Harris's house. City friends crowded the living room and stairway, and along the walls stood a scattering of brown-faced men and women from the neighboring hills and coves. The pallbearers assembled: John Paschall, Angus Perkerson, Bill Rains,

Fountain Williams, and Doctors Allen Bunce and Everett Banker. Warren Candler watched stolidly from behind the coffin, his mind, most likely, on the Oxford days of years ago.

Silence settled upon the little room. Candler raised his head and began to speak. His words carried a faint note of irony. "We admired and respected her so much we are able to prove our admiration and respect by adhering to the modest service which was her final request." [24]

He read the three passages of Scripture selected for him and recited "Nearer My God to Thee." Then he closed with a brief prayer. The pallbearers shouldered the coffin and led the slow procession down the lawn to a newly-dug grave. There Candler read the Methodist burial service and committed the body of Corra Harris to the earth of her Valley.

As the people around the grave dispersed gradually across the lawn, a Cartersville songstress, without warning, broke into the military dirge "Taps." When she had released the last high note, Candler reminded her that Mrs. Harris had wanted no music. He was hardly the one to deliver the reprimand. Mrs. Harris had requested that "Lead Kindly Light," not "Nearer My God to Thee," be recited. Had he forgotten his instructions? Or had he utilized his last opportunity to contradict his argumentative old friend? [25]

In June 1936 a smaller gathering filed into the little chapel built with native rock and lumber over Mrs. Harris's grave. Passing through the door the men and women took seats on the wooden benches flanking the short aisle. Warm Valley air brought the outside world into the small room. One by one the three speakers went to the flat gravestone at the end of the aisle: Holt, Paschall, and Al Harris. Each told of his love and admiration for the woman resting at his feet. Lorimer had sent regrets. He had always found the *Post* an exacting job. [26]

When the ceremony was over, the audience came forward to read on the stone an inscription composed by Al Harris from directions in his aunt's will.

Corra Harris

1869   1935

It is safe to record here everlastingly that she loved her friend Almighty God, her husband Lundy Howard Harris, and her daughter Faith Harris Leech.

Her belief in immortality was as certain as her wish that her dust sleep out the seasons in the Valley in the mountains of her native Georgia.

The words are truthful. Yet, do they tell the whole truth? One recalls a remark in one of Mrs. Harris's letters: "Life is the big thing, not love, nor praise, nor fame." [27]

Mrs. Harris's will covers twelve legal-size sheets and is heavily divided into divisions, subdivisions, and codicils. Its intent, however, is clear. Small monetary bequests and appropriate mementoes were given friends, Valley neighbors, and such kin as her Uncle Wootten Mathews, brother, half-sister, and Hope's youngest boy who had not turned out as well as his brothers. Faith's portrait by Ella Hergesheimer was to be hung in the Nashville Parthenon. The gift of her correspondence to Emory University in the will of 1934 was revoked in a codicil of the revision the following Christmas. She would decide later what to do with her letters. The Rains girls were to have her clothes and the furnishings and furniture in their rooms. Bettie was to receive two thousand dollars and Trannie twenty-five hundred. Trannie's extra five hundred was compensation for nursing Bettie through an illness without charge to Mrs. Harris. The remainder of the estate was to be divided into four parts: her nephews Al, John, and Fred Harris were each to receive one share. The fourth was put in trust to maintain the house, with all its contents, the chapel, and a tract of designated land as a memorial to Mrs. Harris. [28]

Her "home place," she explained, was to be kept an "open house" for the many people who "have believed in me and the books I have written." She tried to anticipate every contingency that might terminate her proposed shrine. The fourth of her estate was to provide the upkeep for it, and a fee charged for all visitors except certain friends, named elsewhere. Trannie would receive a thousand dollars a year as caretaker, out of which sum Bettie was to be paid for any services rendered. The girls could live in her house, rent free, so long as they carried out the wishes of her will and remained unmarried. If they married or left the Valley for any other reason, the buildings and land around them should be offered to first The Daughters of the American Revolution and then to The Daughters of the Confederacy on condition one of the organizations would administer the gift as "a memorial to American life and civilization and whatever contribution or service my life has rendered to my Country." [29]

The memorial, as Mrs. Harris planned it, has not endured. Like Faith, both Bettie and Trannie chose marriage and left the Valley. Neither of the two women's organizations wanted to take over the shrine, and the Trustees could not support it on the money provided. In 1949 Al Harris's widow, John and Fred Harris, with the consent of the Trustees, cut and marketed the best timber and sold the land and all buildings except the chapel to Trannie Rains Smith.[30]

At first, while the Rains sisters were struggling to keep the memorial going, a number of visitors came. Today, a chance traveler appears to look around in the chapel and ask questions about the woman buried there. Trannie Rains Smith and her husband farm the same land where, at various times, she, Harry Leech and hired men labored to please Mrs. Harris. With the passing years the Valley has become more like its rural, agrarian neighborhood. The remaining pines above Mrs. Harris's house are growing taller and thicker. Even if an industrial civilization obliterates them some day, along with all traces of Corra Harris, they may come again in time to cover the entire hill.

ADDENDUM

With the manuscript of this book already in press, an unexpected piece of information has come to hand. A request to the Nashville Parthenon for a print of Faith's portrait by Ella Hergesheimer brought the following reply: "We have no known (as of now) portrait of F. Harris." The writer, however, went on to say:

We have an unidentified portrait of an elegant young woman in a white gown. This is almost life size and was done, we know, by Miss Hergesheimer. This is a beautiful portrait that we have on display at all times, and we call it simply "Portrait of a Lady." [31]

The portrait was readily identified as Faith's, and the Parthenon's director immediately changed the inscription to read, "Portrait of Faith Harris Leech." Mrs. Harris would have wanted this correction made.[32]

Visitors to the Parthenon will continue to pause before the portrait of the "elegant young woman." Some will undoubtedly ask who Faith Harris Leech was and will be told she was the daughter of Corra Harris, a Georgia novelist.

Notes

CHAPTER I

Mrs. Harris's fiction and articles which were published in periodicals are listed in the Bibliography, in chronological order, under the periodical in which they appeared. Volume and page references to these will therefore not be given in the Notes; complete references will be given only for some short pieces not listed in the Bibliography. All of Mrs. Harris's books were serialized before being brought out in book form; see Bibliography for dates and places of publication.

Abbreviations used for the periodicals are as follows:

American	*— Amer.*	*Metropolitan*	*— Met.*
Country Gentleman	*— C.G.*	*Pictorial Review*	*— P.R.*
Good Housekeeping	*— G.H.*	*Saturday Evening Post*	*— S.E.P.*
Independent	*— Ind.*	*Uncle Remus Magazine*	*— U.R.M.*
Ladies Home Journal	*— L.H.J.*	*Woman's Home Companion*	*— W.H.C.*

1. Corra Harris, *My Book and Heart* (Boston, 1924), pp. 73–74. Page references will be made to the books rather than the serials, for the reader's convenience.

2. L. L. Knight, *Georgia and Georgians* (Chicago, 1917), I, pp. 437–440; Ms. of "Genealogy of the White Family," gift to author from Mary Bondurant Warren; Mrs. Harris's famous obituary of her father in the Atlanta *Journal*, April 29, 1930.

3. *Ibid.;* Tinsley White to Corra Harris, June 23, 1917; Al Harris to Corra Harris, undated. Unless otherwise specified, all letters, newspaper clippings, notebooks, and manuscripts quoted are in the Corra Harris Collection, University of Georgia.

4. *My Book and Heart,* pp. 40–44; Corra Harris, *As A Woman Thinks* (Boston, 1925), pp. 34–37.

5. John H. McIntosh, *The Official History of Elbert County* (Elberton, 1940), pp. 488–490; Corra Harris, "Candle-lit Column," Atlanta *Journal,* Oct. 10, 1933.

6. Corra Harris to Mrs. Rains, June 18, 1932 (copy); Mrs. H. H. Herndon to author, Feb. 24, 1965.

7. Anderson (S. C.) *Independent,* Sept. 10, 1956; Interview with Mrs. Arthur Booth; Real estate deed and will of Dr. Albert Clark Mathews in Elbert County Court House, Elberton, Ga.

8. Notebook; *As A Woman Thinks,* pp. 31–37.

9. Interview with Mrs. Arthur Booth.

10. Corra Harris to Mrs. Rains (copy), June 18, 1932; Corra Harris, *The Happy Pilgrimage* (Boston, 1927), pp. 228–230; "Candle-lit Column," Atlanta *Journal,* July 22, 1932.

11. *Ibid.; My Book and Heart,* pp. 21–24, 34–36.

12. Corra Harris, "Early Recollections of Mortality," notebook.

13. Corra Harris, "Memories of an Early Girlhood," *Ind.,* May 7, 1903; Corra

Harris, "Is the Girl of Today as Bad as She's Painted? I Should Say Not—" *P.R.,* (Jan. 1922) ; Corra Harris to A. W. Mathews, Jan. 28, 1933.

14. Harris, "Early Recollections of Mortality"; Hope Harris to Fred Harris, undated.

15. Herbert Wilcox, "Corra Harris," an unpublished Ms.; Manley Grogan to Corra Harris, Oct. 17, 1932; Nan Jones to Corra Harris, undated; *My Book and Heart,* p. 34.

16. Charles Dobbins, "Corra Harris, Her Life and Works," Atlanta *Journal,* Oct. 18, 1931; *My Book and Heart,* p. 34; Mary Heard to Corra Harris, Oct. 20, 1931; Anderson (S. C.) *Independent,* Sept. 10, 1956.

17. Dobbins, "Corra Harris," Atlanta *Journal,* Oct. 18, 1931. In his biographical serial on Mrs. Harris, which she edited and approved, Dobbins says that she left for Salem in 1883. In *My Book and Heart* (pp. 51, 64) Mrs. Harris says she went to Salem in January of the year in which she would be seventeen in March, which would be 1885. The second date is more likely correct.

18. Interview with Sam Jolley; *My Book and Heart,* pp. 64–65.

19. *Ibid.,* pp. 64–65.

20. Sarah Allen, *Our Children's Ancestry* (Atlanta, 1938) , pp. 305–306; Reverend George Smith, *The History of Georgia Methodism* (Atlanta, 1931) , p. 285.

21. Interviews with Mrs. Carrie Weems and Dr. Charles Jarrell.

22. Atlanta *Georgian,* Sept. 20, 1910.

23. H. M. Bullock, *A History of Emory University, 1836–1936* (Nashville, 1936) , p. 160.

24. A. M. Pierce, *Giant in the Sky, the Life of Warren Akin Candler* (Nashville, 1948) , p. 35; E. F. Dempsey, *Atticus Greene Haygood* (Nashville, 1940) , p. 107; Lundy H. Harris, "Anniversary of the Few Literary Society, Sept. 29, 1875," ms; "The Unpaid Parson," the New York *Times,* Sept. 25, 1910; Harold W. Mann, *Atticus Greene Haygood, Methodist Bishop, Editor and Educator* (Athens, 1965) , pp. 99–100.

25. R. J. Burden to Warren Candler, Apr. 21, 1882, Warren Akin Candler Letters, Emory University.

26. *Ibid.;* Corra Harris to Warren Candler, July 1, 1898, Candler Letters.

27. Lundy Harris to Warren Candler, Apr. 22, July 2, 11, 15, 1882 and undated; Lundy Harris to "Dear Abbott," July 5, 1882, all in Candler Letters.

28. *My Book and Heart,* p. 71.

29. *Ibid.*

30. Dobbins, "Corra Harris," Atlanta *Journal,* Oct. 18, 1931; Mary Heard to Corra Harris, Oct. 20, 1931.

31. Lundy Harris to Warren Candler, Mar. 8, 1886, Candler Letters.

CHAPTER II

1. Susan Myrick, "Retirement of a Circuit Rider," Macon *Telegraph,* Nov. 24, 1929.

2. Corra Harris, *A Circuit Rider's Wife* (Philadelphia, 1910) , pp. 38, 47–56, 71, 82, 140–144, 199, 277.

3. *My Book and Heart,* p. 141; Corra Harris to Stiles Bradley, Nov. 17, 1924 (copy) ; Corra Harris to Adelaide Neall, Nov. 14, 1923 (copy) .

4. *My Book and Heart,* pp. 100–103; Luke Johnson to Warren Candler, June 16, 1898, Candler Letters.

5. *My Book and Heart,* pp. 109–111.

6. Dobbins, "Corra Harris," Atlanta *Journal,* Oct. 25, 1931; George Stone to Corra Harris, Dec. 28, 1924; Lundy Harris to Warren Candler, Mar. 8, 1886, Candler Letters.

7. Dobbins, "Corra Harris," Atlanta *Journal,* Oct. 25, 1931.

8. Emory *Phoenix,* Oct. 1891; W. A. Carlton, *In Memory of Old Emory* (Atlanta, 1962) , pp. 3–27.

9. Bullock, *History of Emory*, p. 223; Elam Dempsey, *Life of Bishop Dickey* (Nashville, 1937), pp. 38–41.

10. Pierce, *Giant in the Sky*, pp. 54, 56.

11. Corra Harris to P. E. More, Apr. 9, 1903, Paul Elmer More Letters, Princeton University.

12. Corra Harris to Mrs. Warren Candler, undated, Candler Letters; Mrs. F. L. Stiler to Corra Harris, Oct. 3, 1923; *My Book and Heart*, pp. 122–126.

13. *My Book and Heart*, p. 157; L. R. Jenkins to Corra Harris, Mar. 31, 1923; I. L. McNair to Corra Harris, May 30, 1929; Ben Neal to Corra Harris, Oct. 10, 1928; Interviews with Dr. Charles Jarrell, L. A. Adams, and Mrs. Nathan Goodyear.

14. Corra Harris to Warren Candler, dated "Thursday," Candler Letters.

15. Interview with Mrs. Nathan Goodyear.

16. Dobbins, "Corra Harris," Atlanta *Journal*, Oct. 25, 1931; Emory *Phoenix*, Jan. 1892.

17. Corra Harris to Faith Leech, Mar. 5, 1919; Corra Harris to E. E. Slosson, Jan. 1, 1904, Hamilton Holt Letters, Rollins College Library, Winter Park, Fla.; *My Book and Heart*, pp. 139–143.

18. *My Book and Heart*, pp. 150–151; D. L. Thomas to Corra Harris, Jan. 6, 1924; Robert Morris to Corra Harris, Sept. 22, 1923; William Hosch to Corra Harris, Nov. 30, 1923; T. C. Conway to Corra Harris, May 25, 1932; Interviews with Nathan Thompson and Dr. Charles Jarrell.

19. Dempsey, *Haygood*, pp. 425–426, 608–609; Mann, *Haygood*, p. 208; Emory *Phoenix*, Feb. 1896.

20. Emory *Phoenix*, Dec. 1895; Interview with L. A. Adams.

21. Corra Harris to Mrs. Warren Candler, May 17, 1898, Candler Letters.

22. Emory *Phoenix*, Oct. 1889, July 1890, Nov. 1894, and Nov. 1896.

23. Corra Harris to Adelaide Neall, Apr. 5, 1923, George Horace Lorimer Letters, Pennsylvania Historical Society, Philadelphia, Pa.

24. *My Book and Heart*, p. 161; Covington *News*, June 1, 1898.

25. Interview with Dr. Charles Jarrell.

CHAPTER III

1. Corra Harris to Warren Candler, dated "Sunday," Candler Letters.

2. *Ibid.*

3. *Ibid.*

4. *Ibid.*

5. *Ibid.*

6. Corra Harris to Warren Candler, June 18, 1898; W. P. Lovejoy to Warren Candler, June 21, 1898, both in Candler Letters.

7. Lundy Harris to Warren Candler, June 14, 1898, Candler Letters.

8. Corra Harris to Warren Candler, June 17, 1898, Candler Letters.

9. Corra Harris to Warren Candler, June 18, 1898, Candler Letters.

10. Interview with Nathan Thompson.

11. *Ibid.*; Henry Harris to Corra Harris, June 22, 1898; Nathan Thompson to Corra Harris, June 22, 1898; Nathan Thompson to Warren Candler, June 22, 1898; Henry Harris to Warren Candler, June 26, 1898, all in Candler Letters.

12. W. P. Lovejoy to Warren Candler, June 21, 1898; W. A. Harris to Warren Candler, June 22, 1898, both in Candler Letters.

13. W. P. Lovejoy to Warren Candler, June 30, 1898, Candler Letters; Interview with Nathan Thompson.

14. W. A. Harris to Corra Harris, June 22, 1898; Corra Harris to Warren Candler, June 24, 1898, both in Candler Letters.

15. Corra Harris to Warren Candler, June 24, 1898, Candler Letters.

16. Corra Harris to Warren Candler, July 1, 1898, Candler Letters.

17. *Ibid.*

18. *Ibid.*

19. *Ibid.*
20. *Ibid.*
21. *Ibid.*
22. Corra Harris to Mrs. Warren Candler, Oct. 29, 1899, Candler Letters.
23. *Ibid.*
24. Lundy Harris to Warren Candler, Oct. 31, 1899, Candler Letters.
25. *Ibid.*
26. W. P. Lovejoy to Warren Candler, June 30, 1898; Henry Harris to Warren Candler, June 26, 1898; Nathan Thompson to Warren Candler, June 24, 1898; W. A. Harris to Warren Candler, June 22, 1898, all in Candler Letters.
27. Lundy Harris to Warren Candler, June 14, 1898; Corra Harris to Warren Candler, July 1, 1898, both in Candler Letters.
28. This poem is written on the back of a letter from Lundy Harris to his wife, written Jan. 23, 1910.
29. W. A. Harris to Warren Candler, June 18, 1898; Lundy Harris to Warren Candler, Oct. 31, 1899; W. P. Lovejoy to Warren Candler, June 30, 1898, all in Candler Letters; C. G. Jung, *Civilization in Transition* (New York, 1964), pp. 460–461.
30. Nathan Thompson to Warren Candler, June 24, 1898, Candler Letters.
31. Corra Harris to Warren Candler, June 17, 24, July 1, 1898, and undated, all in Candler Letters.
32. Corra Harris to Warren Candler, one dated "Sunday" and one undated, both in Candler Letters.
33. Corra Harris to Warren Candler, June 17, 1898, Candler Letters; Corra Harris to E. E. Slosson, July 25, 1904, Holt Letters; *My Book and Heart*, pp. 114, 184.
34. Corra Harris to Warren Candler, June 17, July 8, 1898; Lundy Harris to Warren Candler, Oct. 31, 1899, all in Candler Letters; Corra Harris to Faith Leech, Feb. 24, 1909.
35. Corra Harris to Warren Candler, June 24, 1898, and undated, both in Candler Letters.
36. Corra Harris to Warren Candler, July 1, 8, 9, 1898, and undated, all in Candler Letters.
37. Corra Harris to Warren Candler, July 1, 1898, Candler Letters.

CHAPTER IV

1. Corra Harris to Warren Candler, July 1, 22, 1898; Lundy Harris to Warren Candler, July 27, 1898, all in Candler Letters.
2. Corra Harris to Warren Candler, July 1, 1898, June 29, 1899, both in Candler Letters.
3. *My Book and Heart*, pp. 176–179.
4. Atlanta *Constitution*, Apr. 13, 1899; T. G. Steward, "The Reign of the Mob," and W. P. Lovejoy, "Georgia's Record of Blood," *Ind.*, LI (May 11, 1899), 1296–1300; Editorial, *Ind.*, LI (May 11, 1899), 1316–1317.
5. Hamilton Holt, "A Circuit Rider's Wife in Literature," *Literary Digest International Book Review*, II, n. 12 (Nov. 1924), 871–873; Corra Harris, "A Southern Woman's View," *Ind.*, May 18, 1899.
6. Editorial, *Ind.*, LI (May 18, 1899), 1385; *My Book and Heart*, p. 182.
7. Corra Harris, "Negro Womanhood," *Ind.*, June 22, 1899; Editorial, *Ind.*, LI (June 29, 1899), 1773.
8. Hamilton Holt to Corra Harris, June 29, 1899.
9. Corra Harris, "The Negro Child," *Ind.*, Oct. 26, 1899; Corra Harris, "The White Man in the South," *Ind.*, Dec. 28, 1899; Corra Harris, "The Southern White Woman," *Ind.*, Feb. 15, 1900.
10. Corra Harris, "The Poor Man in the Mountains," *Ind.*, May 10, 1900; Corra Harris, "The Country Doctor of the South," *Ind.*, July 19, 1900; Corra Harris, "The Circuit Rider in the South," *Ind.*, May 23, 1901.

11. Book review by Corra Harris of "An English Woman's Love Letters," (anon.) *Ind.*, LIII (Jan. 10, 1901) , 101–102; Holt, "Circuit Rider's Wife in Literature."

12. E. E. Slosson to Corra Harris, Oct. 4, Nov. 27, 1906, Jan. 12, 1909; Corra Harris to E. E. Slosson, Aug. 27, 1904, in Holt Letters.

13. Corra Harris, "Fungus Fiction," *Ind.*, May 3, 1906.

14. Corra Harris, "Literature," *Ind.*, LIII (May 2, 1901) , 1019, and *Ind.*, LIII (Aug. 8, 1901) , 1868; Corra Harris, "Our Novelists," *Ind.*, Nov. 16, 1905.

15. Corra Harris, "Heroes and Heroines in Recent Fiction," *Ind.*, Sept. 3, 1903; Corra Harris, "Neurotic Symptoms in Recent Fiction," *Ind.*, Nov. 19, 1903; Corra Harris, "Fungus Fiction"; Corra Harris, "Our Novelists"; Corra Harris, "To License Novelists," *Ind.*, Nov. 21, 1907; Corra Harris, "The Year's Curriculum in Fiction," *Ind.*, Nov. 18, 1909.

16. Corra Harris to P. E. More, Dec. 2, 1902, and dated "Sunday," both in More Letters.

17. Jack London to Corra Harris, Sept. 17, 1906.

18. Corra Harris, "Literature," *Ind.*, LX (Mar. 29, 1906) , 740–741; Corra Harris, "Literature," *Ind.*, LXV (Nov. 19, 1908) , 1167; Corra Harris, "Our Novelists"; Corra Harris to Upton Sinclair, Jan. 14, 1909, Upton Sinclair Letters, Lilly Library, Indiana University; Corra Harris, "Upton Sinclair and Helicon Hall," *Ind.*, Mar. 28, 1907; Upton Sinclair, "A Protest," *Ind.*, LXVI (Jan. 9, 1909) , 84; Hamilton Holt to Corra Harris, Feb. 27, 1909.

19. Corra Harris, "Books for Christmas," *Ind.*, Nov. 26, 1908; Charlotte Gilman and Corra Harris, "The Future of the Home," *Ind.*, LXI (Oct. 4, 1906) ; Ida Husted Harper to Hamilton Holt, Feb. 18, 1910, Holt Letters; Hamilton Holt to Corra Harris, Mar. 4, 1910.

20. Corra Harris, "The Pike," *Ind.*, Aug. 4, 1904; Corra Harris, "People at the Fair," *Ind.*, Aug. 11, 1904; Corra Harris, "General Impressions of the Fair," *Ind.*, Aug. 18, 1904; Hamilton Holt to Corra Harris, Oct. 26, 1906; W. H. Ward to Corra Harris, Dec. 17, 1906; Corra Harris to Faith Leech, undated.

21. Corra Harris to P. E. More, Oct. 8, 29, 1903, Feb. 3, 1904, all in More Letters; Corra Harris to E. E. Slosson, Jan. 4, Apr. 24, May 29, July 11, Aug. 4, 1904, and May 4, 1906, all in Holt Letters.

22. Arthur Dakin, *Paul Elmer More* (Princeton, 1960) , pp. 7–34.

23. Corra Harris to P. E. More, Apr. 10, June 7, July 12, Nov. 10, 1901, Sept. 4, 1903, Mar. 12, 1909, all in More Letters; P. E. More to Corra Harris, Dec. 17, 1906, Jan. 2, 1907, and Mar. 8, 1909.

24. Corra Harris to P. E. More, May 4, 10, Sept. 6, Dec. 13, 1901, and undated, all in More Letters.

25. Corra Harris to P. E. More, May 28, June 3, 1902, both in More Letters.

26. Corra Harris to P. E. More, Apr. 9, 15, 1903, and undated, all in More Letters.

27. Paul Elmer More and Corra Harris, *The Jessica Letters* (New York, 1904) , pp. 63, 80–83, 109, 141, 230, 180–181; Corra Harris to P. E. More, Nov. 2, 1902, Apr. 9, 15, 1903, all in More Letters.

28. Book review by E. E. Slosson, of *The Jessica Letters, Ind.*, LVI (May 5, 1904) , 1084–1085; Corra Harris to E. E. Slosson, undated, Holt Letters.

29. Corra Harris to P. E. More, Oct. 8, 29, 1903, both in More Letters.

CHAPTER V

1. Corra Harris to Faith Leech, Jan. 17, 1918.

2. Interviews with L. A. Adams, Bettie Rains Upshaw and Nathan Thompson.

3. Dobbins, "Corra Harris," Atlanta *Journal*, Oct. 25, 1931; *My Book and Heart*, pp. 190–193.

4. Corra Harris to Faith Harris, Feb. 11, Dec. 22, 1908; Lundy Harris to P. E. More, Jan. 31, 1902, More Letters.

5. Corra Harris to Faith Harris, Apr. 15, 1909; Corra Harris to Warren Candler, July 1, 1898, June 29, 1899, both in Candler Letters; *My Book and Heart*, p. 252.

6. Lundy Harris to Corra Harris, Jan. 23, 25, 29, 30, 1908.

7. Four notes in Mr. Harris's handwriting, all threatening or indicating an attempted suicide, are found in the Harris Papers: 1) "Memoranda," undated, 2) "Dear Austin," undated, 3) "Dear Corrie," Mar. 3, 1908, and 4) undated and unaddressed, contains instructions on people to notify and tells of collecting morphine; Charles Dobbins, "Corra Harris, Her Life and Works," Unpublished Master's Thesis, Columbia University, 1931, pp. 20, 25.

8. Corra Harris, "Famous Book in New Edition," Atlanta *Journal*, July 30, 1933; Corra Harris to John Paschall, Nov. 7, 1931; Ms. in Harris Papers. Heavy hospital bills for Harris in March and April of 1908 substantiate the date of his violent act.

9. Corra Harris to Faith Harris, Mar. 22, 1909; Corra Harris to Warren Candler, Apr. 3, 1909, Candler Letters.

10. Hamilton Holt to Corra Harris, Nov. 12, 1906; Corra Harris to P. E. More, Dec. 13, 1906, More Letters; Corra Harris to Faith Harris, Jan. 2, 1909.

11. Corra Harris to Faith Harris, Nov. 18, Dec. 10, 1908, Jan. 2, 30, Feb. 11, 1909 and undated; Faith Harris to Corra Harris, Jan. 18, July 27, Sept. 22, 1907, Sept. 27, Oct. 18, Dec. 13, 1908.

12. Corra Harris to E. E. Slosson, undated, Holt Letters.

13. Corra Harris to P. E. More, Oct. 14, 1907, More Letters; "Sid" to Faith Harris, June 16, 1908; Faith Harris to Corra Harris, Nov. 1, 1908.

14. Corra Harris to E. E. Slosson, Aug. 4, 1905, Nov. 12, 1907, Holt Letters; Corra Harris to P. E. More, Dec. 7, 1905, More Letters.

15. Faith Harris to Corra Harris, Mar. 14, 1909.

16. Corra Harris to Faith Harris, Mar. 22, 1909.

17. Corra Harris to P. E. More, Mar. 12, 26, 1909, More Letters.

18. Woods White to Corra Harris, Dec. 3, 30, 1907; Corra Harris to P. E. More, Mar. 12, 26, 1909, More Letters.

19. The "Brasstown" stories are: "The Palingenesis of Billy Meriwether," *Ind.*, July 18, 1901, "Buck Simmons of Brasstown," *Ind.*, Mar. 26, 1903, "Jesse James's Church Collection in Brasstown Valley," *Ind.*, June 24, 1909, "Pappy's Plan of Salvation," *Amer.*, Nov. 1905, "Law in the Valley," *Amer.*, Nov. 1907.

20. P. E. More to Corra Harris, Mar. 16, 1909; Faith Harris to Corra Harris, Mar. 29, 1909.

21. Churchill Williams to Corra Harris, Mar. 18, 24, 31, 1909.

22. *Ibid.*, June 1, 1909.

CHAPTER VI

1. *My Book and Heart*, pp. 259–260.

2. *Ibid.*, p. 262; G. H. Lorimer to Corra Harris, June 8, 10, 1909.

3. John Tebbel, *George Horace Lorimer* (Garden City, 1948), pp. 15, 20–21, 41–42, 44–45, 214–15.

4. *My Book and Heart*, pp. 262–264.

5. *Ibid.*, p. 264.

6. Hamilton Holt to Corra Harris, Aug. 10, 24, 1909; E. E. Slosson to Corra Harris, June 30, 1909.

7. G. H. Lorimer to Corra Harris, July 13, Aug. 13, 1909; Churchill Williams to Corra Harris, July 6, 1909.

8. G. H. Lorimer to Corra Harris, Aug. 13, 1909.

9. *Ibid.*, Aug. 13, 18, 1909.

10. Corra Harris, "A Circuit Rider's Wife," *S.E.P.*, Jan. 22, 1910.

11. Corra Harris, *A Circuit Rider's Wife* (Philadelphia, 1910), pp. 76–77, 99–102, 110, 127–131, 157, 193–195.

12. Corra Harris, "Famous Book in a New Edition"; *My Book and Heart*, p. 270.

13. A. B. Willets to the *S.E.P.*, Feb. 20, 1910; Lee Young to *S.E.P.*, Feb. 14, 1910; Frank Thompson to *S.E.P.*, undated; J. A. Stowe to *S.E.P.*, Feb. 20, 1910; book

reviews in the San Francisco *Bulletin,* Aug. 10, 1910, the *Bookman,* Oct. 1910, and the Chicago *Record-Herald,* Aug. 17, 1910.

14. W. H. Popplewell to *S.E.P.,* Feb. 18, 1910; Lee Young to *S.E.P.,* Feb. 14, 1910; F. W. McCullochy to *S.E.P.,* Feb. 26, 1910; Hiram Phillips to *S.E.P.,* Feb. 26, 1910; L. H. Colvin to *S.E.P.,* Feb. 1, 1910; R. C. Price to *S.E.P.,* Mar. 18, 1910.

15. William Burtcher to Corra Harris, Feb. 22, 1910; *A Circuit Rider's Wife,* p. 334.

16. Book reviews in the New York *Herald,* Aug. 27, 1910, the New York *Times,* Sept. 25, 1910, the *Methodist Quarterly Review,* Oct. 1, 1910, the *Methodist Advocate,* Oct. 6, 1910.

17. Corra Harris to John Paschall, Jan. 7, 1931.

18. Atlanta *Constitution,* Feb. 28, Mar. 6, 1910; Atlanta *Journal,* Feb. 21, 22, 1910.

CHAPTER VII

1. G. H. Lorimer to Corra Harris, Aug. 13, 1909.

2. G. H. Lorimer to Corra Harris, Sept. 10, 24, Nov. 5, 1909, Jan. 4, 14, 25, Mar. 10, 1910; Corra Harris to G. H. Lorimer (copy of wire) Mar. 12, 1910; H. H. Howland to Corra Harris, Jan. 13, 1910; Henry Altemus to Corra Harris, Feb. 1, 3, 7, 18, 21, 1910; Ms. of Altemus contract.

3. See bibliography for titles published at this time.

4. G. H. Lorimer to Corra Harris, Apr. 5, 9, 28, May 4, June 3, 1910; Hamilton Holt to Corra Harris, Apr. 27, May 13, 1910.

5. G. H. Lorimer to Corra Harris, Mar. 10, 1910; E. E. Slosson to Corra Harris, undated; Corra Harris to Faith Leech, undated.

6. Corra Harris to Faith Harris, undated.

7. *Ibid.;* Faith Harris to Harry Leech, July 5, 1910; Faith Harris to Corra Harris, July 5, 1910.

8. Edwin Mims, *Chancellor Kirkland* (Nashville, 1940), pp. 170–180.

9. Lundy Harris to Corra Harris, Jan. 8, 11, 14, 18, 21, 23, 1910; W. A. Harris to Corra Harris, Feb. 4, 1910; Notebook in Harris Papers.

10. *My Book and Heart,* pp. 275–276; Faith Harris to Corra Harris, July 5, 1910.

11. G. H. Lorimer to Corra Harris, Apr. 5, June 16, July 7, 20, Aug. 2, 8, 12, 22, Sept. 6, 12, 1910.

12. Hamilton Holt to Corra Harris, July 22, 1910; *Minutes, Methodist Board of Education, 1910* (Nashville, 1910), p. 61.

13. Lundy Harris to Corra Harris, Sept. 10, 13, 14, 17, 1910.

14. Faith Harris to Harry Leech, Sept. 22, 1910.

15. Faith Harris to Harry Leech, Sept. 19, 22, 1910.

16. Interview with Mrs. Linnie Anthony Crowe.

17. Ms. in Harris Papers.

18. Faith Harris to Harry Leech, Sept. 22, 1910.

19. S. J. Anderson to Corra Harris, Sept. 22, 1910; Corra Harris to S. J. Anderson, (copy) Sept. 24, 1910.

20. *My Book and Heart,* p. 276; Corra Harris to Paul Akin, Sept. 8, 1918, Paul Akin Letters, in possession of Warren Akin, Cartersville, Ga. Mrs. Harris told Lorimer that Candler deserted Lundy in his last years.

21. Corra Harris to Paul Akin, Sept. 22, 1918, Akin Letters; Faith Harris to Harry Leech, Nov. 15, 1910.

22. G. H. Lorimer to Corra Harris, Oct. 21, 1910; Corra Harris, "Eve's Second Husband," *S.E.P.,* Dec. 3, 1910.

CHAPTER VIII

1. Susan Leech to Harry Leech, Feb. 22, 1911.

2. Faith Harris to Harry Leech, Sept. 26, Oct. 5, 1910; Harry Leech to Faith Harris, Oct. 4, 6, 24, Nov. 5, 14, 18, 19, Dec. 17, 1910.

3. Faith Harris to Harry Leech, Oct. 3, 4, 10, 13, Nov. 6, 12 (wire) , 28, 1910.

4. Corra Harris to Faith Leech, Feb. 9, 1911; Faith Leech to Corra Harris, Feb. 16, 1911; Susan Leech to Harry Leech, Feb. 22, 1911.

5. Corra Harris to Faith Leech, Dec. 26, 1910.

6. Faith Leech to Corra Harris, Dec. 26, 1910, Jan. 3, 5, 7, 1911.

7. Corra Harris to Faith Leech, Jan. 6, 10, Feb. 2, 4, 7, 1911.

8. Corra Harris to Faith Leech, Feb. 9, 1911; Faith Leech to Corra Harris, Feb. 7, 14, 16, 1911; Susan Leech to Harry Leech, Feb. 22, 28, 1911.

9. Corra Harris to Faith Leech, Mar. 7, May 3, 1911; G. H. Lorimer to Corra Harris, Jan. 18, Apr. 11, 1911; Corra Harris, "The Recording Angel," *S.E.P.,* Feb. 17, 1924.

10. Corra Harris to Faith Leech, May 10, 1910.

11. Corra Harris to Faith Leech, May 10, 1911; Corra Harris to Harry Leech, May 10, 1911.

12. Corra Harris to Faith Leech, May 15, 1911 and undated.

13. Ms. in Harris Papers; Faith Leech to Harry Leech, July 22, 1911.

14. Faith Leech to Harry Leech, July 22, Aug. 4, 6, 8, 25, 26, 29, 1911; Faith Leech to Susan Leech, Aug. 31, 1911.

15. Faith Leech to Harry Leech, Aug. 19, 1911; Harry Leech to Faith Leech, Aug. 4, 8, 15, 18, 20, 30, 1911.

16. Corra Harris to Faith Leech, undated.

17. *Ibid.*

18. Thomas Cuerton to Corra Harris, Feb. 21, 1930; Corra Harris to Faith Leech, Oct. 5, 12, 29, 31, Nov. 2, 18, 1911; Faith Leech to Corra Harris, undated.

19. Corra Harris, "An Old Woman and a New One in the Old World," *S.E.P.,* Jan. 6, 1912; Corra Harris, "An Old Woman in the Old World," *S.E.P.,* Feb. 3, 1912.

20. Atlanta *Journal,* Apr. 14, 1912; Corra Harris to Faith Leech, Mar. 3, 1911.

21. Atlanta *Journal,* Apr. 14, 1912; Corra Harris to Faith Leech, undated.

22. Faith Harris to Corra Harris, Oct. 27, 1910; Corra Harris to Faith Leech, May 24, 1912; *My Book and Heart,* p. 292.

23. Corra Harris to Faith Leech, May 6, 24, 1912; Interview with Mrs. Linnie Anthony Crowe.

24. Faith Harris to Corra Harris, Oct. 27, 1910.

25. Corra Harris to Faith Leech, May 24, 1911.

26. *Ibid.;* Elberton *Star,* Apr. 9, 1912.

27. Corra Harris to Faith Leech, Apr. 24, May 2, 6, 16, 23, 24, 1912.

28. *My Book and Heart,* pp. 292–293.

CHAPTER IX

1. Corra Harris to Faith Leech, May 24, 1911; when Harry's current job was in danger three years later, Mrs. Harris wrote her daughter that "you and Harry are invited to the Valley to make your home there"; Corra Harris to Faith Leech, Sept. 22, 1914.

2. Paul Akin to Corra Harris, Jan. 19, 1913.

3. Corra Harris to Faith Leech, July 29, 1912; G. H. Lorimer to Corra Harris, July 17, Sept. 11, 1912.

4. Corra Harris to Faith Leech, Aug. 1, 9, 27, 1912.

5. Wallace Steger to Corra Harris, Aug. 14, Oct. 21, 22 (wire) , 1912; Corra Harris to Faith Leech, Sept. 6, Oct. 24, 30, 1912.

6. Corra Harris to Faith Leech, Nov. 25, Dec. 11 (wire) , 1912.

7. Paul Akin to Corra Harris, Jan. 19, 1913; Atlanta *Constitution,* Jan. 26, 1913.

8. Corra Harris to Faith Leech, Dec. 2, 9, 29, 1912, Jan. 1, 9, 12, 13, 16, 1913; Russell Doubleday to Corra Harris, Jan. 6 (wire) , 20, 28, Feb. 3, Mar. 13 (wire) , 1913.

9. G. H. Lorimer to Corra Harris, Dec. 13, 1912; Corra Harris to Faith Leech, Dec. 9, 1912.

10. Corra Harris to Faith Leech, Dec. 11, 13, 14, 18, 1912, Apr. 7, 18, 1913.

11. Corra Harris to Faith Leech, May 28, 29, June 3, 26, July 12, 28, 1913.

12. Corra Harris to Faith Leech, Aug. 4, 9, 19, Sept. 1, 1913.

13. Corra Harris to Faith Leech, Oct. 9, 13, 16, Nov. 4, 1913; W. F. Bigelow to Corra Harris, Sept. 22, 1913.

14. Hamilton Holt to Corra Harris, June 24, July 9, 1913.

15. Mrs. Harris wrote eight articles on New York for the *Independent:* see bibliography; Corra Harris to Faith Leech, Jan. 9, 16, 28, 1914; Norman Hapgood to Corra Harris, June 24, Nov. 26, 1913; Paul Reynolds to Corra Harris, Jan. 29, 1914.

16. G. H. Lorimer to Corra Harris, Jan. 13, Feb. 16, 1914.

17. Corra Harris to Faith Leech, Jan. 9, 23, Feb. 6, 16, 1914; Eric Schuler to Corra Harris, June 23, 1914; *My Book and Heart*, pp. 296–297.

18. The five stories are as follows: "The Scarlet Flower," *Met.*, June, 1914, "The Biography of Mary According to Martha," *Met.*, Aug. 1914, "Man's Word," *G.H.*, Nov. 1914, "Other People," *Harper's* Dec. 1914, and "The Wife Who Waited," *P.R.*, Sept. 1914; *My Book and Heart*, p. 288.

19. Corra Harris to Faith Leech, Mar. 29, May 14, 1914.

20. *Ibid.*, June 23, 24, 1914.

21. *Ibid.*, July 30, 1914.

22. G. H. Lorimer to Corra Harris, Aug. 3, 1914.

23. Corra Harris to Faith Leech, Sept. 13, 1914.

24. *Ibid.*, Sept. 13, 1914, and undated.

25. *Ibid.*, three undated letters.

26. Faith Leech to Corra Harris, Sept. 24, 1914.

27. Corra Harris to Faith Leech, Oct. 1, 1914.

28. Corra Harris to Faith Leech, Oct. 10, 15, 1914; Ms in Harris Papers, "From London in the Dark."

29. Corra Harris, "The New Militants," *S.E.P.*, Nov. 21, 1914; Corra Harris, "The Woman's Defense Army of England," was paid for by Lorimer, but never published: statement in Harris Papers.

30. Corra Harris, "The Women of France," *S.E.P.*, Dec. 12, 1914.

31. Corra Harris, "When the Germans Came," *S.E.P.*, Dec. 19, 1914; Corra Harris, "The Bravest of the Brave," *S.E.P.*, Jan. 16, 1915; Corra Harris to Faith Leech, Nov. 8, 9, 10, 1914.

32. Harris, "Bravest of the Brave,"; Corra Harris to Faith Leech, Nov. 10, 1914.

33. Corra Harris to Faith Leech, Nov. 12, 13, 14, 21, 1914.

34. Mrs. L. M. Grove to Corra Harris, Nov. 28, 1914; newspaper clipping.

35. Annie Ontwater to Corra Harris, undated; "A German Woman" to Corra Harris, Jan. 17, 1915; C. Berg to Corra Harris, Jan. 26, 1915; H. Braan to the *S.E.P.*, Feb. 23, 1915; G. H. Lorimer to Corra Harris, Jan. 6, 22, 1915; Tebbel, *Lorimer*, p. 56.

36. *My Book and Heart*, p. 290.

CHAPTER X

1. Faith Leech to Harry Leech, Jan. 1, 1915.

2. Corra Harris to Harry Leech, Feb. 14, 1911, Apr. 28, 1913, Feb. 17, Mar. 4, 24, 1914; Susan Leech to Faith Leech, Aug. 16, 1911.

3. Harry Leech to Faith Leech, Dec. 9, 17, 1914.

4. Faith Leech to Corra Harris, Jan. 7, 21, 27, 1915; Corra Harris to Faith Leech, Jan. 31, Feb. 1, 1915.

5. Faith Leech to Corra Harris, Feb. 17, 19, 23, 28, 1915; Corra Harris to Faith Leech, Feb. 1, 1915.

6. Corra Harris to Faith Leech, Feb. 17, 19, 1915 and undated.

7. Faith Leech to Corra Harris, Mar. 5, 1915.

8. Corra Harris to Faith Leech, Oct. 29, 1914, Mar. 1, 4, 6, 1915.

9. Faith Leech to Corra Harris, Feb. 28, June 3, 5, 8, 14, 1915.

10. A letter from W. F. Bigelow to Mrs. Harris on Sept. 24, 1915, refers to a story he has bought from her, but it has not been located in *G.H.;* the other stories referred to are: "Sally Domesticates Sam," *P.R.,* Oct. 1915, "Adventures in Hay Fever," *S.E.P.,* June 20, 1915, "A Circuit Rider's Widow," *S.E.P.,* Sept. 2, 1916; G. H. Lorimer to Corra Harris, June 25, 1915; Corra Harris to Faith Leech, June 30, 1915.

11. Corra Harris to Faith Leech, Mar. 1, July 21, 1915; Faith Leech to Corra Harris, July 16, 19, 1915.

12. Faith Leech to Corra Harris, June 3, 4, 5, 14, 17, July 3, 1915.

13. Faith Leech to Corra Harris, July 16, 18, 1915.

14. Corra Harris to Harry and Faith Leech, July 21, 1915.

15. Faith Leech to Harry Leech, Sept. 21, 1915.

16. Corra Harris to A. M. Soule (copies), Dec. 5, 1915, Mar. 18, 1921.

17. Corra Harris to Harry Leech, Mar. 31, 1916; Corra Harris to Faith Leech, Jan. 16, 1916.

18. Corra Harris to Harry Leech, Mar. 31, 1916.

19. Corra Harris to Faith Leech, Apr. 5, 16, May 1, 1916.

20. Faith Leech to Corra Harris, Apr. 24, 28, May 5, 10, 21, 22, June 6, 1916; Corra Harris to Faith Leech, Apr. 30, May 1, 9, 1916.

21. Corra Harris to Faith Leech, June 2, 9, 1916.

22. Harry Leech to Corra Harris, June 7, 1915 (wire); Corra Harris to Faith Leech, June 7, 1915; Faith Leech to Corra Harris, June 5, 9, 10 (wire), 1915.

23. Corra Harris to Mrs. McCrory, July 30, 1916.

24. Harry Leech to Faith Leech, Mar. 29, July 12, 13, 14, 1916.

25. Harry Leech to Faith Leech, July 17, 1916; Notebook in Harris Papers.

26. Corra Harris to Harry Leech, July 21 (wire), 1916; Notebook.

27. Notebook.

28. Corra Harris to Faith Leech, Aug. 15, 1916.

CHAPTER XI

1. Corra Harris to Faith Leech, July 24, 1917.

2. Corra Harris to Faith Leech, July 21, 1917 and undated.

3. Corra Harris to Faith Leech, Aug. 22, Sept. 4, 12, 17, Oct. 17, Nov. 3, Dec. 1, 1916, and undated.

4. Faith Leech to Corra Harris, Aug. 15, 23, Sept. 4, 5, 19, 1916.

5. Faith Leech to Corra Harris, Sept. 20, 1916; Corra Harris to Faith Leech, Sept. 20, 22, 1916 and undated.

6. Corra Harris to Faith Leech, Dec. 19, 1916 and undated.

7. Corra Harris to Faith Leech, Jan. 1, 5, 9, 22, 1917.

8. Corra Harris to Faith Leech, Feb. 7, 15, 21, 1917.

9. The serial published was "The Co-Citizens," *P.R.,* May, 1915; the serial accepted was "The Solution," *P.R.,* Apr. 1918; the serial ordered was "Making Her His Wife," *P.R.,* Aug. 1917. For stories see bibliography.

10. G. H. Lorimer to Corra Harris, May 17, June 2, 1916; Arthur Vance to Corra Harris, May 22, 1916; Paul Reynolds to Corra Harris, May 27, 1916.

11. Corra Harris to Faith Leech, Apr. 10, 19, 1917.

12. Corra Harris to Faith Leech, Apr. 4, 6, 1917.

13. Corra Harris to Faith Leech, Apr. 5, 7, 8, 19, 1917.

14. Corra Harris to Faith Leech, Apr. 28, May 4, 1917, Jan. 17, July 3, 15, 1918 and undated; Hope Harris to Corra Harris, undated; Oscar Price to Corra Harris, Nov. 22, Dec. 12, 1917.

15. Corra Harris to Faith Leech, Apr. 6, May 22, June 10, 1917; Faith Leech to Corra Harris, Apr. 9, 30, May 19, June 25, 1917.

16. Faith Leech to Corra Harris, July 21, 1917.

17. Corra Harris to Faith Leech, July 21, 22, 1917.

18. Faith Leech to Corra Harris, Aug. 15, 19, 21, 1917.

19. Faith Leech to Corra Harris, Aug. 21, 1917.

20. Faith Leech to Corra Harris, June 28, 1917; Corra Harris to Faith Leech, July 24, 1917; Faith Leech, "Perfect Pigs," *C.G.*, Oct. 13, 1917.

21. G. H. Lorimer to Faith Leech, Aug. 22, 1917; G. H. Lorimer to Corra Harris, Aug. 22, 1917.

22. See Mrs. Harris's note on the envelope of Lorimer's letter of Aug. 22, 1917, forwarded to Faith.

CHAPTER XII

1. Corra Harris to Faith Leech, undated.

2. Corra Harris to Faith Leech, Aug. 31, 1917, Sept. 29, 1917.

3. G. H. Lorimer to Corra Harris, Oct. 2, 1917.

4. Faith Leech to Corra Harris, Sept. 12, Oct. 22, 1917; Corra Harris to Faith Leech, Sept. 29, Oct. 23, 24, 1917.

5. G. H. Lorimer to Faith Leech, Nov. 30, 1917, Jan. 9, 1918.

6. Faith Leech to Corra Harris, Jan. 24, Feb. 28, Apr. 2, 3, 1918; Corra Harris to Faith Leech, Jan. 21, 1918.

7. Corra Harris to Faith Leech, Jan. 21, 1918 and undated.

8. G. H. Lorimer to Corra Harris, Jan. 25, 29, 1918.

9. Faith Leech to Corra Harris, Jan. 28, Feb. 26, Apr. 4, 10, 1918; Corra Harris to Faith Leech, Apr. 5, 1918; Joseph Gains to Corra Harris, Apr. 11, 1918.

10. Barton Currie to Corra Harris, Oct. 14, 1918.

11. Corra Harris and Faith Leech, "From Sun-up to Sun-down," *C.G.*, Mar. 16, 1918.

12. Corra Harris and Faith Leech, *From Sun-up to Sun-down* (Garden City, 1919), pp. 5, 10, 109, 115, 282; *My Book and Heart*, p. 297.

13. G. H. Lorimer to Faith Leech, Jan. 9, 1918; G. H. Lorimer to Corra Harris, Mar. 27, Apr. 11, 1918.

14. Faith Leech to Corra Harris, Jan. 10, 20, 1918; Corra Harris to Faith Leech, Nov. 3, 15, 1918 and undated.

15. G. H. Lorimer to Corra Harris, Apr. 29, June 6, Dec. 3, 21, 1918; Corra Harris, "The Will Maker," *S.E.P.*, Mar. 9, 1918.

16. Corra Harris to Faith Leech, undated; Arthur Vance to Corra Harris, June 11, 24, July 20, Dec. 16, 1918; Corra Harris, "Happily Married," *P.R.*, Sept. 1919; Corra Harris, "What Are We Fighting For?" *Ind.*, June 29, 1918.

17. Corra Harris to Faith Leech, June 6, 8, Oct. 7, 10, 14, 24, Nov. 11, 12, 1918; G. H. Lorimer to Corra Harris, Feb. 28, 1918.

18. Faith Leech to Corra Harris, Aug. 2, 4, 1918; Corra Harris to Faith Leech, Apr. 19, 22, June 6, 1918.

19. Corra Harris to Faith Leech, Dec. 24, 1918; Faith Leech to Corra Harris, Dec. 25, 1918; Diary of Alma McClain, Harris Papers.

20. B. W. Currie to Faith Leech, Dec. 11, 1918; Corra Harris to Faith Leech, Jan. 3, 17, 1919; Faith Leech to Corra Harris, Jan. 21, 1919 and undated fragment.

21. Corra Harris to Faith Leech, Feb. 6, 10, 1919.

22. Corra Harris to Faith Leech, Feb. 3, Mar. 20, 1919; G. H. Doran to Corra Harris, Mar. 5, 1919; Russell Doubleday to Corra Harris, Apr. 28, 1919.

23. Corra Harris to Faith Leech, Mar. 31, 1919; McClain Diary.

24. Corra Harris to Faith Leech, Apr. 4, 8, 23, 1919; B. W. Currie to Faith Leech, Mar. 19, 1919.

25. Faith Leech to Corra Harris, Apr. 11, 18, 21, 1919; Corra Harris to Faith Leech, Apr. 23, 1919.

26. Paul Akin to Corra Harris, Apr. 28, 1919; Interview with Effie Morgan; Atlanta *Journal*, May 3, 1919.

27. Isma Dooley to Corra Harris, May 12, 1919; Corra Harris to Hope Harris, Apr. 30, 1919.

28. Genella Neff to Corra Harris, May 8, 1919.

29. Corra Harris to Faith Leech, Apr. 29, 1918.

30. Interview with Minnie Porter; mss in Harris Papers.

31. Fragment of a letter dated June 8, 1919.

32. Interview with Effie Morgan; Hope Harris to Corra Harris, May 1, 1919; Isma Dooley to Corra Harris (wire), May 2, 1919; Henry Harris to Corra Harris, May 6, 1919; Corra Harris to John Paschall, Dec. 15, 1934.

33. Corra Harris to Harry Leech, May 9, 1919; Harry Leech to Corra Harris, May 10, July 8, 1919, Mar. 11, 1927; Corra Harris to Bettie Rains, July 29, 1925; Corra Harris to Fred Harris, undated.

34. J. S. Calhoun to Corra Harris, May 8, 1919; R. L. Griffin to Corra Harris, June 28, 1919; P. R. Reynolds to Corra Harris, July 24, 1919; G. H. Lorimer to Corra Harris, Oct. 16, 1919.

35. Corra Harris to G. H. Lorimer, Oct. 21, 1920.

CHAPTER XIII

1. G. H. Lorimer to Corra Harris, Mar. 20, 1912, Lorimer Papers.

2. These five titles are: "My Son," "The Eyes of Love," "A Daughter of Adam," "The House of Helen," and "Flapper Ann." See bibliography for publication dates of serials.

3. Elberton *Star*, Apr. 9, 1912; Corra Harris to Faith Leech, July 21, 1915; Corra Harris to Medora Perkerson, undated; G. H. Lorimer to Corra Harris, Feb. 4, 1920.

4. Walter Blackstock, *Corra Harris, An Analytical Study of Her Novels* (Tallahassee, 1951), p. 49.

5. Esther Howard to Corra Harris, Oct. 20, 1916; Leonard Jenkins to Corra Harris, Mar. 31, 1922; Frank McLean to Corra Harris, Mar. 12, 1918.

6. G. H. Lorimer to Corra Harris, Nov. 30, 1910; Corra Harris, *The Recording Angel* (Garden City, 1912), p. 319; Corra Harris, "Practical Politics for Gentlewomen," *L.H.J.*, Sept. 1921; Corra Harris, *The Co-Citizens* (Garden City, 1915), pp. 215–216.

7. Corra Harris to P. E. More, Feb. 3, 1904, More Letters.

8. Corra Harris, *Making Her His Wife* (Garden City, 1918), pp. 274–276; Corra Harris, *In Search of a Husband* (Garden City, 1913), p. 291.

9. Corra Harris, "The Single Woman Problem," *Amer.*, Aug. 1906; Elberton *Star*, Apr. 9, 1912; Corra Harris to Arthur Vance, Aug. 3, 1915 (copy); Corra Harris, *Flapper Ann* (Boston, 1926), p. 263.

10. Corra Harris to G. H. Lorimer (copy), Mar. 4, 1926; Arthur Vance to Corra Harris, June 6, 1922.

11. Faith Leech to Corra Harris, undated; Corra Harris to Faith Leech, undated.

12. G. H. Lorimer to Corra Harris, July 17, 1912; George Doran to Corra Harris, June 10, 1920; Corra Harris to Faith Leech, undated.

13. Corra Harris to P. E. More, May 28, 1902, More Letters; Corra Harris to G. H. Lorimer (copy), Oct. 21, 1920.

14. Harris, *As A Woman Thinks*, pp. 123–124.

15. Harris, *Recording Angel*, pp. 177–180; Harris, *The House of Helen*, p. 261; Harris, *My Son*, pp. 129–131; Harris, *Making Her His Wife*, p. 206.

16. G. H. Lorimer to Corra Harris, Feb. 4, 1920; Arthur Vance to Corra Harris, June 18, 1915; George Doran to Corra Harris, Mar. 5, 1919.

17. Adelaide Austin to Corra Harris, Oct. 5, 1913; J. W. Gardner to Corra Harris, undated; Linda Loy to Corra Harris, Dec. 10, 1922; J. B. Dame to Corra Harris, Sept. 9, 1919; Mrs. Susan Hines to Corra Harris, Nov. 11, 1925; B. B. Osborn to Corra Harris, Oct. 26, 1916; S. M. Emery to Corra Harris, Apr. 5, 1912; Richard Obee to Corra Harris, July 26, 1922; Dorothy Love to Corra Harris, July 7, 1920; Grace Davidson to Corra Harris, Aug. 24, 1925.

18. Mrs. Willis Fleming to Corra Harris, Mar. 18, 1912.

CHAPTER XIV

1. Hamilton Holt to Corra Harris, Dec. 9, 1916; Holt, "Circuit Rider's Wife in Literature"; G. H. Lorimer to Corra Harris, Dec. 8, 1921.
2. Corra Harris to Adelaide Neall, Jan. 14, Feb. 3, 1923, Lorimer Letters.
3. *My Book and Heart*, p. 264; Corra Harris to Adelaide Neall, Jan. 14, Feb. 3, 1923, Corra Harris to G. H. Lorimer, Mar. 21, 1923, all in Lorimer Letters.
4. Corra Harris to Adelaide Neall, Jan. 14, Feb. 3, 1923, Lorimer Letters.
5. Corra Harris to G. H. Lorimer, Mar. 9, 1923, Lorimer Letters.
6. G. H. Lorimer to Corra Harris, May 4, 1923, Lorimer Letters.
7. Corra Harris to Adelaide Neall, Feb. 3, 1923 and undated; Corra Harris to G. H. Lorimer, Mar. 9, June 9 (wire), 1923; all in Lorimer Letters.
8. G. H. Lorimer to Corra Harris, Feb. 9 (wire), 12, Mar. 14, May 22, 1923; Adelaide Neall to Corra Harris, Jan. 19, Feb. 12, 1923; Corra Harris to Adelaide Neall, Feb. 3, 1923; all in Lorimer Letters.
9. Corra Harris to G. H. Lorimer, Mar. 9, 21, 1923; G. H. Lorimer to Corra Harris, May 4, 1923 (wire); all in Lorimer Letters.
10. Corra Harris to Adelaide Neall, Nov. 8, 21 (wire), 1923; Adelaide Neall to Corra Harris, Nov. 7, 1923 (wire); G. H. Lorimer to Corra Harris, Sept. 27, Oct. 4, 22, 1923, all in Lorimer Letters.
11. *My Book and Heart*, pp. 148, 225, 246, 296.
12. *Ibid.*, pp. 77–78, 161.
13. *Ibid.*, pp. 252–253.
14. *Ibid.*, p. 276.
15. *Ibid.*, pp. 273, 277.
16. *Ibid.*, pp. 294, 297.
17. Seven folders of letters dated from Sept. 1 to Dec. 31, 1923, are largely made up of responses to this serial.
18. *Ibid.*
19. Springfield *Republican*, Apr. 13, 1924; New York *Times*, June 29, 1924; London *Times*, July 31, 1924.
20. Corra Harris to Paul Akin, Sept. 18, 1918, Akin Letters; Corra Harris to Adelaide Neall, Feb. 23, 1923, Lorimer Letters; *My Book and Heart*, p. 282; Holt, "Circuit Rider's Wife in Literature."
21. Corra Harris to Adelaide Neall, Sept. 9, Nov. 21, Dec. 9, 1923; Corra Harris to G. H. Lorimer, May 17, 1924; folders in Harris Papers; Irby Henderson to Corra Harris, July 28, 1924.
22. Corra Harris to Adelaide Neall, Sept. 9, 1923; G. H. Lorimer to Corra Harris, Oct. 11 (wire), 1923, both in Lorimer Letters.
23. G. H. Lorimer to Corra Harris, May 13 (wire), July 15, 1924; Adelaide Neall to Corra Harris, Oct. 3, 1924.
24. *As a Woman Thinks*, p. 4.
25. *Ibid.*, pp. 7–8, 128, 131.
26. *Ibid.*, pp. 147, 206, 278, 281–282, 310.
27. Corra Harris to Adelaide Neall, Dec. 2, 1924, Lorimer Letters.
28. *As A Woman Thinks*, pp. 310, 312–313.
29. Dr. C. H. Holmes to Corra Harris, Oct. 13, 1925.
30. G. H. Lorimer to Corra Harris, Oct. 1, 1924.

CHAPTER XV

1. Corra Harris to Bettie Rains, Apr. 18, 1925.
2. Corra Harris to Paul Akin, Feb. 13, 1921, Akin Letters.
3. Corra Harris to Bettie Rains, Apr. 5, 11, 18, 29, 1925.
4. *Ibid.*, Apr. 29, May 13, 1925.

5. *Ibid.*, May 13, 16, 1925; Arthur Bryan to Corra Harris, June 1, 1925.

6. Corra Harris to Al and Mary Harris (copy) , June 28, 1925.

7. Corra Harris to Adelaide Neall (copy) , June 30, 1925.

8. Corra Harris to Bettie Rains, June 24, 27, 1925; Corra Harris to Joseph Gains, June 28, 1925 (copy) .

9. Corra Harris to Bettie Rains (wire) , June 29, 1925.

10. Al Harris to Corra Harris (wire) , July 11, 1925; Fred Harris to Corra Harris, July 16, 1925; Adelaide Neall to Corra Harris, July 7, 1925; Arthur Vance to Corra Harris, July 1, 14 (wires) , 1925.

11. Corra Harris to Bettie Rains, July 29, Aug. 8, 1925; G. H. Lorimer to Corra Harris (wire) , Aug. 21, 1925.

12. Corra Harris to Bettie Rains, Aug. 8, 10, 11, 24, Sept. 9, 17, 29, 1925.

13. Corra Harris to Bettie Rains, Aug. 8, 10, Sept. 29, 1925.

14. Corra Harris to Bettie Rains, Sept. 2, 1925.

15. Corra Harris to Bettie Rains, Sept. 27, 1925.

16. Corra Harris to Hamilton Holt, Sept. 1, 1926; Corra Harris to Medora Perkerson, Dec. 27, 1925.

17. G. H. Lorimer to Corra Harris, May 21, Oct. 6, Nov. 2, 1926; Corra Harris to Hamilton Holt, Oct. 23, 1926, Holt Letters.

18. References here are to the serial, not the book, since changes made in the latter must be pointed out. Corra Harris, "The Happy Pilgrimage," *S.E.P.* Dec. 4, 1926.

19. "The Happy Pilgrimage," *S.E.P.*, Dec. 11, 1926; Mary Heard to J. S. Cohen, Oct. 22, 1931.

20. "The Happy Pilgrimage," *S.E.P.*, Jan. 29, 1927.

21. *Ibid.*

22. *Ibid.*, Jan. 8, 29, 1927.

23. *Ibid.*, Jan. 15, 1927.

24. Stella Hailstone to Corra Harris, Feb. 1, 1927; Elizabeth Much to Corra Harris, Apr. 17, 1927; W. M. Wilson to Corra Harris, Jan. 28, 1927. Carol Libenstein to Corra Harris, Jan. 14, 1927.

25. D. F. McGarry to G. H. Lorimer, Jan. 24, 1927; G. H. Lorimer to Corra Harris, Feb. 4, 1927.

26. G. H. Lorimer to Corra Harris, Feb. 4, Mar. 2, 1927; G. H. Lorimer to D. F. McGarry, Feb. 2, 1927 (copy) ; Corra Harris to G. H. Lorimer, Feb. 7, 1927 (copy) .

27. Mary Todd to Corra Harris, June 29, 1925.

28. Adelaide Neall to Corra Harris, Feb. 16, 1926; *The Happy Pilgrimage*, p. 299; James Rolph to Corra Harris, Sept. 8, 1927.

29. The Boston *Transcript*, Sept. 28, 1927; New York *Evening Post*, Oct. 8, 1927; *Saturday Review of Literature*, Sept. 24, 1927; *Independent*, Oct. 29, 1927.

CHAPTER XVI

1. G. H. Lorimer to Corra Harris, Nov. 2, 1926; Hamilton Holt to Corra Harris (copies) , Nov. 5, 27, 1926, Holt Letters.

2. Corra Harris to Hamilton Holt, Dec. 18, 24, 1926; Hamilton Holt to Corra Harris (copy) , Dec. 22, 1926, all in Holt Letters.

3. Corra Harris to Bettie Rains, Jan. 6, 1927.

4. Corra Harris to Bettie Rains, Jan. 9, 18, Feb. 1, 12, 17, 1927; Corra Harris to "My Dear Little Girls," Jan. 6, 1927.

5. Orlando (Florida) *Sentinel*, Mar. 6, 1927.

6. Corra Harris to Bettie Rains, Feb. 5, 11, 14, 1927.

7. Hamilton Holt to Corra Harris, Jan. 26, 1929 (copy) , Holt Letters; ms in Harris Papers, dated Jan. 9, 1928.

8. Corra Harris to Marjorie McClain, May 31, 1930.

9. Corra Harris to Bettie Rains, Feb. 17, 1928.

10. Libbie Morrow to Corra Harris, Jan. 13, 1927.

11. Corra Harris to Bettie Rains, July 29, Aug. 21, 1925; Jan. 29, 1927; Feb. 1, 9,

17, 1928; Bill Rains to Corra Harris, undated; Ellis Jones to Corra Harris, Mar. 17, 1928.

12. *My Book and Heart*, p. 266; Corra Harris to "Dear Mr. Field," Oct. 19, 1917; R. E. Adair to Corra Harris, Oct. 12, 1921.

13. Ed Howe to Corra Harris, Mar. 8, 1927, Mar. 2, 21, Apr. 4, May 3, 9, 1928; Corra Harris to Marjorie McClain, Jan. 3, 1927, Mar. 17, 1929.

14. See bibliography for Mrs. Harris's *Forum* articles; Corra Harris to Edwin Mims, Sept. 26, 1926 (copy).

15. Corra Harris to G. H. Lorimer, Oct. 5, 1927 (copy); G. H. Lorimer to Corra Harris, Oct. 14, 1927.

16. Corra Harris, "Behind the Times," *S.E.P.*, Sept. 15, 1928; Corra Harris, "Obsolete Womanhood," *S.E.P.*, Aug. 24, 1929; Corra Harris, "Last Leaves," *S.E.P.*, Nov. 23, 1929; "The Editor" to Corra Harris, Feb. 22, 1929 (copy); Corra Harris to "Dear Mr. Lorimer," Mar. 17, 1929 (copy); G. H. Lorimer to Corra Harris, Apr. 25, 1929.

17. Hamilton Holt to Corra Harris, Oct. 21, 1929; Corra Harris to Hamilton Holt, Oct. 26, 1929; Corra Harris to Mr. Clark, Dec. 9 (copy), 1929, all in Holt Letters.

18. Corra Harris to Bettie Rains, Feb. 7, 13, 1930, and undated.

19. Corra Harris to Bettie and Trannie Rains, Feb. 22, Mar. 5, 1930.

20. Lecture notes in Harris Papers; student notes in Holt Letters.

21. "The Chair of Evil," *Forum*, Aug. 1930.

22. Virginia Jarrell to Corra Harris, May 5, 1930; James Phelphs to Corra Harris, Feb. 27, 1930; Stella Dale to Corra Harris, Apr. 1, 1930; William Hurlbut to Corra Harris, Feb. 20, 1930; *Independent*, Mar. 22, 1930; Buffalo *Courier Express*, Feb. 22, 1930; London *Times*, Feb. 22, 1930; Atlanta *Georgian*, May 4, 1930; Hamilton Holt to Margaret Walsh, Mar. 5, 1929 (copy), Holt Letters.

23. Ed Howe to Bettie Rains, undated; Adelaide Neall to Corra Harris, Feb. 25, 1930 (wire); E. O. Groover to Corra Harris, Mar. 3, 1930.

24. Atlanta *Journal*, Apr. 29, 1930.

25. Corra Harris to Medora Perkerson, June 18, 1930; Corra Harris to Marjorie McClain, Sept. 1, 1930.

26. Corra Harris to Medora Perkerson, Feb. 17, Mar. 18, 1931; Corra Harris to Adelaide Neall, Apr. 25, 1931 (copy).

27. Corra Harris, "A Woman Takes a Look at Politics," *S.E.P.*, June 13, 1931; Corra Harris to Medora Perkerson, June 26, 1931.

28. Charles Dobbins to Corra Harris, Nov. 25, Dec. 5, 1930, Jan. 8, May 7, 1931; Corra Harris to Medora Perkerson, June 15, 26, Sept. 14, 1931.

29. Dobbins, "Corra Harris," Master's Thesis, pp. 20, 35.

30. *Ibid.*, p. 35.

31. Dobbins, "Corra Harris," Atlanta *Journal*, Nov. 11, 1931.

32. Dobbins, "Corra Harris," Master's Thesis, p. 69.

33. Corra Harris to Medora Perkerson, Sept. 14, 1931; Paul Cousins to Corra Harris, Sept. 7, 1931.

34. John Paschall to Corra Harris, Sept. 28, 1931 (copy).

CHAPTER XVII

1. Corra Harris to Adelaide Neall, Sept. 12, 1931 (copy); Corra Harris to A. W. Mathews, Nov. 19, 1931, Dec. 3, 1932; Bettie Rains to Mrs. A. W. Mathews, Nov. 22, 1932.

2. W. T. Perkerson to Corra Harris, Mar. 8, 1933; Statement in Harris Papers; Corra Harris to Hamilton Holt, Jan. 28, 1933, Holt Letters.

3. Bettie Rains to Corra Harris, Mar. 30, 1934; Corra Harris to John Paschall, Nov. 11, 1931; Corra Harris to Mary Bachellor, Jan. 15, 1934 (copy).

4. Corra Harris to John Paschall, July 3, 1934; Interviews with William Tate and Edwin M. Everett.

5. Corra Harris to John Paschall, Aug. 28, 1933; John Harris to Corra Harris, Aug. 16, 1934; Undated clipping, Atlanta *Journal,* in Harris Papers.

6. Corra Harris to "Dear Governor," undated (copy); Theodore Dreiser to Corra Harris, undated; Circular in Harris Papers; Corra Harris to Hamilton Holt, May 17, 1932, Holt Letters.

7. Adelaide Neall to Corra Harris, May 23, 1933; Corra Harris to Adelaide Neall, Sept. 19, 1931.

8. Ferris Greenslet to Corra Harris, Feb. 7, Mar. 25, 1933; Henry Altemus to Corra Harris, Feb. 23, 1933; Stanley Johnson to Corra Harris, Feb. 25, 1932.

9. Ethel Bryan to Corra Harris, July 5, 1925 (wire); R. L. Griffin to Corra Harris, July 18, 19, 24, 1919 (wires); Harry Lee to Corra Harris, Aug. 2, 1931; Atlanta *Journal,* Mar. 14, Apr. 25, 1920, July 23, 1950.

10. Corra Harris to Adelaide Neall, Apr. 23, 1932 (copy); Angus Perkerson to Corra Harris, Sept. 28, 1931; Corra Harris, "Candlelit Column," Atlanta *Journal,* Dec. 11, 23, 1931, Feb. 19, 21, June 22, July 29, 1932, Jan. 13, Feb. 15, Apr. 14, 21, Aug. 2, 1933.

11. Corra Harris to Marjorie McClain, undated; Corra Harris to John Paschall, June 19, 1934; "Candlelit Column," Apr. 9, 11, Aug. 3, 31, 1934.

12. Corra Harris to John Paschall, Nov. 20, 1933.

13. "Candlelit Column," Apr. 20, 22, 27, 29, May 4, 11, 1932.

14. *Ibid.,* Feb. 10, 1933; Corra Harris to Marjorie McClain, June 5, 1933; Corra Harris to John Paschall, June 2, 1933; Interview with Bettie Rains Upshaw.

15. Corra Harris to John Paschall, Mar. 1, 8, 14, 22, 23, 1934 and undated; Ms of speech in Holt Letters; *Happy Pilgrimage,* p. 115; Bettie Rains to Corra Harris, Mar. 26, 1934; Hamilton Holt to Corra Harris, Nov. 21, 1933.

16. Corra Harris to Marjorie McClain, Aug. 1, 25, 1934; Mrs. H. H. Stone to Corra Harris, Nov. 20, 1934; L. M. Hartman to Corra Harris, Nov. 13, 1934; Adelaide Neall to Corra Harris, Dec. 5, 1934; Corra Harris to John Paschall, Aug. 25, 1934.

17. Corra Harris to Hamilton Holt, May 26, 1934, Holt Letters; Corra Harris to John Paschall, July 11, Oct. 28, Nov. 24, 1934 and undated.

18. Bettie Rains to Mrs. A. W. Mathews, Dec. 22, 1934.

19. Adelaide Neall to Corra Harris, July 18, 1930; J. C. Rogers to Corra Harris, Oct. 2, 1934; A. E. Hoyle to Corra Harris, Dec. 28, 1934.

20. Corra Harris to Al Harris, Jan. 1, 1935 (copy).

21. Corra Harris to John Paschall, Jan. 1, 1934.

22. Interviews with Dr. H. B. Bradford, Bettie Rains Upshaw and Frank Daniel.

23. Interviews with Bettie Rains Upshaw and Marjorie McClain.

24. Interview with Bettie Rains Upshaw; Atlanta *Journal,* Feb. 12, 1935.

25. Interviews with Bettie Rains Upshaw and Marie Vaughan.

26. Atlanta *Journal,* June 7, 1936.

27. Corra Harris to John Paschall, undated.

28. Mrs. Harris's will in Bartow County Courthouse.

29. *Ibid.*

30. Harold Patterson to author, Feb. 16, 1965.

31. Carl Strobel to author, Feb. 13, 21, 1968.

32. *Ibid.,* March 12, 1968.

Bibliography

I. PRIMARY SOURCES

1. MANUSCRIPTS AND PERSONAL PAPERS

Corra Harris Collection, University of Georgia Library. The vast assortment of material in this collection furnished most of the information for this biography. It contains approximately 1700 letters, manuscripts of most of Mrs. Harris's writings, newspaper clippings, and a great variety of miscellaneous papers. The unbroken correspondence between Mrs. Harris and her daughter Faith Harris Leech gives perhaps the best insight into the characters of the two women. The letters of Lundy Howard Harris, Mrs. Harris's husband, were invaluable for the book's first division. The correspondence between Mrs. Harris and the Rains sisters, Trannie and Bettie, threw light upon the life in her Valley home. To the original collection given by John Harris and General Frederick Harris, Mrs. Harris's nephews, three of Mrs. Harris's friends, John Paschall, Medora Field Perkerson, and Marjorie (Mrs. Douglas S.) McClain, have added letters from Mrs. Harris which are needed for an understanding of her later life. Also, forty letters from Mrs. Harris to her uncle A. W. Mathews of Comer, Georgia, are on loan to the University of Georgia Library. The original collection includes letters from George Horace Lorimer, Hamilton Holt, Paul Elmer More, Joel Chandler Harris, Warren Candler, William Hayes Ward, and Edwin E. Slosson, all of whom figured prominently in Mrs. Harris's life.

Fortunately there is a surprisingly large number of Mrs. Harris's own letters to people outside her family and household. She frequently requested correspondents, for various reasons, to return her letters.

Warren Akin Candler Papers, Emory University Library. The letters from Corra and Lundy Harris to Warren Candler in 1898–99 are the only source of information on Mr. Harris's tragic breakdown and flight to Texas. A few letters before and after that period contribute little to the story of Mrs. Harris's life.

Hamilton Holt Papers, Rollins College. Holt's letters to Mrs. Harris from 1926 to 1935 supply information on her unfortunate "Chair of Evil" lectures and her several Florida trips. Also in this collection is a sheaf of letters from Mrs. Harris to Edwin E. Slosson during 1904–05, which help to reveal her relations with the *Independent* Magazine.

Paul Elmer More Papers, Princeton University Library. Mrs. Harris's chatty, confessional letters to More tell much about her family life in Nashville, her literary ambition, and the genesis of *A Circuit Rider's Wife.* She wrote to More frequently and at great length from 1901 to 1906. The few letters from 1906 to 1909 help explain her developing literary objectives.

George Horace Lorimer Papers, Pennsylvania Historical Society. This collection contains many, but not all, of her letters to Lorimer and his *Post* assistant, Adelaide Neall, from 1911 to 1928. It also includes several copies of letters from Lorimer and Miss Neall to Mrs. Harris. This correspondence traces Mrs. Harris's determined efforts to publish in the *Post* and Lorimer's shrewd handling of a difficult contributor.

Paul F. Akin Letters, in possession of Warren Akin, Cartersville, Georgia. Mrs. Harris's letters to her lawyer from 1913 to 1923 afford an insight into her business problems and methods.

Arthur T. Vance Letters, Southern Historical Collection, University of North Carolina Library. Two of the three letters from Mrs. Harris to the editor of *Pictorial Review* magazine in 1920–21 show her demanding methods in dealing with an editor more pliable than George Lorimer.

Upton Sinclair Letters, Lilly Library, University of Indiana. A letter of Mrs. Harris's written in 1909 and another in 1922 deal with two of the lively literary controversies between her and Sinclair.

Walter Hines Page Letters, Houghton Library, Harvard University. Three letters from Mrs. Harris to Ambassador Page give an idea of her frame of mind before leaving London for France during her brief career as a war correspondent in 1914.

William Lyon Phelps Letters, Yale University Library. A single letter from Mrs. Harris to Professor Phelps gives the educational views of the Rollins Professor of Evil.

2. Mrs. Harris's Works

(a) *Novels*

Harris, Corra. *A Circuit Rider's Wife.* Philadelphia, 1910. Serial in *Saturday Evening Post,* Jan. 22, 29, Feb. 5, 12, 19, 26, 1910.

————. *A Circuit Rider's Widow.* Garden City, 1916. Serial in *Saturday Evening Post,* Sept. 2, 9, 16, 23, 30, Oct. 7, 14, 21, 1916.

————. *A Daughter of Adam.* New York, 1922. Serial in *Country Gentleman,* Oct. 21, 28, Nov. 4, 11, 18, 25, Dec. 2, 9, 1922.

————. *Eve's Second Husband.* Philadelphia, 1911. Serial in *Saturday Evening Post,* Dec. 3, 10, 17, 24, 31, 1910, Jan. 7, 14, 21, 1911.

————. *Flapper Ann.* Boston, 1926. Serial in *Ladies Home Journal,* Sept., Oct., Nov., Dec., 1925.

————. *Happily Married.* New York, 1920. Serial in *Pictorial Review,* Sept., Oct., Nov., 1919.

————. *In Search of a Husband.* Garden City, 1913. Serial in *Saturday Evening Post,* Aug. 30, Sept. 6, 13, 20, 27, Oct. 4, 11, 1913.

————. *Justice.* New York, 1915. Published in *Good Housekeeping,* May, 1915.

————. *Making Her His Wife.* Garden City, 1918. Serial in *Pictorial Review,* Aug., Sept., Oct., 1917.

————. *My Son.* New York, 1921. Serial in *Saturday Evening Post,* Dec. 11, 18, 25, 1920, Jan. 1, 8, 1921.

————. *The Co-Citizens.* Garden City, 1915. Serial in *Pictorial Review,* May, June, July, 1915.

————. *The Eyes of Love.* New York, 1922. Serial in *Pictorial Review,* Sept., Oct., Nov., 1921.

————. *The House of Helen.* New York, 1923. Serial in *Ladies Home Journal,* Dec., 1922, Jan., Feb., Mar., 1923.

————. *The Recording Angel.* Garden City, 1912. Serial in *Saturday Evening Post,* Feb. 17, 24, Mar. 2, 9, 16, 23, 30, 1912.

Collaborations

Harris, Corra, with Paul Elmer More, *The Jessica Letters.* New York, 1904. Serial in *The Critic,* Oct., Nov., Dec., 1903, Feb., Apr., 1904.

————, with Faith Harris Leech. *From Sun-up to Sun-down.* Garden City, 1919. Serial in *Country Gentleman,* Mar. 16, 23, 30, Apr. 6, 13, 20, May 4, 18, Aug. 31, Sept. 21, Oct. 12, Nov. 9, 1918.

(b) *Autobiographical*

Harris, Corra. *As A Woman Thinks.* Boston, 1925. Serial in *Saturday Evening Post,* Aug. 15, 22, 29, Sept. 5, 12, 19, 26, Oct. 3, 10, 1925.

————. *Happy Pilgrimage.* Boston, 1927. Serial in *Saturday Evening Post,* Dec. 4, 11, 18, 25, 1926, Jan. 1, 8, 15, 22, 29, 1927.

————. *My Book and Heart.* Boston, 1924. Serial in *Saturday Evening Post,* Sept. 1, 8, 15, 22, 29, Oct. 6, 13, 20, 27, 1923.

(c) *Periodical Fiction and Articles*

Country Gentleman:

"Diary of a Country Woman," LXXXVIII (Dec. 1, 1923), 7; (Dec. 8, 1923), 8; (Dec. 15, 1923), 8; (Dec. 22, 1923), 8; (Dec. 29, 1923), 8; LXXXIX (Jan. 5, 1924), 6; (Jan. 12, 1924), 8; (Jan. 19, 1924), 8; (Jan. 26, 1924), 8; (Feb. 2, 1924), 6; (Feb. 9, 1924), 8; (Feb. 16, 1924), 10; (Aug. 9, 1924), 3; (Sept. 6, 1924), 7; XC (Jan. 31, 1925), 23; (Mar. 7, 1925), 19; (May 16, 1925), 21; (June 6, 1925), 19; (July 18, 1925), 23; (Aug. 8, 1925), 21.

"Eden Mothers," XCII (July 1927), 21.

"Strut Your Stuff," XCII (Sept. 1927), 25.
"Real Life," XCII (Dec. 1927), 22.
"Good Little Lives," XCIII (Feb. 1928), 30.
"Farmer's Blues," XCIII (Apr. 1928), 30.
"My Garden," XCIII (June 1928), 22.
"The Weaning of Boys," XCIII (Sept. 1928), 24.
"Good Things to Eat," XCIII (Oct. 1928), 30.
"Christmas in the Valley," XCIII (Dec. 1928), 22.
"Letters to a Young Mother," XCIII (Dec. 1928), 22.
"First Babies and Weaned Husbands," XCIV (Apr. 1929), 32.
"The Man in the Garden," XCIV (June 1929), 23.
"Etiquette with Animals," XCIV (Aug. 1929), 22.
"The Circuit Rider's Wife's First Thanksgiving Dinner," XCIV (Nov.
    1929), 23.
"Two Days," XCV (Mar. 1930), 28.
"Parsing the Land with a Plow," XCV (Apr. 1930), 28.
"Two Girls on a Farm," XCV (Nov. 1930), 24.
"Those Unexpected Visitors," XCVI (May 1931), 22.

Good Housekeeping:

"Sabbath Webster's Lover," LVII (Oct. 1913), 464–475.
"Taming the Hawk," LVIII (Jan. 1914), 15–26.
"Azalee's Valentine," LVIII (Feb. 1914), 159–169.
"Man's Word," LIX (Nov. 1914), 548–559.
"Miss Apsylla's Furlough," LXVII (Oct. 1918), 33–34.

Harper's:

"Other People," CXXX (Dec. 1914), 54–57.
"Buying Caskets on the Installment Plan," CXXVII (Aug. 1913),
    342–353.

Harper's Weekly:

"Ideal," LVIII (Sept. 27, 1913), 12–13.
"New Wine in Old Bottles," LVIII (Jan. 17, 1914), 24–25.

Independent Magazine:

"A Southern Woman's View," LI[1] (May 18, 1899), 1354–55.
"Negro Womanhood," LI[1] (June 22, 1899), 1687–89.
"The Negro Child," LI[2] (Oct. 26, 1899), 2884–86.
"White Man in the South," LI[2] (Dec. 28, 1899), 3475–77.
"Southern White Women," LII[1] (Feb. 15, 1900), 430–32.
"Posy," LII[1] (Mar. 8, 1900), 594–97.
"The Poor Man in the Mountains," LII[1] (May 10, 1900), 1115–16.
"Country Doctor of the South," LII[2] (July 19, 1900), 1728–30.
"Colonel's Last Campaign," LII[2] (Nov. 8, 1900), 2673–75.
"The Circuit Rider in the South," LIII[1] (May 23, 1901), 1184–85.
"Palingenesis of Billy Merriwether," LIII[2] (July 18, 1901), 1670–76.

"Confederate Veteran," LIII² (Oct. 3, 1901), 2357–58.

"New Pigeon Holes for Novels," LIV¹ (Feb. 13, 1902), 394–96.

"A Southern Woman's View of Southern Women," LIV¹ (Apr. 17, 1902), 922–24.

"Partners," LIV² (Dec. 4, 1902), 2874–76.

"Buck Simmons of Brasstown," LV¹ (Mar. 26, 1903), 723–25.

"Memories of an Early Girlhood," LV (May 7, 1903), 1071–75.

"Heroes and Heroines in Recent Fiction," LV² (Sept. 3, 1903), 2111–15.

"Neurotic Symptoms in Recent Fiction," LV² (Nov. 19, 1903), 2725–28.

"Uncle Jimmie and the X-Ray Doctor," LV² (Dec. 10, 1903), 2907–09.

"A Woman's Relation to the Two Sexes," LVI (Apr. 21, 1904), 906–08.

"A Man's Relation to the Two Sexes," LVI (May 26, 1904), 1188–90.

"The Pike," LVII (Aug. 4, 1904), 249–54.

"The People at the Fair," LVII (Aug. 11, 1904), 305–08.

"General Impressions of the Fair," LVII (Aug. 18, 1904), 363–66.

"Novels and Novelists," LVII (Nov. 17, 1904), 1131–35.

"Reflections Upon Old Bachelors in New England," LVII (Dec. 29, 1904), 1492–94.

"North and South—The Difference," LVIII (June 15, 1905), 1348–50.

"Fashions in Fiction," LVIII (June 22, 1905), 1407–11.

"Cheerful Life in the South," LIX (July 20, 1905), 137–39.

"Our Novelists," LIX (Nov. 16, 1905), 1171–75.

"The Serpent and the Woman in Fiction," LIX (Dec. 7, 1905), 1332–33.

"A Southern Woman's Impression of New York City," LX (Feb. 22, 1906), 430–34.

"Fungus Fiction," LX (May 3, 1906), 1040–44.

"The Walking Delegate Novelist," LX (May 24, 1906), 1213–16.

"Southern Manners," LXI (Aug. 9, 1906), 321–25.

"Gossip About Novels and Novelists," LXI (Sept. 6, 1906), 557–64.

"Monstrous Altruism," LXI (Oct. 4, 1906), 792–98.

"Future of the Home," with C. Gilman, LXI (Oct. 4, 1906), 788–798.

"Advice to Literary Aspirants," LXII (Jan. 10, 1907), 79–84.

"Superwoman," LXII (Feb. 21, 1907), 426–28.

"The Rise and Fall of Popular Novels During 1906," LXII (Mar. 7, 1907), 544–46.

"Upton Sinclair and Helicon Hall," LXII (Mar. 28, 1907), 711–13.

"Yeast-Stirrers in New York City," LXII (Apr. 18, 1907), 891–95.

"How New York Appears to a Southern Woman," LXII (June 13, 1907), 1400–02.

"The Passing of Brother Milam," LXIII (Sept. 5, 1907), 552–56.

"A Forty Days' Troth with the Forest," LXIII (Sept. 19, 1907), 674–77.

"To License Novelists," LXIII (Nov. 21, 1907), 1247–50.

"Literature, Literaturites and Literalism," LXIV (Jan. 23, 1908), 182–84.

"Hindering the Children," LXIV (Mar. 12, 1908), 582–83.

"The Great Kinship," LXIV (Apr. 23, 1908), 899–900.

"The Women and the Future," LXIV (May 14, 1908), 1090–92.

"The Mind of the Child," LXIV (June 19, 1908), 1398–99.

"The Passing of Uncle Remus," LXV (July 23, 1908), 190–92.

"The Advance of Civilization in Fiction," LXV (Nov. 19, 1908), 1166–72.

"Sanitariums and Sanitarium Women," LXV (Nov. 26, 1908), 1240–41.

"The South's Ways," LXV (Dec. 3, 1908), 1274–77.

"The Willipus Wallipus in Tennessee Politics," LXVI (Feb. 25, 1909), 622–26.

"Jesse James's Church Collection in Brasstown Valley," LXVI (June 24, 1909), 1386–89.

"The Year's Curriculum in Fiction," LXVII (Nov. 18, 1909), 1149–54.

"A Southern Woman in New York," LXVIII (Feb. 17, 1910), 346–52.

"The Crab Apple Adams," LXIX (Nov. 3, 1910), 967–970.

"Be Sweet, Clever Maid," LXX (May 11, 1911), 1007–08.

"Moving Pictures of English and American Women," LXXII (Apr. 4, 1912), 715–18.

"The Recording Angel," LXXIII (July 18, 1912), 146–48.

"Jeff," LXXIII (Sept. 26, 1912), 715–24.

"New York as Seen from a Georgia Valley," LXXVII (Jan. 19, 1914), 97–99.

"The Abomination of Cities, "LXXVII (Jan. 26, 1914), 129–31.

"Men and Women—and the Woman Question," LXXVII (Feb. 2, 1914), 164–65.

"Marriage—New Profession or Old Miracle?" LXXVII (Feb. 16, 1914), 234–35.

"The Streets of the City," LXXVII (Mar. 2, 1914), 306–08.

"How New York Amuses Itself," LXXVII (Mar. 16, 1914), 374–76.

"Literary Spectrum of New York," LXXVII (Mar. 30, 1914), 341–43.

"If You Must Come to New York," LXXVIII (Apr. 6, 1914), 29–33.

"The Valley—After New York," LXXIX (July 13, 1914), 63–66.

"From the Peace Zone in the Valley," LXXXII (May 3, 1915), 190–92.

"War and Brides in June," LXXXII (June 21, 1915), 506.

"Why We Should Read Books," LXXXV (Jan. 24, 1916), 117–18.

"What Men Know About Women," LXXXV (Mar. 13, 1916), 379.

"June Brides," LXXXVI (June 5, 1916), 377.

"The Woman of Yesterday," LXXXVI (June 19, 1916), 484.

"In the Valley," LXXXVII (July 24, 1916), 123–24.

"Politics and Prayers in the Valley," LXXXVII (July 31, 1916), 155–56.

"Dr. William Hayes Ward," LXXXVII (Sept. 11, 1916), 375.

"War Time in the Valley," XCII (Dec. 8, 1917), 471.

"What Are We Fighting For," XCIV (June 29, 1918), 502.
"Marrying Off the American Army," XCVII (Feb. 22, 1919), 260–61.
"Was Eve a Feminist?" XCVII (Mar. 8, 1919), 338.
"Spring Days in the Valley," CII (May 8, 1920), 200.
"That Secret Marriage," CII (June 5, 1920), 311.

Ladies Home Journal:

"Widow Ambrose," XXXVII (Aug. 1920), 7–9.
"Concerning Widows, or, How to be a Widow," XXXVII (Sept. 1920),
    13.
"Practical Politics for Gentlewomen," XXXVIII (Sept. 1921), 16.
"My Aunt Clarinda's Orphan," XXXVIII (Oct. 1921), 10–13.
"On How to Choose a Husband," XXXVIII (Nov. 1921), 38.
"Pageant Widow," XXXIX (Apr. 1922), 10–11.
"Unknown Great American Women," XL (Jan. 1923), 25.
"Bonneted Hornets," XL (Oct. 1923), 18.
"Happy Women," XL (Nov. 1923), 33.
"Has the World Got Us at Last?" XLI (July 1924), 21.
"Political Preparedness for Women," XLI (Oct. 1924), 29.
"Sob Sister Citizens," XLII (Feb. 1925), 29.
"On the Management of a Husband," XLII (Mar. 1925), 30.
"These Husbands," XLII (June 1925), 27.
"Happy Days?" XLII (July 1925), 27.
"Our Family Album," XLII (Sept. 1925), 34.
"Renaissance of the Ruffle," XLIII (Mar. 1926), 35.
"Fortune Telling for Old People," XLIII (May 1926), 33.
"Woman Wins," XLIII (June 1926), 6–7.
"Borrowed Timers," XLIII (Sept. 1926), 35.
"Synthetic Girls," XLV (Apr. 1928), 37.
"Care and Dieting of Guests," XLVI (Dec. 1929), 10–11.

Metropolitan:

"The Scarlet Flower," XL (June 1914), 10–12.
"The Biography of Mary According to Martha," XL (Aug. 1914), 5–
    8.

Pictorial Review:

"The Wife Who Waited," XV (Sept. 1914), 4–6.
"Sally Domesticates Sam," XVII (Oct. 1915), 7–8.
"Epsie of Blue Sky," XVII (Apr. 1916), 14–15.
"Enoch's Great Temptation," XVII (May 1916), 15–16.
"Serena's Mary's and Martha's Hands," XVII (June 1916), 15–16.
"The Windmills of Love," XIX (Nov. 1917), 19–21.
"The Solution," XIX (April, 1918), 6–11; (May 1918), 17–22; (June
    1918), 22–27.
"Is the Girl of To-day as Bad as She's Painted? I Should Say Not—"
    XXIII (Jan. 1922), 5.

"Has the World Conquered the Church?" XXIII (July 1922), 5.
"What Marriage Was and What It Is Not," XXIV (Jan. 1923), 2.
"Yes, If Love Always Rules," XXVII (Jan. 1926), 11.

Saturday Evening Post:

"Jim Bledsoe's Courtship," CLXXX (Sept. 21, 1907), 12-13.
"Price of Suffrage for American Women," CLXXXII (Oct. 23, 1909), 10-11.
"Sally in New York," CLXXXII (Dec. 18, 1909), 3-5.
"The Pendergrass Sanitarium for Incurables," CLXXXII (Mar. 26, 1910), 9-11.
"The Son of Old Blood," CLXXXII (May 7, 1910), 13-15.
"An Old Woman and a New One in the Old World," CLXXXIV (Jan. 6, 1912), 14-15; (Jan. 13, 1912), 16-17; (Jan. 20, 1912), 16-18; (Jan. 27, 1912), 16-18.
"An Old Woman in the Old World," CLXXXIV (Feb. 3, 1912), 24-25.
"Autobiography of a Mother-in-law" (Appeared under the name of Mary Bain Wright), CLXXXV (Mar. 8, 1913), 8-10.
"The Turkey Trot," CLXXXV (June 14, 1913), 10-11.
"The New Militants," CLXXXVII (Nov. 21, 1914), 3-5.
"The Women of France," CLXXXVII (Dec. 12, 1914), 11-12.
"When the Germans Came," CLXXXVII (Dec. 19, 1914), 11-12.
"The Bravest of the Brave," CLXXXVII (Jan. 16, 1915), 6-8.
"A Communiqué," CLXXXVII (Jan. 23, 1915), 14-15.
"War and Hallucination," CLXXXVII (Feb. 13, 1915), 23.
"Adventures in Hay Fever," CLXXXVII (June 20, 1915), 7.
"The Other Unit," CLXXXIX (July 15, 1916), 3-4.
"Superparents," CLXXXIX (Nov. 11, 1916), 15-17.
"Corra Harris—Herself," CXC (July 28, 1917), 23.
"Her Last Affair," CXC (Sept. 1, 1917), 16-19.
"The Other Soldiers in France," CXC (Nov. 3, 1917), 28.
"The Will Maker," CXC (Mar. 9, 1918), 26.
"Demobilizing the American Women," CXCI (Apr. 26, 1919), 10-11.
"Taking Over the Problem," CXCI (May 31, 1919), 10-11.
"Sentimental Citizens," CXCV (Nov. 11, 1922), 16.
"Back to the Hills," CXCV (Feb. 17, 1923), 16.
"When the Tide Turns," CXCVIII (Nov. 7, 1925), 41.
"Prosody of Old Age," CXCVIII (May 8, 1926), 35.
"Student Government for the Country," CXCIX (June 4, 1927), 5.
"Manual of Education for the Educated," CC (Aug. 20, 1927), 27.
"Behind the Times," CCI (Sept. 15, 1928), 37.
"Obsolete Womanhood," CCII (Aug. 24, 1929), 6-7.
"Last Leaves," CCII (Nov. 23, 1929), 10-11; (Jan. 4, 1930), 14; (Feb. 22, 1930), 42; (Mar. 15, 1930), 29; (Apr. 12, 1930), 26; (June 28, 1930), 14-15; CCIII (Sept. 20, 1930), 18.
"Black and White," CCIII (Nov. 29, 1930), 21.

"The Old Penitentiary School of Childhood," CCIII (Feb. 21, 1931), 29–30.
"A Woman Takes a Look at Politics," CCIII (June 13, 1931), 25.
"A Change for the Better," CCIV (Sept. 12, 1931), 25.
"Pharisee's Lament," CCIV (Dec. 19, 1931), 32.
"Parents and Children, Yesterday and Today," CCIV (May 28, 1932), 24.

The American:

"Budd Sockwell's Courtship," LX (Sept. 1905), 533–37.
"Mary Frances," LX (Oct. 1905), 615–22.
"Pappy's Plan of Salvation," LXI (Nov. 1905), 17–22.
"Little April," LXI (Apr. 1906), 628–33.
"Mrs. Teasley's Summer Boarder," LXII (July 1906), 239–46.
"Single Woman's Problem: Why It Exists," LXII (Aug. 1906), 426–27.
"Love in the Valley," LXIII (Feb. 1907), 438–43.
"Seth Carter's Wife," LXIV (May 1907), 73–77.
"Law in the Valley," LXV (Nov. 1907), 20–24.
"God's Lonesome Man in Brasstown Valley," LXVII (Mar. 1909), 450–58.
"Brother Milam's Story," LXVIII (Sept. 1909), 450–55.
"Taming of Tom Purcell," LXIX (Nov. 1909), 91–98.

The Atlanta *Journal:*

"Candlelit Column." A tri-weekly column in the Atlanta *Journal* from Nov. 15, 1931 to Apr. 28, 1935.

The Critic:

"Fiction, North and South," XLIII (Sept. 1903), 273–75.
"Patriotic Criticism in the South," XLIV (June 1904), 548–50.
"Southern Writers," XLVII (Sept. 1905), 260–63.

The Forum:

"South," LXXIX (Feb. 1928), 177–180.
"Are We Happier Than Our Grandmothers?" LXXX (Dec. 1928), 816–22.

Uncle Remus Magazine:

"On Becoming a Man," I (Sept. 1907), 29.
"Literary Horror Hunters," I (Oct. 1907), 21.
"The Year's Fiction," I (Dec. 1907), 32.

Woman's Home Companion:

"Colonel Wilkie and the Ladies," XLVI (Mar. 1929), 10–11; (Apr. 1929), 14–15.

II. SECONDARY SOURCES

1. CRITICAL WORKS

Blackstock, Walter. *Corra Harris, An Analytical Study of Her Novels.* Tallahassee, 1951.

Dobbins, Charles. "Corra Harris, Her Life and Work." Unpublished M.A. thesis, Columbia University, 1931.

Reeves, Ruby. "Corra Harris, Her Life and Works." Unpublished M.A. thesis, University of Georgia, 1940.

Talmadge, John E. "Corra Harris Goes to War," *Georgia Review* XVIII (Summer, 1964), 150–156.

Tate, William. "A Neighbor's Recollection of Corra Harris," *Georgia Review,* V (Spring, 1951), 22–33.

Wilcox, Herbert. "Corra Harris." An unpublished MS. in Corra Harris Collection, University of Georgia.

2. BOOKS

Allen, Sarah. *Our Children's Ancestry.* Atlanta, 1938.

Bullock, H. M. *A History of Emory University, 1836–1936.* Nashville, 1936.

Carlton, W. A. *In Memory of Old Emory.* Atlanta, 1962.

Dakin, Arthur. *Paul Elmer More.* Princeton, 1960.

Dempsey, E. F. *Atticus Greene Haygood. He Took the Kingdom by Violence, Matthew 11:12.* Nashville, 1940.

————. *Life of Bishop Dickey, Bishop of the Methodist Episcopal Church, South.* Nashville, 1937.

Farish, Hunter Dickinson. *The Circuit Rider Dismounts: A Social History of Southern Methodism.* Richmond, Va., 1938.

Knight, L. L. *Georgia and Georgians. Vol. I.* Chicago, 1917.

Kuehl, Warren F. *Hamilton Holt, Journalist, Internationalist and Educator.* Gainesville, Fla., 1960.

McIntosh, John H. *The Official History of Elbert County.* Elberton, Ga., 1940.

Mann, Harold W. *Atticus Greene Haygood, Methodist Bishop, Editor and Educator.* Athens, 1965.

Mims, Edwin, *Chancellor Kirkland.* Nashville, 1950.

Minutes, Methodist Board of Education, 1910. Nashville, 1910.

Pierce, Alfred M. *Giant Against the Sky.* Nashville, 1948.

Smith, George. *The History of Georgia Methodism.* Atlanta, 1913.

Tebbel, John. *George Horace Lorimer.* Garden City, 1948.

Index